easy

Quicken® 2004

Sherry Kinkoph

Contents

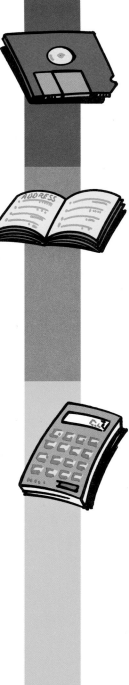

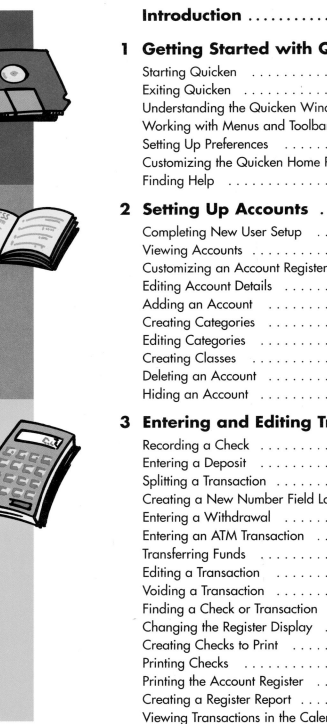

Easy Quicken® 2004
Copyright © 2004 by Que Publishing

International Standard Book Number: 0-7897-3073-1

Library of Congress Catalog Card Number: 029236730734

Printed in the United States of America

First Printing: November 2003

06   05   04   4   3   2

Trademarks

All terms mentioned in this book that are known to be trademarks or service marks have been appropriately capitalized. Que Publishing cannot attest to the accuracy of this information. Use of a term in this book should not be regarded as affecting the validity of any trademark or service mark.

Warning and Disclaimer

Quicken is a registered trademark of Inuit, Inc.

Bulk Sales

Que Publishing offers excellent discounts on this book when ordered in quantity for bulk purchases or special sales. For more information, please contact

U.S. Corporate and Government Sales

1-800-382-3419

corpsales@pearsontechgroup.com

For sales outside of the U.S., please contact

International Sales

1-317-428-3341

international@pearsontechgroup.com

Associate Publisher
Greg Wiegand

Acquisitions Editor
Michelle Newcomb

Development Editor
Laura Norman

Managing Editor
Charlotte Clapp

Project Editor
Tricia Liebig

Copy Editor
Barbara Hacha

Technical Editor
Cari Skaggs

Team Coordinator
Sharry Lee Gregory

Interior Designer
Anne Jones

Cover Designer
Anne Jones

Page Layout
Michelle Mitchell

Dedication

To my dear friend, Lisa Bell Jamison, for her continued support and encouragement.

About the Author

Sherry Kinkoph has authored more than 60 computer books over the past 10 years on a variety of topics. *How to Use Microsoft Office XP, Easy PowerPoint 2003, The Complete Idiot's Guide to Excel 2000, Master Visually Dreamweaver MX and Flash MX,* and *Teach Yourself Adobe Premiere 6 VISUALLY* are just a few of Sherry's recent publications. A native of the Midwest, Sherry currently resides in the Indianapolis area and continues in her quest to help users of all levels and ages master ever-changing computer technologies.

Acknowledgments

I would like to say thanks to the team at Que Publishing for all their efforts in producing this book. Special thanks go to Michelle Newcomb for her fine acquisitions work; to Laura Norman for her skills and dedication in developing this project; to Tricia Liebig for shepherding this book every step of the way until its final form; to Barbara Hacha for dotting the Is and crossing the Ts; and to Cari Skaggs for checking to make sure everything is technically accurate. Extra special thanks to the production group for assembling this visual masterpiece and to the sales and marketing staff for bringing it to bookshelves everywhere.

We Want to Hear from You!

As the reader of this book, *you* are our most important critic and commentator. We value your opinion and want to know what we're doing right, what we could do better, what areas you'd like to see us publish in, and any other words of wisdom you're willing to pass our way.

As an associate publisher for Que, I welcome your comments. You can email or write me directly to let me know what you did or didn't like about this book—as well as what we can do to make our books better.

Please note that I cannot help you with technical problems related to the topic of this book. We do have a User Services group, however, where I will forward specific technical questions related to the book.

When you write, please be sure to include this book's title and author as well as your name, email address, and phone number. I will carefully review your comments and share them with the author and editors who worked on the book.

Email: feedback@quepublishing.com

Mail: Greg Wiegand
           Associate Publisher
           Que Publishing
           800 East 96th Street
           Indianapolis, IN 46240 USA

For more information about this book or another Que title, visit our Web site at **www.quepublishing.com**. Type the ISBN (excluding hyphens) or the title of a book in the Search field to find the page you're looking for.

1 Each step is fully illustrated to show you how it looks onscreen.

It's as Easy as 1-2-3
Each part of this book is made up of a series of short, instructional lessons, designed to help you understand basic information that you need to get the most out of your computer hardware and software.

2 Each task includes a series of quick, easy steps designed to guide you through the procedure.

3 Items that you select or click in menus, dialog boxes, tabs, and windows are shown in **bold**.

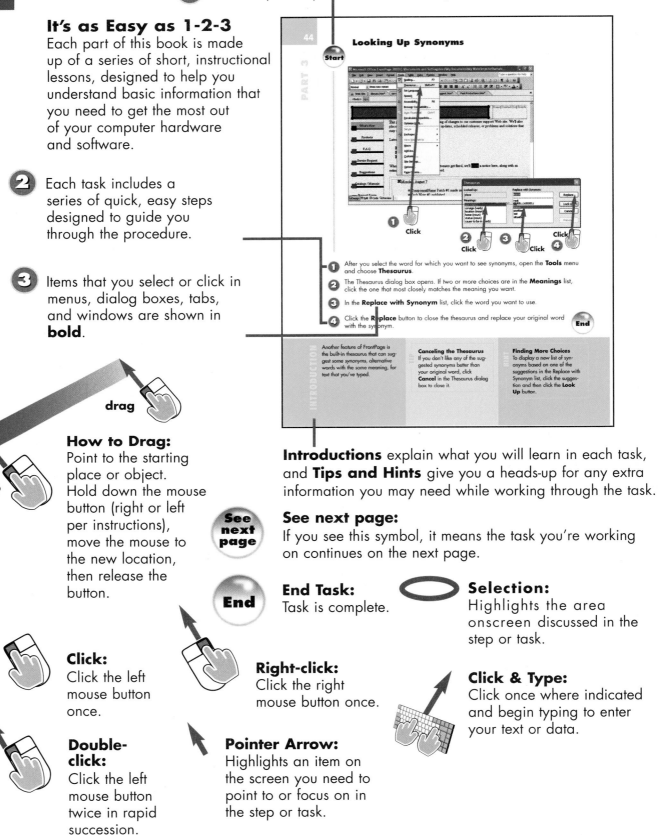

Introductions explain what you will learn in each task, and **Tips and Hints** give you a heads-up for any extra information you may need while working through the task.

How to Drag:
Point to the starting place or object. Hold down the mouse button (right or left per instructions), move the mouse to the new location, then release the button.

drag

drop

See next page

See next page:
If you see this symbol, it means the task you're working on continues on the next page.

End

End Task:
Task is complete.

Selection:
Highlights the area onscreen discussed in the step or task.

Click:
Click the left mouse button once.

Right-click:
Click the right mouse button once.

Click & Type:
Click once where indicated and begin typing to enter your text or data.

Double-click:
Click the left mouse button twice in rapid succession.

Pointer Arrow:
Highlights an item on the screen you need to point to or focus on in the step or task.

Introduction to Easy Quicken 2004

Whether you're learning a program for the first time or getting acquainted with the latest upgrade, finding your way around new tools, dialog boxes, and program features can be daunting as well as time consuming. *Easy Quicken 2004* can help you get up and running fast.

Quicken 2004 comes in several editions: Basic, Deluxe, Premier, and Premier Home & Business. All editions include features for tracking your checking and savings accounts, and Deluxe, Premier, and Premier Home & Business include additional features for managing tax information, investments, or business finances. No matter which edition you are using, *Easy Quicken 2004* shows you how to make the program work best for you.

Easy Quicken 2004 gives you simple, step-by-step instructions that show you exactly what to expect on your own computer screen. Most people are visual learners, so seeing how to perform a task is a much faster way to learn about a program than wading through pages of text. With *Easy Quicken 2004*, you'll learn all the basics for creating and working with your own financial accounts. You'll find out how to create a checking account register, populate it with transactions, add accounts to track your credit card debt, and reconcile an account to make sure your amounts and the bank's amounts agree. You'll find out how to use online banking features, download stocks and manage your investments, set up a budget, and plan for taxes. Along the way, you'll pick up valuable skills and tips for making Quicken work the way you want.

You can start in Part 1 and read through to the end of the book, or you can skip around and tackle just the tasks that interest you. You can also use the book as a reference for times when you need just a bit of extra help with the program. With the *Easy* visual format, you'll feel confident and up-to-date with Quicken 2004 in no time at all.

Getting Started with Quicken

Quicken is the most popular personal finance package on the market today. You can use Quicken to manage your checking and saving accounts, plan for taxes, create and balance a budget, track investments, conduct transactions online, and much more. Whether you are using Quicken at home or with a small business, you can put its many features to work to help you oversee and control your finances.

Before you begin creating and working with accounts in Quicken, first acquaint yourself with the various program elements and how they work. The Quicken program window comprises a menu bar, a toolbar, and several panes and windows, such as the Account bar, which lists your Quicken accounts. The first step to mastering the program is knowing how to navigate the onscreen elements.

If you run into a problem or have a question about a Quicken command or task, you can consult the Quicken Help files for assistance. The Help files offer quick instructions and explanations for using the program, along with links to online Help sources on the Web.

When you start Quicken for the first time after installing the program, you will be prompted to set up an initial account. See Part 2, "Setting Up Accounts," to learn more about types of accounts and how to proceed through the setup steps.

The Quicken Program Window

The toolbar offers short-cuts to useful features and commands.

The home page displays alerts, scheduled transactions, and other information.

The Account bar shows your different accounts.

Quicken 2004 Premier - MY FINANCES - [Quicken Home]

File   Edit   Tools   Online   Cash Flow   Investing   Property & Debt   Planning   Tax   Reports   Help

Back   Update   Reports   Setup   Brokerage   Services   Quicken.com   Customize

Quicken Home

Quicken Home

Customize ▼   How Do I?

Welcome, Sherry & Greg

Cash Flow Center
Checking   5,000.00
Savings   8,000.00
                $13,000.00

Investing Center
                $0.00

Property & Debt Center
                $0.00

Alerts   Options ▼
Date   Message
7/10/2003   Online: Fifth Third Bank now offers online services
7/10/2003   Investments: Send your portfolio to Quicken.com, so you can track i...
6/30/2003   Maximum Balance: Your Savings is at or over the $5,000.00 balance ...
[Show All Alerts]   [Set Up Alerts]

Current Bills and Scheduled Transactions

Scheduling your recurring payments and deposits allows Quicken to remind you when they are coming due.

Add a bill or other scheduled transaction.

[Go to Cash Flow Center]

Next Steps to Meet Your Financial Goals   Options ▼

Finish setting up Quicken:
Enter your bills with Quicken Guided Setup.

Net Worth $13,000.00

Financial Overview

[Customize]   [Hide Amounts]

Online Updates   ▼
[One Step Update]
Never connected.
Schedule Updates

Save time -- download from your brokerage.
[Set Up Now]

Quicken Tips
Separate business from personal expenses - get the big picture of what you've spent, when and where

Quicken Services
Quicken Bill Pay
Order Checks & Supplies
Protect Your Quicken Data
Quicken MasterCard

Protect your Quicken data with easy online backups

Starting Quicken

Start

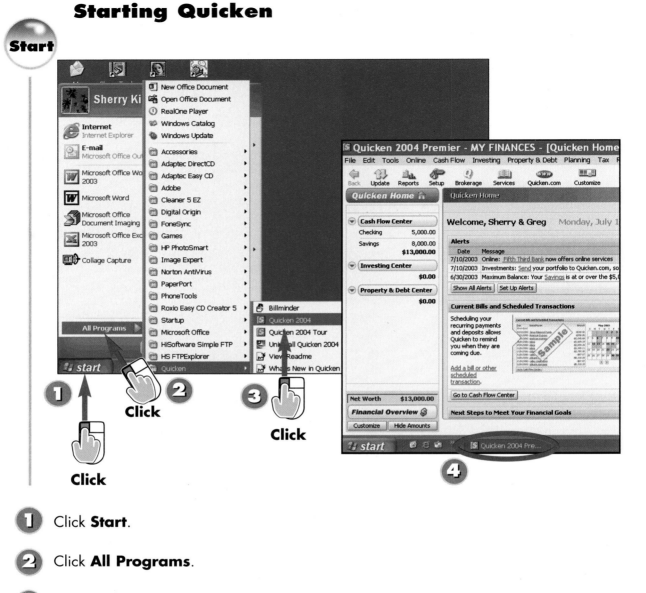

Click

Click

Click

1 Click **Start**.

2 Click **All Programs**.

3 Click **Quicken**, and then click **Quicken 2004**.

4 Quicken opens and a taskbar button appears on the Windows desktop taskbar.

End

INTRODUCTION

There are several ways to start Quicken. As you get more comfortable you might choose another method, but for now, just start Quicken using the Windows Start menu.

TIP

Starting Your First Account

The very first time you open Quicken after installing the software, dialog boxes appear to help you set up your first account. See Part 2 to learn more about setting up your Quicken accounts.

Exiting Quicken

Start

1 Click **File**.

2 Click **Exit**.

3 The Quicken window closes and the taskbar button for the program no longer appears on the Windows desktop taskbar.

End

Understanding the Quicken Window

Start

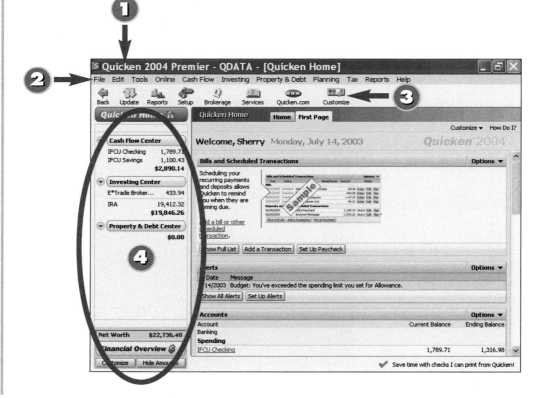

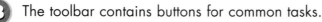

1 The title bar displays the name of the program and the name of the current file.

2 The menu bar displays menus that list all the commands available in Quicken.

3 The toolbar contains buttons for common tasks.

4 The Account bar lists each account.

INTRODUCTION

The Quicken program window contains several elements—some of which are unique to Quicken, such as the Account bar and home page. Other elements, such as the menu bar and toolbar, are common among most programs. The various onscreen elements enable you to quickly perform tasks and activate commands.

TIP

Quicken Feature Windows
Many features you open in Quicken display in their own windows. Click the window's **Minimize** button to minimize the window to an icon that sits at the bottom of the Quicken program window. To view the window in full again, click the window name.

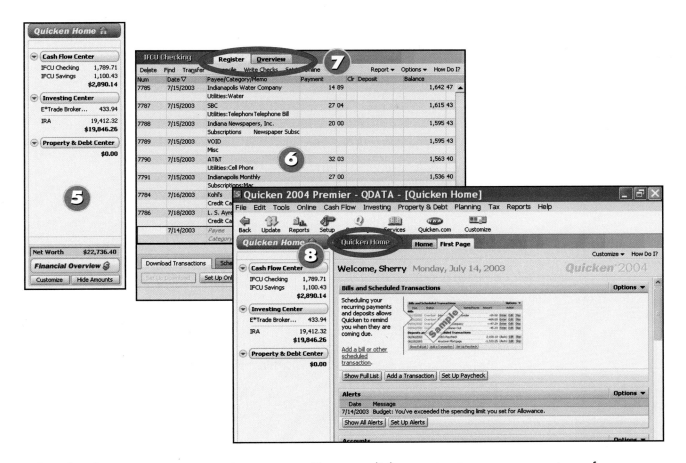

5 Quicken groups accounts into centers. You can click a center to see an overview of an account.

6 Depending on the account you are viewing, you can use the work area to display account registers and other information.

7 Switch between different views by using the tabs at the top of the page.

8 By default, the home page is displayed in the work area when you open Quicken; it offers links to frequently used features.

Customize It
The Quicken Home page appears whenever you open Quicken, but you can customize which window you see at startup. See the task "Setting Up Preferences" later in this chapter to learn more.

Your Window May Look Different
Depending on your monitor's screen resolution setting, the arrangement of Quicken program elements on your computer may differ from those shown in this book. If you share your computer with other users, various features may be turned on or off by someone else.

Working with Menus and Toolbars

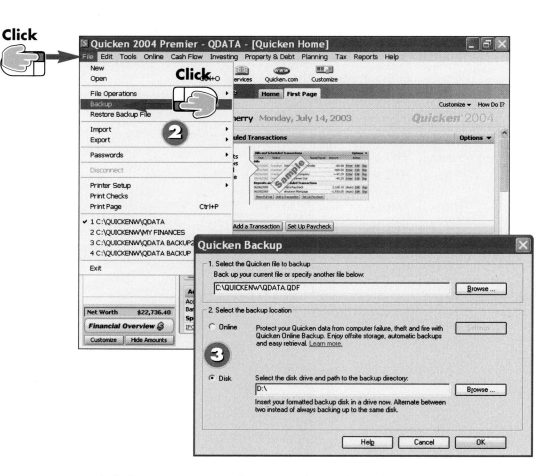

To view a menu, click the menu name. The menu drops down from the menu bar to reveal a list of commands.

To activate a command, click the command name.

Selecting a command sometimes involves selecting additional options from a separate dialog box.

INTRODUCTION

Use Quicken's menus and toolbars to activate commands and tasks. The menu bar groups related commands and tasks under menu names. For example, the File menu includes commands to help you work with Quicken files. Toolbars contain clickable shortcuts to common features.

TIP

Keyboard Commands
You can also use the keyboard to activate menu commands in Quicken. Press the **Alt** key along with the underlined letter of the menu to open the menu onscreen. Then press the corresponding underlined letter shown in the command name to activate a particular command.

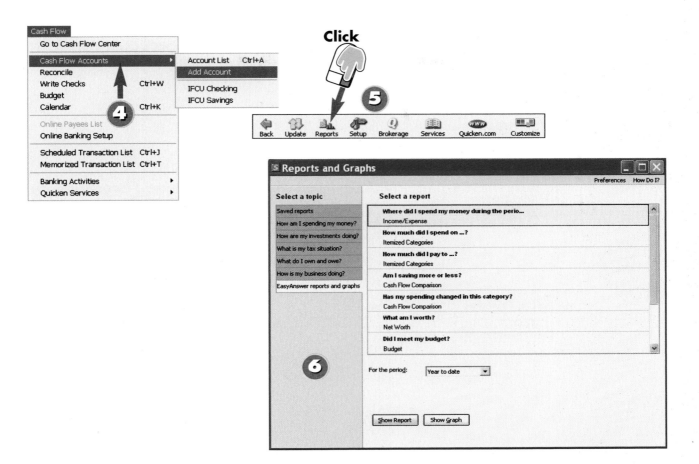

Click

④ Some commands reveal an additional submenu of commands. Move the mouse pointer over the command to view a submenu.

⑤ To activate a toolbar command, click a toolbar button.

⑥ Quicken carries out the command, which may involve opening a new window.

Shortcut Keys
TIP Look for various shortcut keys throughout the Quicken menus. Shortcut keys appear next to the command names and enable you to activate the feature without using a menu.

Shortcut Menus
TIP You can also right-click over various features in Quicken to display a pop-up or shortcut menu that lists commands related to the task at hand.

Setting Up Preferences

Start

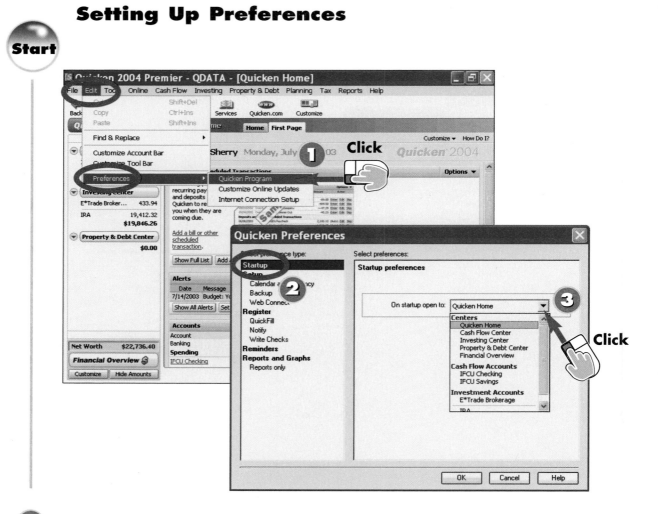

1 Click **Edit**, **Preferences**, **Quicken Program**.

2 The Quicken Preferences dialog box opens. The Startup preference is selected by default.

3 Click the drop-down arrow and select which window you want to view in the work area at startup.

The Quicken Preferences dialog box is used to customize how Quicken runs on your computer. You can use the Quicken Preferences dialog box to change which window appears at startup, turn off Quicken sounds, set reminders for backing up data, control how account registers are displayed, and more.

Can the Account Bar Be Closed?
No. The Account bar is always onscreen; however, using the Setup preferences, you can choose on which side of the screen it appears.

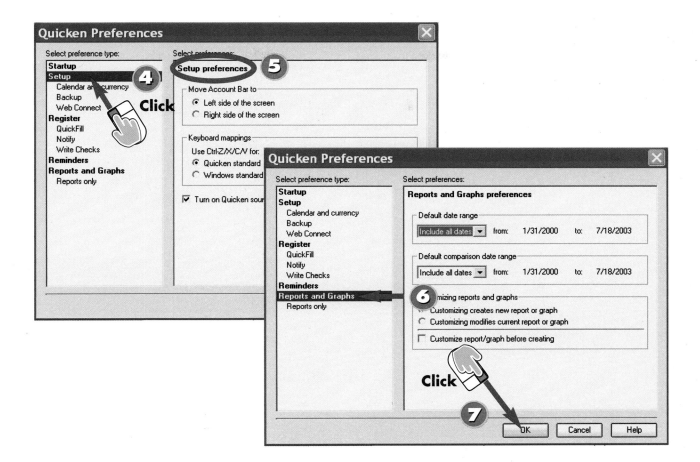

4 Click another preference to customize.

5 Related customizing options appear. You can change an option as needed. In this example, the Setup Preferences appear.

6 You can continue selecting different preferences and editing the options.

7 When finished, click **OK** to close the dialog box and apply the new settings.

Customize Online Updates
Click **Edit**, **Preferences**, **Customize Online Updates** to open the Customize Online Updates dialog box, where you can customize the way in which online updates work in Quicken.

Change Your Online Connection
If you ever need to change the way in which Quicken connects to the Internet and your online accounts, open the guided Internet Connection Setup Wizard. Click **Edit**, **Preferences**, **Internet**.

Customizing the Quicken Home Page

Start

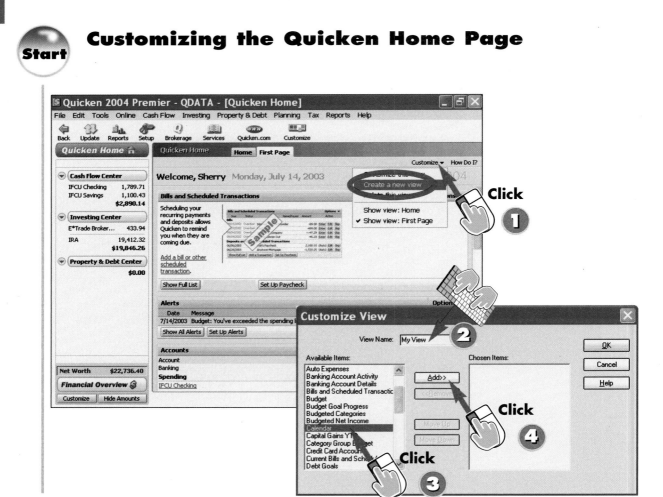

1. Click the **Customize** button on the home page, and then click **Create a New View**.

2. The Customize View dialog box opens. Type a name for the new view.

3. Select the feature you want to add to the new view.

4. Click the **Add** button.

The Quicken Home page offers you quick access to alerts, current bills and scheduled transactions, online updates, and more. Although you cannot edit the default home page, you can create a new view of the page and customize it to show only the features you use the most. Each view appears as a tab at the top of the work area.

TIP

Rearrange the Items
With the Customize View dialog box open, you can use the **Move Up** and **Move Down** buttons to change the order in which items appear in the view.

Customize View

View Name: My View

Available Items:
Portfolio Value Graph
Portfolio Value vs. Cost Basis
Projected Tax
Property & Debt Accounts
Returns
Savings Analysis
Savings Goal Progress
Security Holding Period
Set Up Paycheck
Spending & Savin
Tax Calendar
Taxable Income
Tax-Related Expens
Watch List

Click

Review how much you're saving

Add>>
<<Remove

Move Up
Move Down

Chosen Items:
Calendar
Income Year-to-Date
Savings Analysis

OK
Cancel
Help

Click

Quicken Home | Home | First Page | **My View**

Customize ▾ How Do I?

Welcome, Sherry Monday, July 14, 2003   *Quicken* 2004

| 20 | 21 | 22 | 23 | 24 | 25 | 26 |
| 27 | 28 | 29 | 30 | 31 | | |

Full Calendar   ◄ ►

Income Year-to-Date
Interest Inc	41.61
Other Inc	7,445.87
Salary	27,675.17
TOTAL	35,162.65

Add Paycheck

Savings Analysis   Options ▾
Total Savings:	22,736.40
Emergency Fund:	unknown
Savings Rate (last 30 days):	-5.66%

⬇ The Debt Reduction Planner helps you become debt free

---

5 The item is added to the new view.

6 Repeat steps 3 and 4 to add more items to the view.

7 Click **OK** when finished.

8 Quicken creates the new view and displays a tab for the view at the top of the work area.

End

TIP

Remove an Item
To remove an item you no longer need, reopen the Customize View dialog box, select the item from the Chosen Items list and click the **Remove** button.

TIP

Remove a View
To delete a view you no longer need, click the View tab to display the view, and then click the **Customize** button and select **Delete This View**. Click **Yes** to confirm the deletion, and the view is removed.

Finding Help

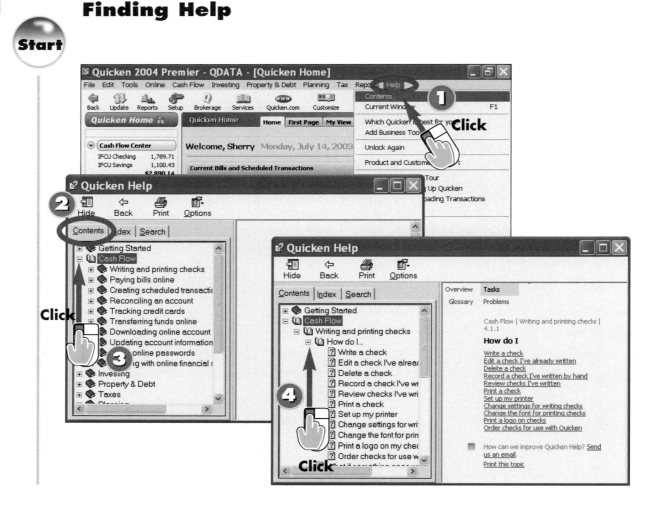

① Click **Help**, **Contents**.

② The Help window opens and displays the Contents tab.

③ Click a Help category to expand the list of topics.

④ Continue expanding the category until all the topics are listed.

INTRODUCTION

From time to time, you may find yourself needing some additional help with the Quicken program. Quicken offers several ways you can look up information about a particular task or feature. For example, the Help menu lists a variety of features you can tap into to find assistance.

TIP

Find Help on the Web
Click **Help**, **Product and Customer Support** to open the Product and Customer Support window. Click the **Quicken Technical Support Home Page** link to open your Web browser and view the Intuit Web site for additional help. You must be logged on to your Internet account to access this site.

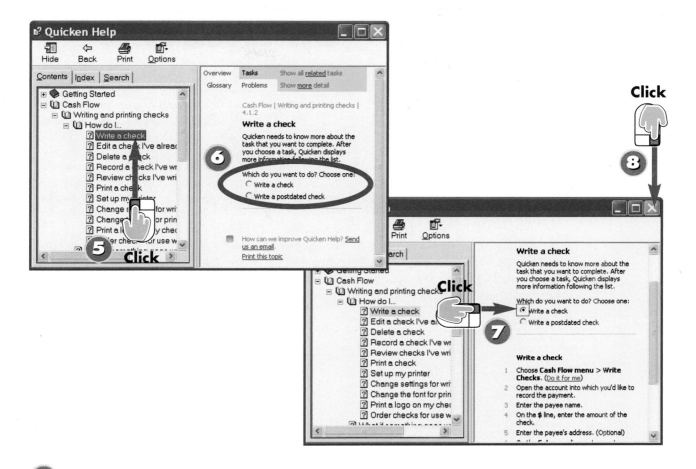

5 Click a topic.

6 Information on the topic appears in the right pane of the Help window.

7 Some topics include additional information. Simply click the option you want to read more about.

8 Click the **Close** button to exit the Help window and return to Quicken.

End

Help at Hand
Numerous Quicken features include a button for directly accessing help related to the topic at hand. Click the **How Do I?** button to quickly open the Help window to topics related to your current task.

Conduct a Search
To look up a specific topic, click the **Search** tab in the Help window and type in the keyword or words you want to search for. Click the **List Topics** button and Quicken generates a list of possible matches you can search through.

Setting Up Accounts

You can create different types of accounts in Quicken 2004. An *account* in Quicken holds financial information for a corresponding checking, savings, or other account at a bank or financial institution. Most users start out tracking checking and savings accounts in Quicken. You can also add other types of accounts at any time, such as accounts to keep track of your credit cards.

You can create accounts to track assets and liabilities. *Assets* are things you own, such as a house, a car, or investments. *Liabilities* are things you owe, such as a mortgage or car loan. You can add numerous types of accounts to a single Quicken data file.

After setting up your accounts, you can begin entering transactions into your account registers. Much like a paper register that comes with your checkbook, a Quicken register is a listing of all the actions pertaining to your account. Understanding how to create and work with accounts is a key part of learning how to use the Quicken program.

Quicken's Guided Setup Wizard

The Add Accounts window in the Setup Wizard enables you to add all kinds of accounts to your Quicken file.

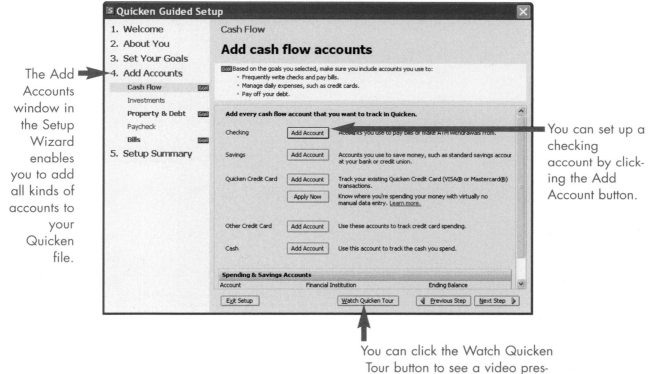

You can set up a checking account by clicking the Add Account button.

You can click the Watch Quicken Tour button to see a video presentation about Quicken.

Completing New User Setup

Start

Quicken Guided Setup

1. Welcome
2. About You
3. Set Your Goals
4. Add Accounts
   Cash Flow
   Investments
   Property & Debt
   Paycheck
   Bills
5. Setup Summary

Welcome to Quicken Guided Setup

Before you start using Quicken...

Quicken Guided Setup helps you get the most from Quicken. After you select your financial goals, Quicken Guided Setup leads you through a personalized setup process so that you set up only the parts of Quicken you need to meet your goals.

Quicken Guided Setup will help you:
- Enter some basic information about yourself.
- Select your financial goals.
- Set up the parts of Quicken you need to meet your goals.

To learn more about what Quicken can do for you, watch the video.   [Watch Quicken Tour]

[Next Step ▶]

Quicken Guided Setup

1. Welcome
2. About You
3. Set Your Goals
4. Add Accounts
   Cash Flow
   Investments
   Property & Debt
   Paycheck
   Bills
5. Setup Summary

About You

Tell us about yourself

This information will be used to personalize Quicken and to generate categories that best fit your needs.

	First	Last
Your Name:	Robin	Oglesby
Your Birth Date:	3/14/1975	

Are you married?   ○ Yes   ● No

Name: First _____   Last _____

Birth Date: 1/1/1960

How many dependents do you have?   0

Do you own a home?   ○ Yes   ● No
Do you own any rental properties?   ○ Yes   ● No
Do you want to use Quicken to track a business?   ○ Yes   ● No

Your Company Name: _____ (Optional)

[Exit Setup]   [Watch Quicken Tour]   [◀ Previous Step] [Next Step ▶]

2

Click

1

Click

1 Start Quicken and click **Next Step** at the Quicken Guided Setup Welcome window.

2 On the About You page, fill in the personal information fields and then click **Next Step**.

When you start Quicken for the very first time, the Quicken Guided Setup Wizard opens to walk you through the process of setting up your financial accounts. Quicken collects a variety of information about you to generate categories to suit your financial situation. After you finish entering personal information, the Guided Setup Wizard can help you set up your basic accounts.

TIP

No Desktop Shortcut?
If you don't see the Quicken 2004 desktop shortcut icon, you also can choose **Start**, **Programs**, **Quicken**, **Quicken 2004** from the Windows desktop to open Quicken.

Quicken Guided Setup

Set Your Goals

What do you want to get out of Quicken?

Quicken Guided Setup uses this icon to highlight the areas of setup that are most important for addressing your goals.

Information about setup that relates to your goals will appear in a box like this one.

I want Quicken to help me:

☑ **Manage my checkbook and bills.**
- Use Quicken to balance your checkbook.
- Have Quicken remind you when bills are due.

☑ **Know where my money is going.**
- Identify how much you spend in areas like housing and entertainment.
- Save time by downloading transactions from your bank and categorizing them automatically.

☐ **Save more money.**
- See where you're spending your money and identify areas where you can save.

Next Step ▶

Cash Flow

Add cash flow accounts

Based on the goals you selected, make sure you include accounts you use to:
- Frequently write checks and pay bills.
- Manage daily expenses, such as credit cards.
- Pay off your debt.

Click cash flow account that you want to track in Quicken.

	Add Account	Accounts you use to pay bills or make ATM withdrawals from.
Savings	Add Account	Accounts you use to save money, such as standard savings accounts at your bank or credit union.
Quicken Credit Card	Add Account	Track your existing Quicken transactions.
	Apply Now	Know where you're spending manual data entry. Learn
Other Credit Card	Add Account	Use these accounts to trac
Cash	Add Account	Use this account to track t

Exit Setup   Finish Later   Watch Qui

Quicken Account Setup

What is the financial institution for this account? **Click**

◉ This account is held at the following institution:

Bank |

BANK 21
Bank First
Bank Independent
Bank Midwest, Minnesota Iowa, NA
Bank of Alabama
Bank of Alameda
Bank of Albuquerque
Bank of America - California
Bank of America - Oregon
Bank of America -All Other States

Cancel   Help   Next

---

3 On the Set Your Goals window, select the check boxes for the areas in which you want to track information and click **Next Step**.

4 Click the **Add Account** button next to the checking account option.

5 Type the name of your bank or select the bank name from the list that appears when you start typing in the field. Then click **Next** to continue.

See next page

More Setups
You'll encounter the Quicken Guided Setup Wizard any time you create a new data file. To learn more about creating new files, see Part 13, "Managing Quicken Data Files."

Take a Tour
If you are new to Quicken, you can click the **Watch Quicken Tour** button on the Welcome window to see a video tour about the program.

Where's My Bank?
If your bank doesn't appear on the Financial Institution drop-down list in step 5, you can type the name of your bank into the text box. The bank you choose here determines which online banking features you'll be able to use in Quicken.

Completing New User Setup Continued

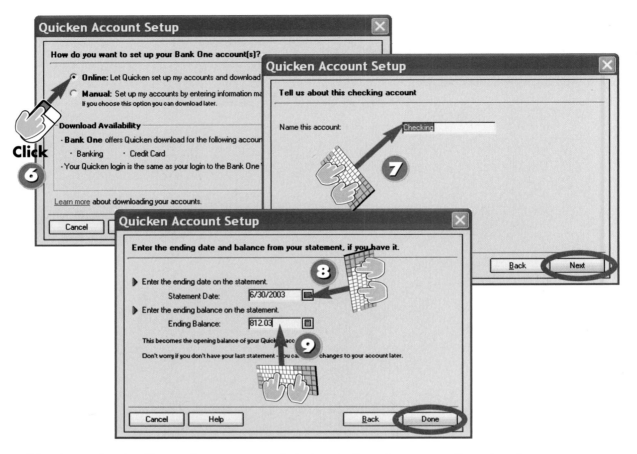

6. If your bank offers online options, click the **Online** button to allow Quicken to set up your checking account; otherwise, choose to set up the account manually. Click **Next**.

7. Enter a descriptive name for the account and then click **Next**.

8. Enter the ending date found on your most recent bank statement into the **Statement Date** field.

9. Type in the statement **Ending Balance** and click **Done**. Repeat steps 5–10 to set up additional accounts, if needed.

Quicken Guided Setup

1. Welcome
2. About You
3. Set Your Goals
4. Add Accounts
   Cash Flow
   Investments
   Property & Debt
   Paycheck
   Bills
5. Setup Summary

Setup Summary

Review your data

To add additional items, click the appropriate Add button in the lower-left corner of each section. When you have finished adding accounts, bills, and paychecks, click Done to go to Quicken.

Spending & Savings Accounts

Account	Financial Institution	Ending Balance		
Spending				
Checking	Bank One	812.03	Edit	Delete

Add Account

Credit Card Accounts
Track your credit card spending. Add credit card accounts.
Add Account

Investment & Retirement Accounts
Track your investments. Add investment accounts.
Add Account

Property & Debt Accounts
Track the value of your assets (property) and manage your liabilities (debt). Add asset and liability accounts.
Add Account

Set Up Paycheck

Watch Quicken Tour   Previous Step   Done

Click

en 2004

...ken can now help you manage your finances. Follow the Next Steps listed ...the Quicken Home page to help you realize the goals you've selected.

Next Steps to Meet Your Financial Goals
Finish setting up Quicken:
Add your paycheck with Quicken Guided Setu...
Remember to secure your data with a file bac...
Go to the Cash Flow Center
How do I categorize transactions and track m...
How do I download transactions from my fina...
Go to Guided Setup   Review Your Goals

Quicken Home

Click

Click

OK

(10) When you are finished setting up accounts, click **Setup Summary**.

(11) A summary window appears, listing all the accounts you created. Verify the account information and then click **Done**.

(12) Quicken tells you that the Setup Wizard is complete. Click **OK** and Quicken opens the account.

End

No Statement?
HINT
If you don't have your last bank statement and did not enter a balance in step 10, Quicken enters **0** as the starting balance. You can later edit the Deposit column entry for the Opening Balance transaction in the register.

Oops!
TIP
If you entered a wrong amount when setting up an account, you can correct the amount in the Summary window.

Register Me
TIP
If Quicken displays the Product Registration dialog box, click the **Register** button and follow the prompts to register your copy of the software. Registration has many benefits, including free product updates available from Quicken.com.

Viewing Accounts

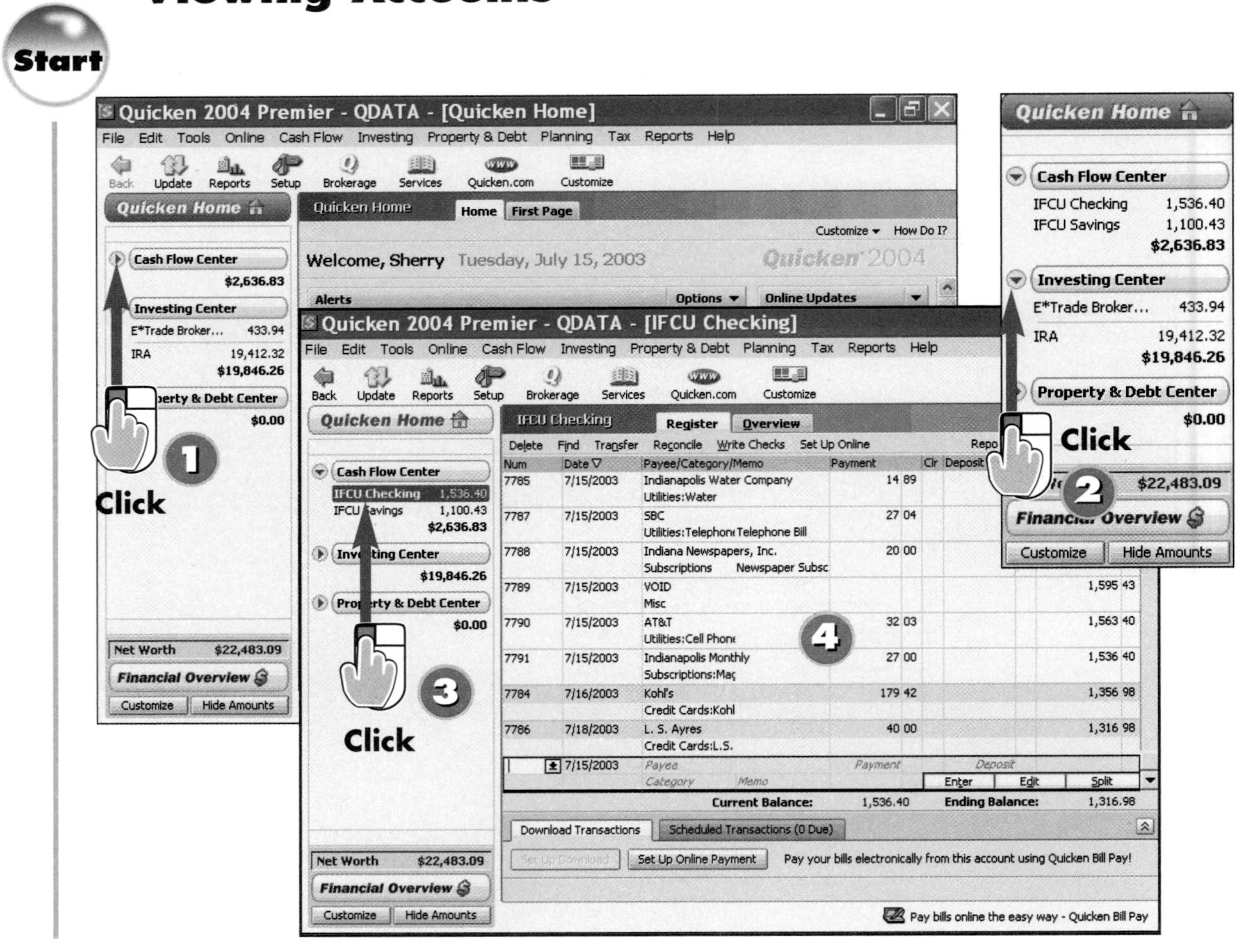

Start

1 To expand a center, click the **Expand** arrow.

2 To collapse a center, click the **Collapse** arrow.

3 To view an account register, click the account name.

4 Quicken displays the account register.

INTRODUCTION

The Account bar lists your accounts in the appropriate center group along with the account's total amount. For example, checking and savings accounts appear under the Cash Flow Center, investment accounts appear under the Investing Center. You can expand and collapse the account listing displayed in the Account bar. With a simple mouse click, you can also display the register for any account.

TIP

The Cash Flow Center
To learn more about using the Cash Flow Center to view information about your cash flow accounts, see Part 7, "Tracking Your Cash Flow."

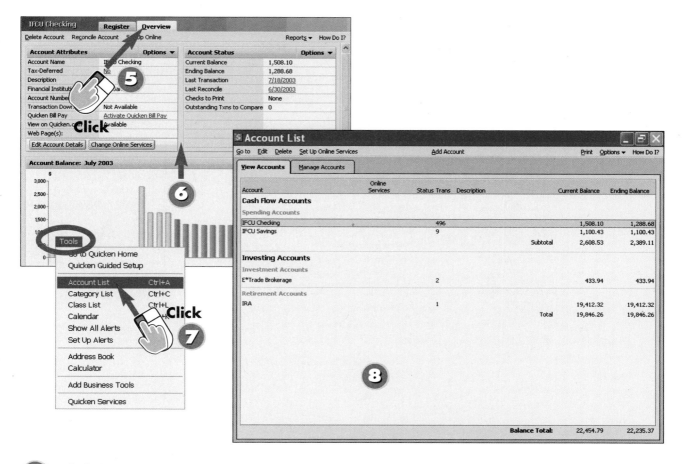

5 Click the **Overview** tab.

6 Quicken displays an overview page for the account showing the account's attributes and status.

7 Click **Tools**, **Account List**.

8 Quicken displays the Account List window, which also lists all the accounts in your data file. To view an account, click the account name.

End

Click a Link
You can also open an account register by clicking the account name link on the Cash Flow Center page.

Customize It
You can customize where the Account bar is located in your Quicken program window. See Part 1, "Getting Started with Quicken," to learn more about customizing Quicken features.

Customizing an Account Register

Start

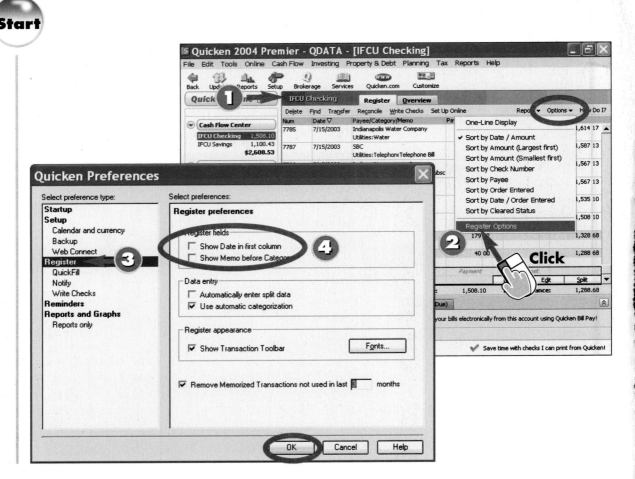

1 Open the account register you want to customize.

2 Click the **Options** button and choose **Register Options**.

3 The Quicken Preferences dialog box opens and displays the register preferences.

4 Select or deselect the register option you want to change and then click **OK** to apply the changes.

End

Editing Account Details

Start

1 Open the register for the account you want to change and click the **Overview** tab.

2 Click the **Edit Account Details** button.

3 The Account Details dialog box opens. Edit the account details as needed.

4 Click **OK** to apply the changes.

End

INTRODUCTION

You can make changes to the details of an account, such as changing the name of the account, the account description, or inserting an account number. You may need to change the account details if you switch banks, for example.

Adding an Account

Start

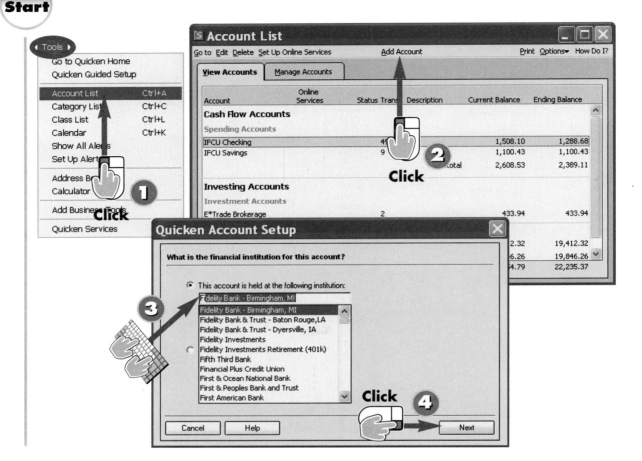

 Click **Tools**, **Account List**.

 The Account List window opens. Click the **Add Account** button.

 Type the name of your bank or select the bank name from the drop-down list that appears when you click in the field.

 Click **Next** to continue.

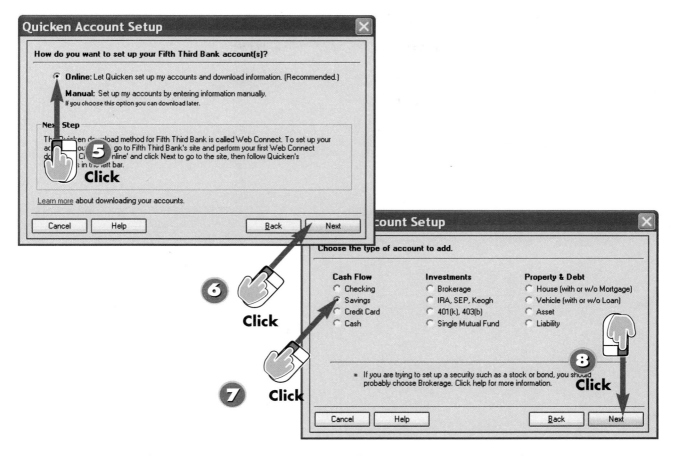

Quicken Account Setup

How do you want to set up your Fifth Third Bank account(s)?

○ **Online:** Let Quicken set up my accounts and download information. (Recommended.)

Manual: Set up my accounts by entering information manually.
If you choose this option you can download later.

Next Step

The Quicken download method for Fifth Third Bank is called Web Connect. To set up your account you... go to Fifth Third Bank's site and perform your first Web Connect d... Click online' and click Next to go to the site, then follow Quicken's ...s in the left bar.

Click

Learn more about downloading your accounts.

Cancel   Help   Back   Next

...count Setup

Choose the type of account to add.

Cash Flow
○ Checking
○ Savings
○ Credit Card
○ Cash

Investments
○ Brokerage
○ IRA, SEP, Keogh
○ 401(k), 403(b)
○ Single Mutual Fund

Property & Debt
○ House (with or w/o Mortgage)
○ Vehicle (with or w/o Loan)
○ Asset
○ Liability

Click

• If you are trying to set up a security such as a stock or bond, you should probably choose Brokerage. Click help for more information.

Click

Cancel   Help   Back   Next

5 If your bank offers online options, click the **Online** option to allow Quicken to set up your checking account; otherwise, choose to set up the account manually.

6 Click **Next** to continue.

7 Select the type of account, such as Savings or Cash.

8 Click **Next** to continue.

See next page

Need a New File?

TIP

Quicken adds all new accounts you create to the current QDATA file. If you want to keep another person's financial information completely separate from yours, create another data file, as described in Part 13.

Adding an Account Continued

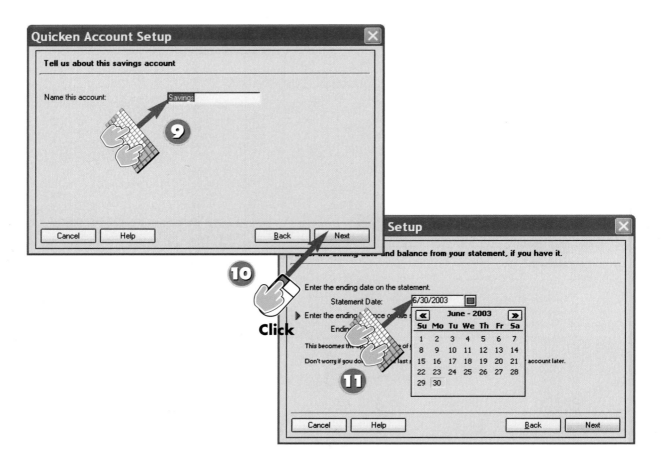

 Type a descriptive name for the account.

 Click **Next** to continue.

 Using your most recent bank statement, locate the statement ending date and type it into the **Statement Date** field. You can also click the Calendar icon to select a date.

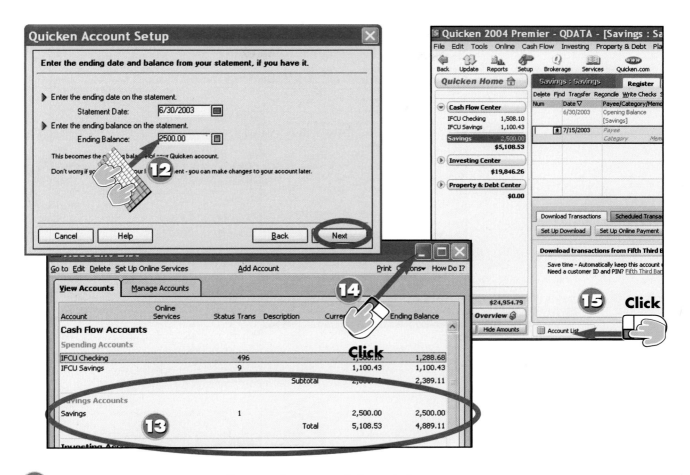

12 Type in the statement **Ending Balance** and then click **Next**.

13 The account is added to the Account List window.

14 Click the **Minimize** button to minimize the Account List window to view the register for the new account.

15 The Account List window appears as a button at the bottom of the program window. Click the button to display the list again.

End

Creating Categories

Start

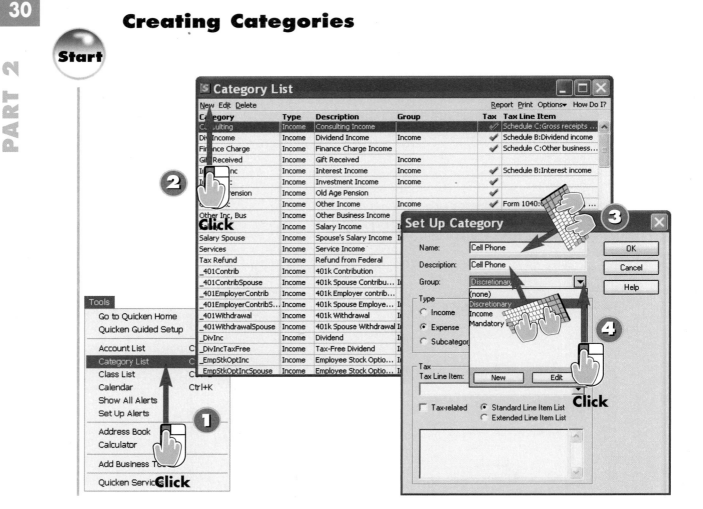

1. Click **Tools**, **Category List**.

2. The Category List window opens. To add a new category, click the **New** button.

3. The Set Up Category dialog box opens. Type in a name and description for your new category.

4. Optionally, to select a group for the new category, open the **Group** drop-down list and click a choice.

INTRODUCTION

To help you organize and track your spending, you can assign categories to the transactions that you record in your account registers. You can assign income or expense categories. Income categories include entries such as *salary, interest income,* and *gifts received.* Expense categories include entries such as *rent, groceries,* and *utilities.* Or you can create a subcategory. A default set of categories is created when you set up a new account, but you can add new categories to suit your own financial tracking needs.

TIP

About Groups
Groups classify similar categories and subcategories. Groups are primarily used for budgeting purposes, so assigning a group to a category is optional.

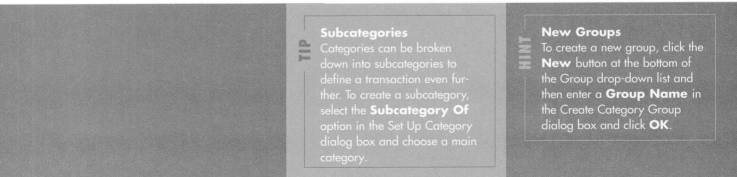

Set Up Category

Name: Cell Phone
Description: Cell Phone
Group: Discretionary

Type
- Income
- Expense   Spending is not discretionary
  Subcategory of

Tax
Tax Line Item:

related   Standard
            Extended

Click 5

Set Up Category

Name: Cell Phone
Description: Cell Phone
Group: Discretionary

OK
Cancel
Help

Type
- Income
- Expense   Spending is not discretionary
- Subcategory of Office Expense

Office Expense
Other Exp
Pension and Profit-Sharing,
Postage and Delivery
Printing and Reproduction
Recreation
Rent on Equip
Subscriptions

ax Line Item:

related
            Extended Line Item List

Click 6   **Click** 7

Edit Category

Name: Cell Phone
Description: Cell Phone
Group:

OK
Cancel
Help

Type
- Income
- Expense   Spending is not discretionary
- Subcategory of Office Expense

Tax
Tax Line Item:
Schedule C:Office expenses

☑ Tax-related   ● Standard Line Item List
                 Extended Line Item List

The cost of consumable office supplies such
as stationery, pens, pencils, computer
supplies, etc. Include cost of postage stamps,
business cards, UPS and Federal Express
charges, rental of postal box or postage

Click 8

---

⑤ Click either **Income** or **Expense** to identify the category's purpose. Also, if appropriate, check **Spending Is Not Discretionary**.

⑥ To turn the new category into a subcategory of an existing category, click the **Subcategory Of** option button.

⑦ Click the down arrow to open the drop-down list, and then select the category.

⑧ For a tax category, check **Tax-Related**, open the **Tax Line Item** drop-down list, and select the appropriate tax form. Click **OK** to finish creating the category.

End

Editing Categories

Start

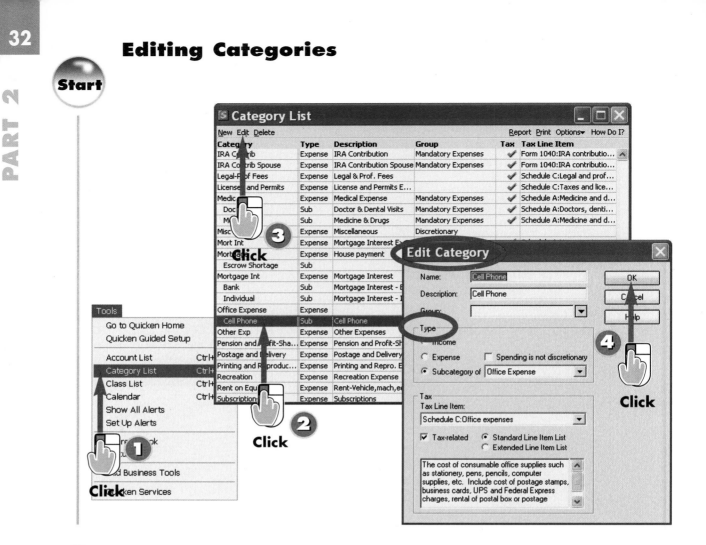

Click

Click

Click

Click

1 Click **Tools**, **Category List**.

2 The Category List window opens. Select the category you want to edit.

3 Click the **Edit** button.

4 The Edit Category dialog box opens. You can make changes to the settings as needed. Click **OK** to apply the changes.

INTRODUCTION

You can fine-tune Quicken's categories list to include just the categories you use the most. By default, Quicken sets up a number of predefined categories. You can remove categories you do not need or edit existing categories to suit the way you want to record account information.

Deleting Is Permanent!
If you delete a category you have already used throughout your account register, all transactions that referenced the category will be uncategorized, making them difficult to track for reports.

Category List

New Edit Delete — Report Print Options How Do I?

Category	Type	Description	Group	Tax	Tax Line Item
IRA Contrib	Expense	IRA Contribution	Mandatory Expenses	✔	Form 1040:IRA c...
IRA Contrib Spouse	Expense	IRA Contribution Spouse	Mandatory Expenses	✔	Form 1040:IRA c...
Legal-Prof Fees	Expense	Legal & Prof. Fees		✔	Schedule C:Lega...
Licenses and Permi...	Expense	License and Permits E...		✔	Schedule C:Taxe...
Medical	Expense	Medical Expense	Mandatory Expenses	✔	Schedule A:Medi...
Doctor	Sub	Doctor & Dental Visits	Mandatory Expenses	✔	Schedule A:Doct...
Medicine	Sub	Medicine & Drugs	Mandatory Expenses	✔	Schedule A:Medi...
Misc	Expense	Miscellaneous	Discre...		
Mort Int	Expense	Mortgage Interest Exp			
Mortgage	Ex				
Escrow Shortage	Su				
Mortgage Int	Ex				
Bank	Su				
Individual	Su				
Cell Phone					
Pension and Profit-Sha...	Ex				
Postage and Delivery	Ex				
Printing and Reproduc...	Ex				
Recreation	Ex				
Rent on Equip	Ex				
Subscriptions	Ex				

Click 5

Delete Category

⚠ You are about to permane...

You can delete the category or repla...
replace the category, select a new o...

Delete Options
◉ Delete Category
○ Replace Category

OK   Cancel

6 **Click**

Quicken 2004 for Win... ✕

⚠ Deleting subcategory.
Merge subcategory with parent?

Yes   No   Cancel

7

Category List

New Edit Delete — Report Print Options How Do I?

Category	Type	Description	Group	Tax	Tax Line Item
Medicine	Sub	Medicine & Drugs	Man...	✔	Schedule A:Medicine and d...
Misc	Expense	Miscellaneous	Disc...		
Mort Int	Expense	Mortgage Interest Exp		✔	Schedule A:Home mortgag..
Mortgage	Expense	House payment			
Escrow Shortage	Sub				
Mortgage Int	Expense	Mortgage Interest	Mandatory Expenses	✔	
Bank	Sub	Mortgage Interest - B...	Mandatory Expenses	✔	Schedule A:Home mortgag...
Individual	Sub	Mortgage Interest - I...	Mandatory Expenses	✔	Schedule A:Home mortgag...
Office Expense	Expense			✔	
Other	Expense	Other Expenses		✔	
Pension and Profit-Sha...	Expense	Pension and Profit-Sh...		✔	Schedule C:Pension/profit ...
Postage and Delivery	Expense	Postage and Delivery ...		✔	Schedule C:Other business...
Printing and Reproduc...	Expense	Printing and Repro. E...		✔	Schedule C:Other business...
Recreation	Expense	Recreation Expense	Discretionary		
Rent on Equip	Expense	Rent-Vehicle,mach,equip		✔	Schedule C:Rent/lease ve...
Subscriptions	Expense	Subscriptions	Discretionary		
Magazine	Sub	Magazine Subscriptions			
Tax	Expense	Taxes	Mandatory Expenses	✔	
Fed	Sub	Federal Tax	Mandatory Expenses	✔	W-2:Federal tax withheld, ...
Medicare	Sub	Medicare Tax	Mandatory Expenses	✔	W-2:Medicare tax withheld...
Other	Sub	Misc. Taxes	Mandatory Expenses	✔	
Prop	Sub	Property Tax		✔	Schedule A:Real estate ta...
Property	Sub	Property Tax	Mandatory Expenses	✔	Schedule A:Real estate ta...

Click   **Click**   8

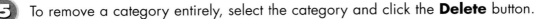

5. To remove a category entirely, select the category and click the **Delete** button.

6. The Delete Category dialog box appears. Leave the **Delete Category** option selected and click **OK**.

7. If you are deleting a subcategory, a different prompt box appears. Click **Yes** to merge the subcategory with the main category, or click **No** to delete.

8. Quicken removes the category from the list. Click the **Close** button to close the Category List window.

End

Watch Out for Subcategories
HINT
You cannot delete a category that has associated subcategories. You can, however, delete a subcategory.

I Need That Category!
TIP
If it turns out you do need a category that you previously removed, you can add it using the steps shown in the previous task.

Creating Classes

Start

Tools
~~Go to~~ Quicken Home
Quicken Guided Setup

Account List   Ctrl+A
Category List   Ctrl+C
Class List   Ctrl+L
Calendar   Ctrl+K
Show All Alerts
Set Up Alerts

Address Book
Calculator

Add Business Tools

Quicken Services

Click

1

S Class List

New Edit Delete   Report Print How Do I?

Class   Description

2

Click

Set Up Class

Name: Chevrolet Astro Van

Description: Expenses for Greg's Work Van

...umber (Optional):

3

Cancel   Help

1 Click **Tools**, **Class List**.

2 The Class List window opens. Click the **New** button.

3 The Set Up Class dialog box opens. Type a name and description for the class into the corresponding fields.

You can use *classes* as optional identifiers for your account transactions. If you have an expense or bill that includes more than one identifier, you can set up a class for each. For example, you might have two vehicles in which you pay expenses. You might create a class for your car and your truck. This way, when you record a transaction related to vehicle expenses, you can identify exactly which vehicle the transaction applies to.

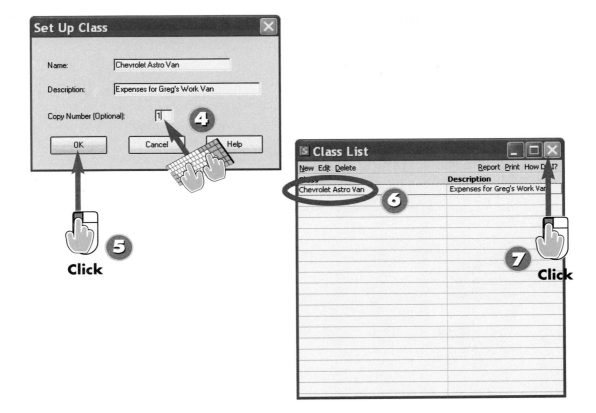

Click

Click

4️⃣ Optionally, if you have more than one use for the class name, enter a copy number.

5️⃣ Click **OK**.

6️⃣ Quicken adds the class to the list.

7️⃣ You can add more classes or click the **Close** button to close the window.

End

Copy Number
Although optional, the Copy Number setting in the Set Up Class dialog box allows you to separate a class into two or more items.

Assign a Class
Record a transaction as you normally do, and assign a category. With the category field still active, open the Class List window and double-click the class you want to assign.

Deleting an Account

Start

1. Click the **Customize** button at the bottom of the Account bar to open the Account List window.

2. Select the account you want to remove and click the **Delete** button.

3. Type **Yes** and click **OK**. Quicken removes the account.

End

Menu Method
Another way to open the Account List window is to click the **Tools** menu and click **Account List**. You can also press **Ctrl+A** on the keyboard.

Hiding an Account

Start

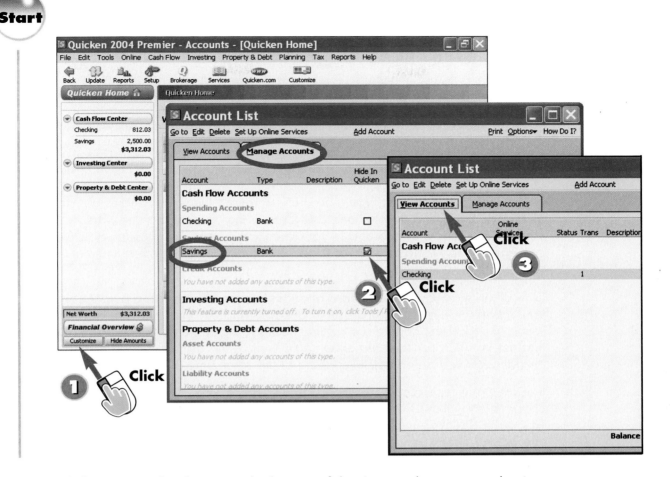

① Click **Click**

② **Click**

③ **Click**

① Click the **Customize** button at the bottom of the Account bar to open the Account List window.

② Click the **Manage Accounts** tab, select the account you want to hide, and click the **Hide In Quicken** check box.

③ Click the **View Accounts** tab to see that the account is no longer listed.

End

INTRODUCTION

You can hide an account so that it is no longer in view in any list in Quicken in which it would normally appear. You might use this feature to hide accounts you no longer use regularly. Unlike deleting an account, hiding it keeps all recorded transactions intact.

TIP

View It Again
To view a hidden account in the Account List window, click the **Options** button and choose **View Hidden Accounts**.

Entering and Editing Transactions

You can record your account activities in Quicken by entering transactions. A *transaction* is any activity that causes money to move in or out of your cash flow accounts. Transactions include deposits, withdrawals, ATM withdrawals, transfers, debit card purchases, and, of course, any checks that you write.

In this section of the book, you learn how to record the various types of transactions, as well as learn how to view and edit them in the account register window. Most of your transactions are recorded in your checking or savings account; however, you can apply these same techniques to record transactions into other types of accounts you create in Quicken.

One of the techniques you'll learn about in this part is recording a *split* transaction. You might, for example, purchase $10 worth of oil for your car and another $20 worth of groceries, but write a single check for all the items. A split transaction enables you to track the auto expense as well as the grocery expense separately, even though you purchased everything at the same time and at the same store.

In addition to recording your account transactions, you can also write out your checks from within Quicken and record them into your register at the same time. The Write Checks window lets you write and enter checks and print them out using specialized check paper you can purchase from Intuit.

Write and Record Checks Simultaneously

You can choose which account to pay from.

Write Checks: IFCU Checking

Delete Find Edit▾ Order Checks Payments Payees   Report▾ Print▾ Options How Do I?

Write checks from: IFCU Checking ▾

Pay to the
Order of Indianapolis Water Company   Date 7/29/2003 $ 22.31

Twenty-Two and 31/100** Dollars

Address 1305 West Main
         Indianapolis, IN 46290

Address...

☐ Online Payment

Quicken bill pay

Memo

Category Utilities:Water   Split   Record Check

When you're ready to record the check, you can press the Record Check button.

Checks to Send

Date	Type	Payee	Category	Amount
7/27/2003				

Ending Balance: 1,519.96   Print

Fill out the check as you normally do with paper checks that you write.

Recording a Check

Start

1 Open the register for the checking or savings account you want to add a transaction to by clicking the checking account link under the Cash Flow Center.

2 In the empty transaction line, type the check date, using the mm/dd/yyyy format.

3 Click the drop-down arrow next to the field in the **Num** column, and then click **Next Check Number**. You can also type a specific check number into the Num field.

4 Click in the **Payee** field and type a payee name.

You can record every check you write as a transaction in your checking account register. Each time you enter a transaction into the register for a checking account, Quicken automatically recalculates the current ending balance for your account, making sure you always have a handle on what your spending limits are. Use the new transaction line to enter your new transaction.

Today's Dateline

If you enter one or more post-dated transactions, a blue high-light line appears above the first postdated transaction. The line sets off the postdated or future transactions from the current transactions.

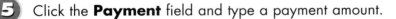

7/25/2003	7809	Marsh		39 72		Deposit		
		Grocer ⬆ Memo			Enter	Edit	Split	
		B...ng	Expense					
		...tertainment	Expense					
		Gifts	Expense					
		Groceries	Expense					
		Hair Cut	Expense					
		Haz. Insurance	Expense					
		Home Equity Loan	Expense					
		Home Repair	Expense					

Split | Transfer | Add Cat

6 **Click** **5**

7/25/2003	7809	Marsh	39 72	Deposit			
		Groceries			Enter	Edit	Split

7 **Click**

IFCU Checking | **Register** | **Overview**

Delete Find Transfer Reconcile Write Checks Update Now   Report ▾ Options ▾ How Do I?

Date	Num ▽	Payee/Category/Memo	Payment	Clr	Deposit	Balance	
7/25/2003	7806	Lowe's	425 31			1,980 20	▲
		Misc New Grill					
7/25/2003	7807	Shell	146 97			1,833 23	
		Auto:Fuel					
7/25/2003	7808	Euro Motorworks	51 53			1,781 70	
		...otive Oil Change					
7/25/2003	7809	Marsh	39 72		**8**	1,741 98	
		Groceries					
7/25/2003	Num	Payee	Payment		Deposit		
		Category Memo		Enter	Edit	Split	▾

Ending Balance: 1,741.98

5 Click the **Payment** field and type a payment amount.

6 Click the **Category** field drop-down arrow and select an expense category or sub-category.

7 Click the **Memo** field and type memo information if desired. Click the **Enter** button.

8 Quicken records the check and adds another empty transaction line to the bottom of the register.

End

Tab It
You can also press the **Tab** key to move from field to field in a transaction.

Name That Payee
Each time you enter a new name in the payee field in the register, the QuickFill feature remembers the transaction information. You can learn more about using QuickFill in Part 4.

Use Those Categories!
Categories are key to tracking where your money goes. Be sure to make full use of Quicken's categories when entering transactions into your account registers (see Part 2, "Setting Up Accounts").

Entering a Deposit

Start

IFCU Checking | Register | Overview

Delete	Find	Transfer	Reconcile	Write Checks	Update Now		Report ▾	Options ▾	How Do I?
Date	Num ▽	Payee/Category/Memo		Payment		Clr	Deposit		Balance	
7/25/2003	7806	Lowe's		425	31				1,980	20 ▲
		Misc	New Grill							
7/25/2003	7807	Shell		146	97				1,833	23
		Auto:Fuel								
7/25/2003	7808	Euro Motorworks		51	53				1,781	70
		Auto:Service Oil Change								
7/25/2003	7809	Marsh		39	72				1,741	98
		Groceries								
7/25/2003	DEP ▲	Payee		Payment			Deposit			

1

Next Check Num
ATM
Deposit
Print Check
Send Online P...
Transfer
EFT

Enter | Edit | Split

Edit List

2

Click

IFCU Checking | Register | Overview

Delete	Find	Transfer	Reconcile	Write Checks	Update Now		Report ▾	Options ▾	How Do I?
Date	Num ▽	Paid By/Category/Memo		Payment		Clr	Deposit		Balance	
7/25/2003	7806	Lowe's		425	31				1,980	20 ▲
		Misc	New Grill							
7/25/2003	7807	Shell		146	97				1,833	23
		Auto:Fuel								
7/25/2003	7808	Euro Motorworks		51	53				1,781	70
		Auto:Service Oil Change								
7/25/2003	7809	Marsh		39	72				1,741	98
		Groceries								
7/25/2003	DEP	Kinkoph Designs		Payment			250.00 ▦			
		Misc	Memo							

...er | Edit | Split

Ending Balance: 1,741.98

3

4

1 In the empty transaction line, type the deposit date using the mm/dd/yyyy format.

2 Click the **Num** field and then click **Deposit** or click **EFT** (if your employer deposits your paycheck electronically rather than giving you a paper check).

3 Click in the **Paid By** field and type the name of the person or company from which you received the funds.

4 Click the **Deposit** field and specify a deposit amount.

The money you deposit into an account can come from your paycheck, interest deposited into your account by the bank, loose cash you deposit via an ATM, gifts you receive from relatives, and so on. Every time you deposit money into your account, be sure to enter a corresponding deposit transaction in the Quicken account.

HINT

No Numbers in the Num Field
When you enter a withdrawal or deposit transaction, make sure you don't type a number into the Num field. Quicken allows this, but doing so creates confusion with the check numbers you enter.

7/25/2003	DEP	Kinkoph Designs	*Payment*	250 00	
		Other Memo		Enter	Edit	Split

Inves Inc	Income			
Old Age Pension	Income			
Other Inc	Income			
Other Inc, Bus	Income			
Royalty	Income			
Salary	Income			
Salary Remodeling				
Salary Spouse	Income			

[Split] [Transfer] [Add Cat]

Click **5**

7/25/2003	DEP	Kinkoph Designs	*Payment*		250 00
		Other Inc *Payment*		Enter	Edit	Split

6

Click **7**

IFCU Checking   Register   Overview

Delete Find Transfer ~~Recond~~   ~~Update Now~~   Options How Do I?

Date	Num	Payee/Category/Memo	Payment	Clr	Deposit	Balance
7/25/2003	DEP	Kinkoph Designs Other Inc Payment for Materials			250 00	2,877 50
7/25/2003	7800	 Insurance	139 27			2,757 23
7/25/2003	7802	Campus Crusade For Christ Charity	10 00			2,747 23
7/25/2003	7803	Cinergy PSI Utilities:Electric	71 09	·		2,676 14
7/25/2003	7804	**VOID**Vectren Energy Delivery Utilities:Gas		c		2,676 14
7/25/2003	7805	Vectren Energy Delivery Utilities:Gas	20 63			2,655 51
7/25/2003	7806	Lowe's Misc New Grill	425 31			2,230 20
7/25/2003	7807	Shell Auto:Fuel	146 97			2,083 23
7/25/2003	7808	Euro Motorworks Auto:Service Oil Change	51 53			2,031 70
		Current Balance:	1,991.98		**Ending Balance:**	1,991.98

8

5 Click the **Category** field and select an income category or subcategory.

6 Click the **Memo** field and type memo information if desired.

7 Click the **Enter** button.

8 Quicken records the transaction. By default, Quicken sorts the transactions based on date entered and then by the Num field, placing this transaction earlier in the register.   **End**

Categorizing Income
Categorizing your income is just as important as categorizing your expenses. For example, if a relative gives you large gifts, you need to track whether the gift amounts total enough to compel you to pay taxes on them.

Paycheck Time
If you categorize a deposit as Salary, a Paycheck Setup dialog box might ask whether you want to use that feature to automate your paycheck entries. For more information on using this feature, see Part 4.

Splitting a Transaction

Start

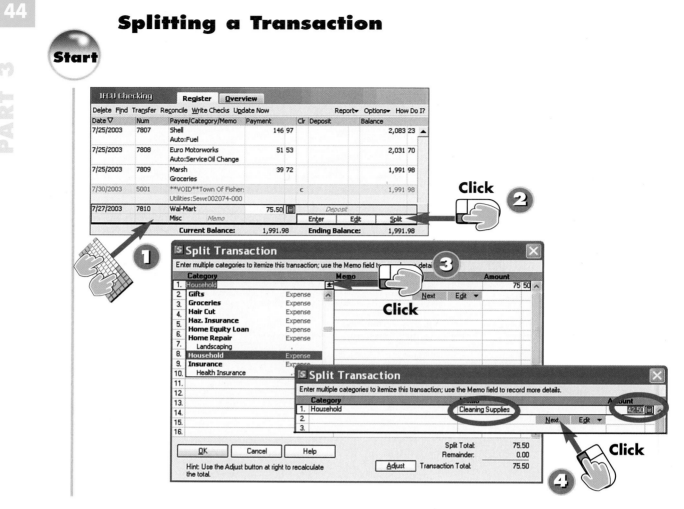

1 Fill in the **Date**, **Num**, **Payee**, and **Payment** or **Deposit** fields for the new transaction you want to split.

2 Click the **Split** button.

3 The Split Transaction window opens. Select a category from the **Category** drop-down list for the first split item.

4 Type **Memo** and **Amount** entries and click **Next**.

Some checking activities require you to write a check that covers several expenses. To handle such situations, Quicken enables you to *split* a transaction. When you split a transaction in a bank account, you apply more than one category or subcategory and specify what portion of the transaction falls into each category or subcategory.

Split Transaction

Enter multiple categories to itemize this transaction; use the Memo field to record more details.

	Category	Memo	Amount
1.	Household	Cleaning Supplies	42 50
2.	Office Expense	Printer Paper and Office Supplies	33 00
3.		Next Edit ▼	
4.			
5.			
6.			
7.			
8.			
9.			
10.			
11.			
12.			
13.			
14.			
15.			
16.			

OK   Cancel   Help

Hint: Use the Adjust button at right to recalculate the total.

Click

⑥ **Click**

⑤

⑦

JF40 Checking   **Register**   **Overview**

Delete Find Transfer Reconcile Write Checks Update Now   Report▼ Options▼ How Do I?

Date ▽	Num	Payee/Category/Memo	Payment	Clr	Deposit	Balance
7/25/2003	7807	Shell	146 97			2,083 23
		Auto:Fuel				
7/25/2003	7808	Euro Motorworks	51 53			2,031 70
		Auto:Service Oil Change				
7/25/2003	7809	Marsh	39 72			1,991 98
		Groceries				
7/30/2003	5001	**VOID**Town Of Fisher:		c		1,991 98
		Utilities:Sewe002074-000				
7/27/2003	7810	Wal-Mart	75 50		Deposit	
		--Split--☑☒			Enter Edit Split	

Current Balance: 1,991.98   Ending Balance: 1,991.98

⑧   **Click**

⑤ Specify the next **Category** and **Memo**. Edit the **Amount** entry or simply continue if the calculated amount is correct.

⑥ Click **Next** and repeat step 5 as many times as necessary to add other categories.

⑦ Click **OK** to finish entering the categories for the split and return to the register.

⑧ Click the **Enter** button to finish recording the entry.

End

TIP

Identifying Split Transactions
When you split a transaction, Quicken enters **Split** as the category for that transaction in the register.

Creating a New Number Field Label

Start

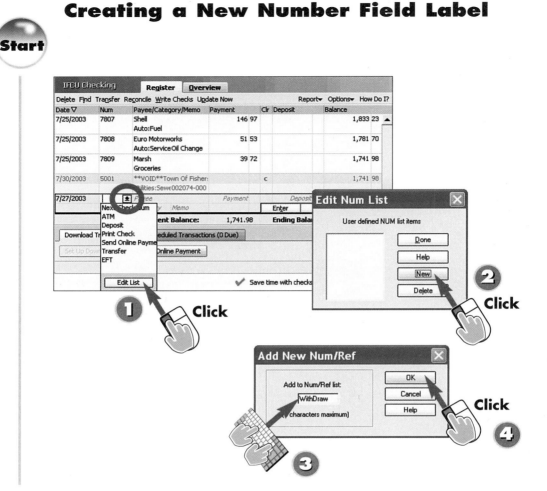

Click

Click

Click

① Click the **Num** field and click the **Edit List** button.

② Quicken opens the Edit Num List dialog box. Click the **New** button.

③ Quicken opens the Add New Num/Ref dialog box. Type up to a 9-character title for the label you want to create.

④ Click **OK**.

When recording your transactions, you can choose from Next Check Num, ATM (automated teller machine), Deposit, Print Check, Send Online Payment, Transfer, and EFT (electronic funds transfer). Some of your transactions, such as withdrawals or debit card purchases, may require a more descriptive field. You can add new fields to the Num list as needed.

Label Ideas
You can add WD for Withdrawal as a label for withdrawals, or Debit as a label for your debit card purchases.

5 The new label appears in the Edit Num List dialog box.

6 Click the **New** button to add another label following step 4, or click **Done** to close the dialog box.

7 The new label is now listed among the Num field choices. Click the **Num** field to view the choices.

End

Remove a Label
To remove a label you no longer want, reopen the Edit Num List dialog box, select the label, and click **Delete**. Click **Done** to close the dialog box again.

Entering a Withdrawal

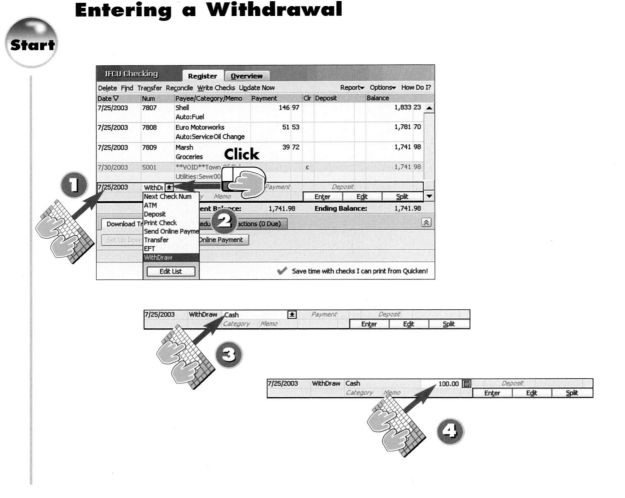

1 In the empty transaction line, type the withdrawal date.

2 Either skip the **Num** field or click the **Num** field and click the name for the withdrawal choice if you created one in the previous task.

3 Click the **Payee** field and type a payee name, such as the cash recipient's name, or something generic, such as **Cash**.

4 Click the **Payment** field and specify a withdrawal amount.

Whenever you walk into a bank and use a withdrawal slip to take money out of a checking, savings, or money market account, you need to enter a corresponding withdrawal transaction in the Quicken account for that real-world account.

Withdrawal Nums
The Num field doesn't include a withdrawal choice. You can add new choices to the list. See the previous task to learn how.

5 **Click**

| 7/25/2003 | WithDraw | Cash | | 100 00 | | *Deposit* | | | |
| | | *Memo* | Enter | E | t | | | | |

		Allowance	Expense	∧
		Auto	Expense	
		Fuel		.
		Insurance		.
		Loan		.
		Service		.
		Bank Charge	Expense	
		Check Printing		. ∨

Split | Transfer | Add Cat

| 7/25/2003 | WithDraw | Cash | | 100 00 | *Deposit* | | | |
| | | Allowance | For trip | | Enter | Edit | Split |

6

Click

7

IFCU Checking   **Register**   **Overview**

Delete Find Transfer Reconcile Write Checks Update Now   Report▾ Options▾ How Do I?

Date	Num	Payee/Category/Memo	Payment		Clr	Deposit		Balance	
7/25/2003	WithDraw	Cash Allowance For Trip	100 00					2,527 50	▲
7/25/2003	7800	State Farm Insurance Insurance	120 27					2,407 23	
7/25/2003	7802	Campus Crusade For Chris Charity	10 00					2,397 23	
7/25/2003	7803	Cinergy PSI Utilities:Elect	71 09					2,326 14	
7/25/2003	7804	**VOID**Vectren Energy Utilities:Gas			c			2,326 14	▼
		Current Balance:	1,641.98			**Ending Balance:**		1,641.98	

Download Transactions | Scheduled Transactions (0 Due)   ≫

Set Up Download | Make an Online Payment

✓ Save time with checks I can print from Quicken!

8

---

5 Click the **Category** field and select an expense category or subcategory.

6 Optionally, click the **Memo** field and type in memo information.

7 Click the **Enter** button.

8 Quicken records the transaction.

End

List of Payees?
If you select the Payee field in any transaction and a list opens, it holds memorized transactions. See Part 4 to learn how to work with memorized transactions. For now, simply type the entry you want.

Withdrawal Category
Quicken provides a category you can use for miscellaneous account withdrawals—the Cash expense category. Otherwise, you should choose the category that best reflects how you spent the money.

Entering an ATM Transaction

Start

IFCU Checking		**Register**	**Overview**				
Delete Find Transfer Reconcile Write Checks Update Now					Report▾	Options▾	How Do I?
Date ▽	Num	Payee/Category/Memo	Payment	Clr	Deposit	Balance	
7/25/2003	7807	Shell	146 97			1,733 23 ▲	
		Auto:Fuel					
7/25/2003	7808	Euro Motorworks	51 53			1,681 70	
		Auto:Service Oil Change					
7/25/2003	7809	Marsh	39 72			1,641 98	
		Groceries					
7/30/2003	5001	**VOID**Town Of Fisher:		c		1,641 98	
		Utilities:Sewe002074-000					
7/27/2003	ATM ▲	Payee	Payment		Deposit		
	Next Check Num	Memo		Enter	Edit	Split	▼
	ATM						
	Deposit	ent Balance:	1,641.98		Ending Balance:	1,641.98	
Download	Print Chec	Transactions (0 Due)				⊼	
	Send Online Payn						
Set Up Dov	Transfer						
	EFT						
	WithDraw						
	Edit List	**Click**	Save time with checks I can print from Quicken! ✓				

IFCU Checking		**Register**	**Overview**				
Delete Find Transfer Reconcile Write Checks Update Now					Report▾	Options▾	How Do I?
Date ▽	Num	Payee/Category/Memo	Payment	Clr	Deposit	Balance	
7/25/2003	7807	Shell	146 97			1,733 23 ▲	
		Auto:Fuel					
7/25/2003	7808	Euro Motorworks	51 53			1,681 70	
		Auto:Service Oil Change					
7/25/2003	7809	Marsh	39 72			1,641 98	
		Groceries					
7/30/2003	5001	**VOID**Town Of Fisher:		c		1,641 98	
		Utilities:Sewe002074-000					
7/27/2003	ATM	Cash	25.00 ▦		Deposit		
		Category Memo		Enter	Edit	Split	▼
		Current	1,641.98		Ending Balance:	1,641.98	

1 Type the ATM transaction date.

2 Click the **Num** field and then click **ATM**.

3 Click the **Payee** field and type a payee name. You can use something generic such as **Cash** or name the deposit source.

4 Click the **Payment** field or **Deposit** field and specify an amount.

Keeping track of all your ATM receipts can require a lot of organizational skills. If you maintain the same discipline you use to record other account transactions to record your ATM transactions, you won't have to worry about the status of your account balance.

TIP

Tossing Your Receipts?
Don't trash your ATM withdrawal receipts. Use those receipts as the basis for ATM transactions you enter into Quicken.

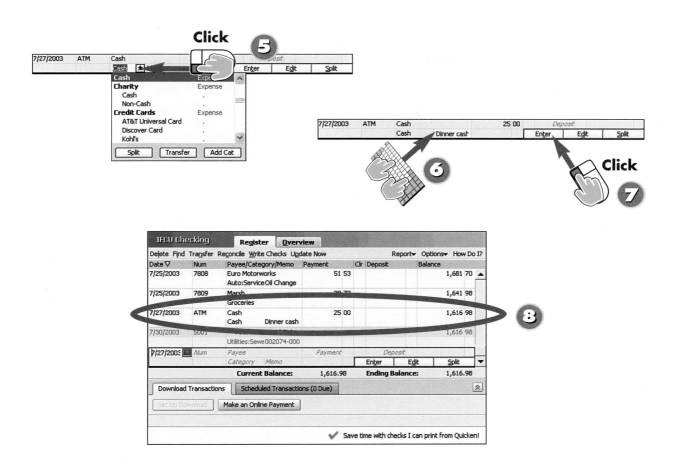

5 Click the **Category** field and select an expense category, such as **Cash**, or a sub-category.

6 Click the **Memo** field and type in any memo information.

7 Click the **Enter** button.

8 Quicken records the transaction.

ATM Fees
Depending on the type of account you have, you might incur a fee each time you use your ATM. This is especially true if you use an ATM at another bank. If you're using your bank's ATM, you might be able to accurately include the ATM fee as part of the ATM transaction; however, to ensure you're entering accurate ATM fees, you should wait until you receive your bank statement and enter a separate transaction for each fee.

Transferring Funds

Start

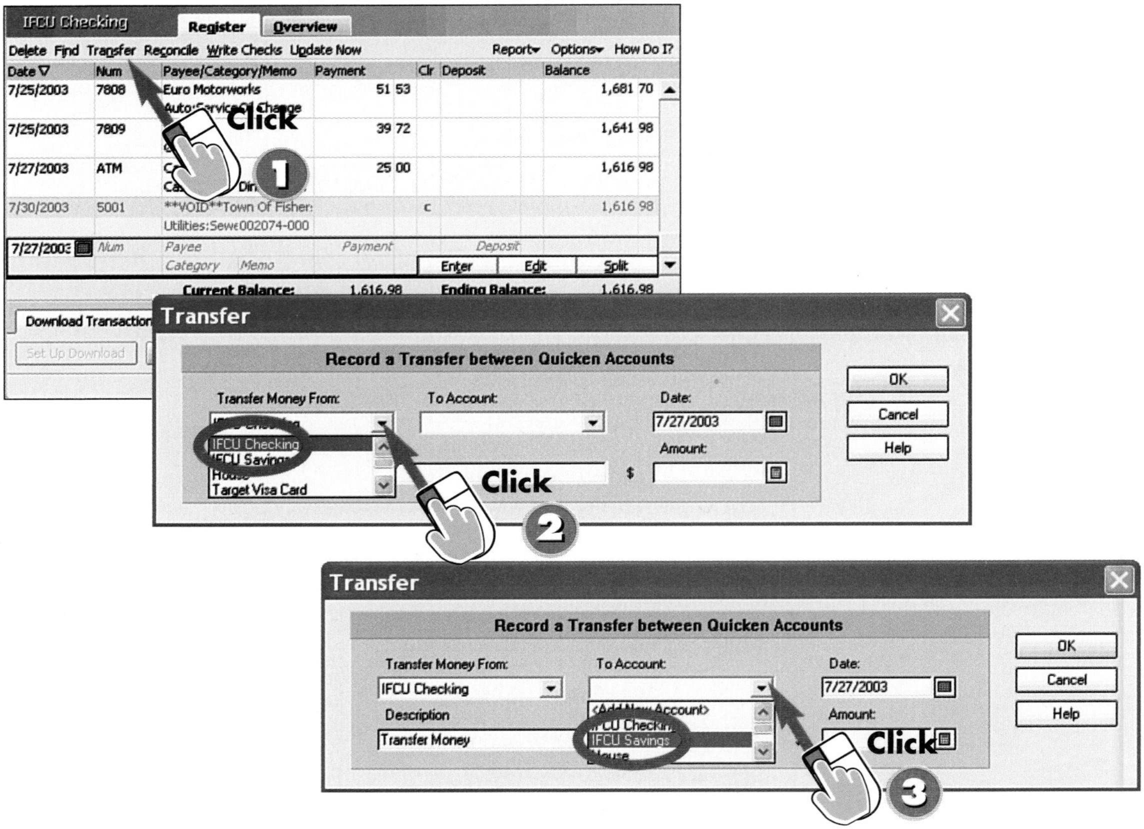

1 Click the **Transfer** button at the top of the register window.

2 Quicken opens the Transfer dialog box. Click the **Transfer Money From** drop-down arrow and select an account.

3 Click the **To Account** drop-down arrow and select an account.

It is quite common to have multiple bank accounts. For example, you might have both a checking and a savings account, or you might have multiple savings accounts—one for yourself and spouse and one for each of your kids. When you move money from one account to another, you can record the transfer in Quicken using the Transfer category.

Transfer Label
To record transfers, fill out the transaction in the register as you normally would, assigning the **Transfer** label in the Num field. Click the **Category** drop-down arrow, scroll to the bottom of the list, and choose a transfer account.

INTRODUCTION

Transfer ✕

Record a Transfer between Quicken Accounts

Transfer Money From:　To Account:
IFCU Checking ▾　IFCU Savings ▾　7/28/2003 ▦

4

Description
Transfer Money　$ 500.00 ▦

OK
Cancel
Help

Click

6

5

IFCU Checking		Register	Overview					
Delete Find Transfer Reconcile Write Checks Update Now						Report▾ Options▾ How Do I?		
Date ▽	Num	Payee/Category/Memo		Payment	Clr	Deposit		Balance
7/25/2003	7803	Cinergy PSI		71 09				2,326 14 ▲
		Utilities:Electric						
7/25/2003	7804	**VOID**Vectren Energy Delivery			c			2,326 14
		Utilities:Gas						
7/25/2003	7805	Vectren Energy Delivery		20 63				2,305 51
		Utilities:Gas						
7/25/2003	7806	Lowe's		425 31				1,880 20
		Misc	New Grill					
7/25/2003	7807	Shell		146 97				1,733 23
		Auto:Fuel						
7/25/2003	7808	Euro Motorworks		51 53				1,681 70
		Auto:Service	Oil Change					
7/25/2003	7809	Marsh		39 72				1,641 98
		Groceries						
7/27/2003	ATM	Cash		25 00				1,616 98
		Cash	Dinner cash					
7/28/2003	TXFR	Transfer Money		500 00				1,116 98
		[IFCU Savings]						
			Current Balance:	1,616.98		Ending Balance:		1,116.98

7

4 Specify a date for the transaction and type a description for the transfer.

5 Type the amount of the transfer into the **Amount** field.

6 Click **OK**.

7 Quicken records the transaction in both the account you are transferring from and the account you are transferring to.

 End

Good Descriptions

You can't assign a category or subcategory to a transfer trans-action, but it's important to use the Description field to describe the reason for the transfer. Such recordkeeping enables you to verify when you've made a needed transfer.

Editing a Transaction

Start

IFCU Checking		Register	Overview					
Delete Find Transfer Reconcile Write Checks Update Now					Report▾ Options▾ How Do I?			
Date ▽	Num	Payee/Category/Memo	Payment		Clr	Deposit	Balance	
7/25/2003	7806	Lowe's	425	31			1,880	20
		Misc New Grill						
7/25/2003	7807	Shell	146	97			1,733	23
		Auto:Fuel						
7/25/2003	7808	Euro Motorworks	51	53			1,681	70
		Auto:Service Oil Change						
7/25/2003	7809	Marsh	39	72			1,641	98
		Groceries						
7/27/2003	ATM	Cash	25.00 🔲			*Deposit*	1,616	98
		Cash Dinner cash			Enter	Edit	Split	
		Current Balance:	1,616.9		**Ending Balance:**		1,116.98	

Click **1**

IFCU Checking		Register	Overview					
Delete Find Transfer Reconcile Write Checks Update Now					Report▾ Options▾ How Do I?			
Date ▽	Num	Payee/Category/Memo	Payment		Clr	Deposit	Balance	
7/25/2003	7806	Lowe's	425	31			1,880	20
		Misc New Grill						
7/25/2003	7807	Shell	146	97			1,733	23
		Auto:Fuel						
7/25/2003	7808	Euro Motorworks	51	53			1,681	70
		Auto:Service Oil Change						
7/25/2003	7809	Marsh	39	72			1,641	98
		Groceries						
7/27/2003	ATM	Cash	45.00 🔲			*Deposit*	1,616	98
		Cash Dinner cash			Enter	Edit	Split	
		Current e:	1,616.98		**Ending lance:**		1,116.98	

2   **Click** **3**

 1 Scroll through the register to find the transaction you want to edit, and click any field in the transaction to select it.

2 Make your changes to the transaction fields, as needed.

3 Click the **Enter** button to finish entering the changes, or press **Esc** to cancel edits.

 End

INTRODUCTION

You can edit a transaction to change the payment or deposit amount, the category, or some other field. For example, if you enter a payment in advance of receiving its bill, you might need to go back and adjust the payment amount before you print the check. Make the change to a transaction right in the register.

TIP

Using the Edit Button
For other types of edits, click the transaction and click the **Edit** button. Select a command from the menu that appears. For example, to delete a transaction, click **Delete Transaction**.

HINT

Watch Out!
Avoid changing a cleared transaction. When you do change a cleared transaction, Quicken asks you to verify the change. See Part 5, "Balancing Accounts," to learn more about reconciling and clearing transactions.

Voiding a Transaction

Start

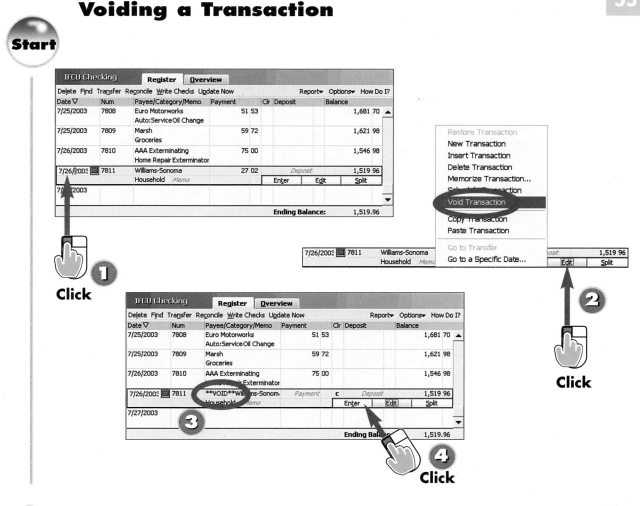

1. Click any field in the transaction to select the transaction.

2. Click the **Edit** button and then click **Void Transaction**.

3. Quicken immediately adds **VOID** in the Payee field.

4. Click the **Enter** button to record the edit.

End

You can void a check and leave the check number recorded, but delete any amounts associated with the transaction. This helps Quicken correctly number later checks and helps you account for the gap between valid check numbers. Quicken inserts **VOID** in the Payee field for a voided check and marks the check as cleared.

Fixing a Printed Check

If you find an error on a check you've printed but not mailed, don't void it. Edit and reprint the check. You can learn more about printing checks later in this section.

Finding a Check or Transaction

Start

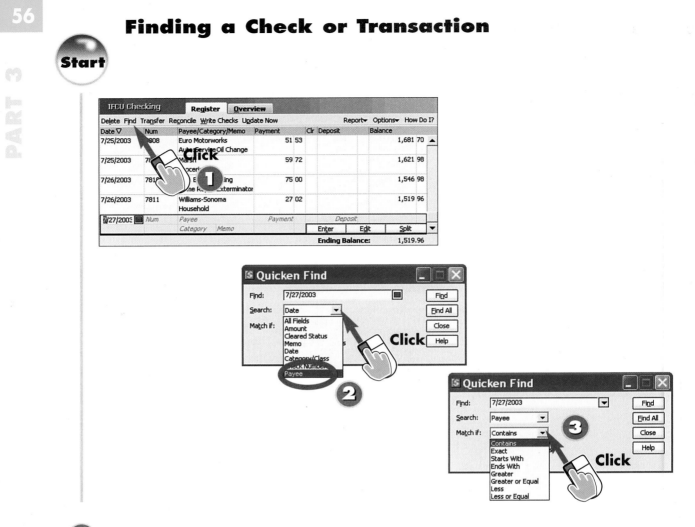

1 Click the **Find** button on the register window's toolbar.

2 The Quicken Find dialog box opens. Click the **Search** drop-down arrow and select the type of information to match.

3 Optionally, select an operator from the **Match If** list to further narrow your search criteria.

When you need to double-check or change the information in a transaction, you can use the Find feature to jump to the transaction you need. When you perform a Find, you enter information that appears in the transaction, such as a specific check number. Quicken takes you to the matching transaction in the register.

Controlling Search Precision
Use the **Match If** choice to specify how narrow or broad the search should be. The **Exactly** choice narrows results the most; found transactions must match exactly when this is selected.

Quicken Find (dialog box)

Find: Lisa Jamison

Search: Payee

Match if: Contains

☑ Search Backwards

Find
Find All
Close
Help

Click

5

IFCU Checking

Register **Overview**

Delete Find Transfer Reconcile Write Checks Update Now   Report▾ Options▾ How Do I?

Date ▽	Num	Payee/Category/Memo	Payment		Clr	Deposit		Balance	
2/14/2003	WithDraw	Allowance Allowance	50 00		R			-517 01	▲
2/15/2003	7441	Town of Fishers Utilities:Sewe	26 00		R			-543 01	
2/17/2003 🔲	7455	Lisa Jamison Charity:Cash Girl Scout Co	15 00		R	Deposit		-558 01	
						Enter	Edit	Split	
2/17/2003	7456	Target Misc							
2/17/2003	7457	Marsh Groceries							

Download Transactions   Sched

Set Up Download   Make an On

🔲 Quicken Find   ✓ Save time wi...s I can print from Quicken!

Quicken Find (dialog box)

Find: Lisa Jamison

Search: Payee

Match if: Contains

☑ Search Backwards

Find
Find All
Close
Help

Click **7**

6 **Click**

---

4 Specify the information to match by typing it into the **Find** text box or by selecting from the text box's list.

5 If you want to search forward through the register, click to remove the check mark from the **Search Backwards** check box.

6 Click **Find** to jump to the first matching record in the register. Repeat to find subsequent matches.

7 Click **Close** to finish the search and work with the found transaction.

End

Finding Multiple Matches
Click **Find All** in the Quicken Find dialog box to display a window listing all matching records in the current account and other accounts in the same Quicken file. To go to a particular transaction in the register, double-click the transaction.

Finding Again
The Quicken Find dialog box remembers your last search settings. If you closed the Quicken Find dialog box, you can click **Find** on the toolbar to redisplay your find choices.

Changing the Register Display

Start

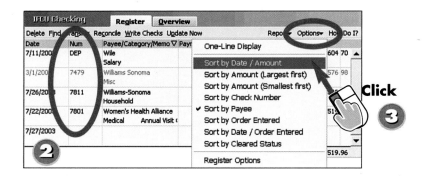

Click 1

Click 3

1 Click the **Options** button on the toolbar and then click a new sort order to use.

2 Quicken applies the new sort to the transactions.

3 To return to the original order, click the **Options** button and click **Sort by Date/Amount**.

By default, the register organizes transactions according to the transaction date. You might want to display the transactions in another order, instead. For example, you might want to sort the transactions by payee, so you can review recent payments to that payee. You can also choose to view transactions on one line instead of two.

Sorting Caution
Some sorting orders cause your balance to calculate incorrectly, so return to the Date/Amount sort order to get an accurate balance calculation.

IFCU Checking | **Register** | **Overview**

Delete Find Transfer Reconcile Write Checks Update Now   Repo ▾ Options▾ Ho Do I?

Date ▽	Num	Payee/Category/Memo	Payr
7/25/2003	7808	Euro Motorworks Auto:Service Oil Change		681 70
7/25/2003	809	Marsh Groceries		
7/26/2003	810	AAA Exterminating Home Repair Exterminator		546 98
7/26/2003	811	Williams-Sonoma Household		519
7/27/2003				

One-Line Display
✔ Sort by Date / Amou
Sort by Amount (Large first)
Sort by Amount (Smalle
Sort by Check Number
Sort by Payee
Sort by Order Entered
Sort by Date / Order Entered
Sort by Cleared Status

Register Options

Click

519.96

④

⑤

IFCU Checking | **Register** | **Overview**

Delete Find Transfer Reconcile Write Checks Update Now   Report▾ Options▾ How Do I?

Date ▽	Num	Payee	Category	Payment	Clr	Deposit	Balance
7/25/2003	7803	Cinergy PSI	Utilities:Elect	71 09			2,326 14
7/25/2003	7804	**VOID**Ve	Utilities:Gas		c		2,326 14
7/25/2003	7805	Vectren Ener	Utilities:Gas	20 63			2,305 51
7/25/2003	7806	Lowe's	Misc	425 31			1,880 20
7/25/2003	7807	Shell	Auto:Fuel	146 97			1,733 23
7/25/2003	7808	Euro Motorw	Auto:Service	51 53			1,681 70
7/25/2003	7809	Marsh	Groceries	59 72			1,621 98
7/26/2003	7810	AAA Extermi	Home Repair	75 00			1,546 98
7/26/2003	7811	Williams-Son	Household	27 02			1,519 96
7/27/2003							

⑥

Ending Balance: 1,519.96

---

④ Quicken sorts the transactions by the date again.

⑤ Click the **Options** button on the toolbar and then click **One-Line Display**.

⑥ Quicken displays the register transactions on a single line instead of the default two.

End

Back to Two Lines
To return to the regular display, click the **Options** button on the toolbar and then click **One-Line Display** again.

As You Like It
You can customize how the register looks and works, including whether Quicken memorizes transaction information you enter. Click the **Options** button and then click **Register Options**.

Creating Checks to Print

Start

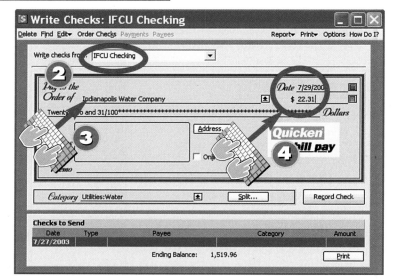

Click

1 Click the **Write Checks** button in any account register window.

2 Quicken opens the Write Checks window. Make sure the correct account is selected in the **Write Checks from** field.

3 Type a date for the check and then click the **Pay to the Order of** field. Type the payee name, or click the drop-down arrow and select a name from the list.

4 Type an amount for the check. Quicken writes the dollar amount out for you.

You can also write and record checks into your account register at the same time. Using the Write Checks window, you can specify which account to use and write your check data just as you do a regular paper check. After writing the checks, you can then instruct Quicken to print the checks.

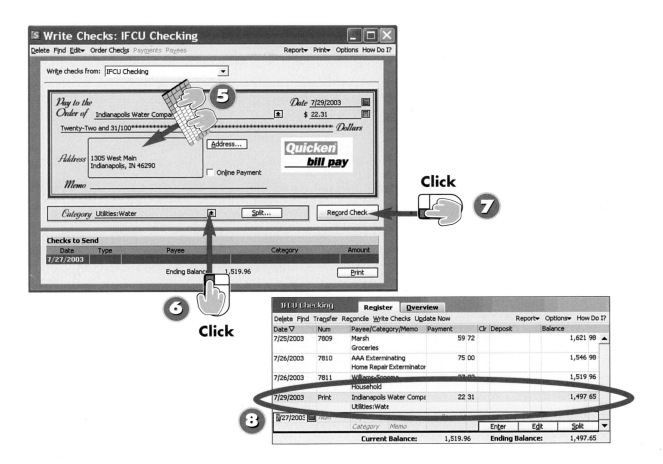

5 If you mail your checks in a window envelope, you can enter the payee's address in the **Address** field.

6 Enter a memo, if needed, and then click the **Category** drop-down arrow and choose a category for the check.

7 Click the **Record Check** button and then click the **Close** button to close the window.

8 Quicken records the check in the account register and identifies it with a Print label in the Num field. The check is also added to the list of checks to print.

End

Made a Mistake?

As long as you haven't printed the check yet, you can press the **PgUp** or **PgDn** key to move back and forth through your check transactions in the Write Checks window and make changes to the entries.

Keep Going

The Write Checks window stays open for as long as you need it. If you want to record several checks, keep entering the check information and then click the **Record Check** button to record each check that you write.

Printing Checks

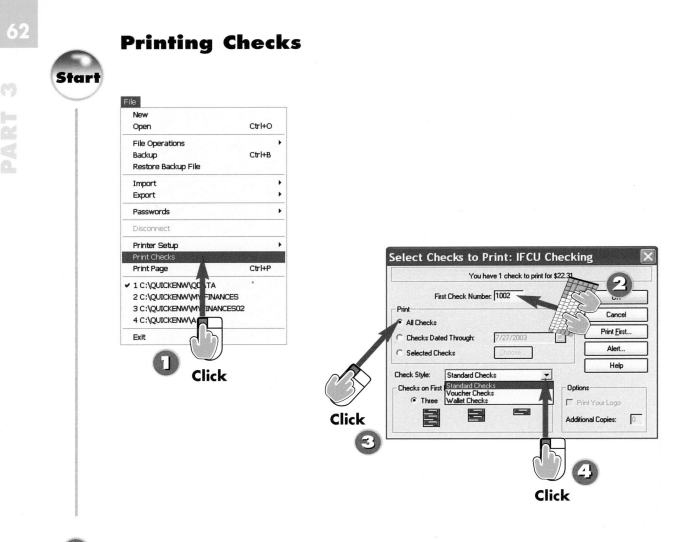

Start

Click

Click

Click

1. Load the check paper into your printer and then click **File**, **Print Checks**.

2. The Select Checks to Print dialog box opens. Type the first check number to be printed.

3. To print all the checks you have written so far, leave the **All Checks** option selected. Choose one of the other print options to specify the checks to be printed.

4. Click the **Check Style** drop-down arrow and select the type of checks you purchased.

Printing checks in Quicken consists of two stages: purchasing paper checks and then setting up your printer for printing them. Visit Quicken's Web site or check the catalog that came with the program to order check paper for your printer. After you've received your checks, you should follow the printer setup process to ensure that your checks print correctly.

Printing Test

To print test checks on blank paper, choose **File**, **Printer Setup**, **For Printing Checks**. Click **Align** and click a check alignment button. Next, click **Print Sample**.

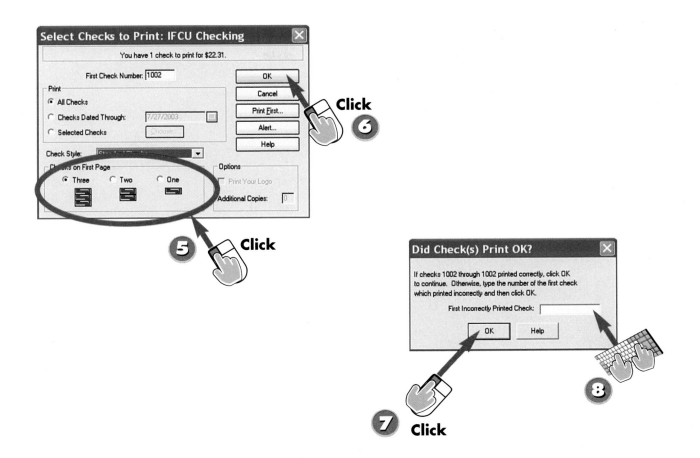

5 If the first page of checks is partial, make a choice in the **Checks on First Page** area.

6 Click **OK** to send the checks to the printer.

7 After the checks print, click **OK** when the Did Check(s) Print OK? message box appears.

8 If you encountered a problem, enter the check number that misprinted and click **OK** to return to the Select Checks to Print dialog box and try again.

End

Reprinting a Check
To later reprint a check, change the check transaction **Num** field entry to **Print Check** and click the transaction **Enter** button. Choose **File, Print Checks**, specify the correct **First Check Number**, and click **OK**.

Use the Write Checks Window
You can also open the Select Checks to Print dialog box from the Write Checks window. Click the **Print** button.

Printing the Account Register

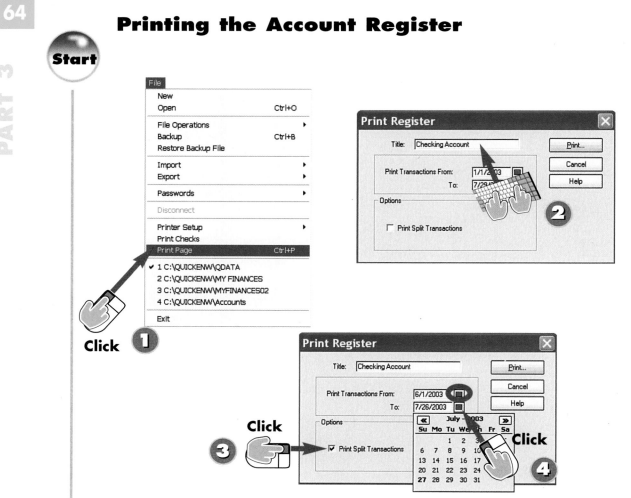

Start

Click **1**

Click **3**

Click **4**

2

 1 Display the register you want to print and then choose **File**, **Print Page**.

 2 The Print Register dialog box opens. In the **Title** text box, type the phrase that you want to display at the top of the printout.

 3 To print only transactions with date entries from a particular period, change the **From** and **To** dates by clicking the **Calendar** icon and selecting a date.

 4 If you want to include all the category information for split transactions, check **Print Split Transactions**.

The register gives you detailed information about each transaction in your account, so you can check the account history anytime you want. For example, if you want to review recent transactions for an account with your spouse or a financial planning professional, you can print the relevant transactions from the register rather than huddling around your computer.

When to Print

You don't have to print your account every week or month to have a safe copy of your data. Instead, back up your Quicken file on disk, as described in Part 13, "Managing Quicken Data Files."

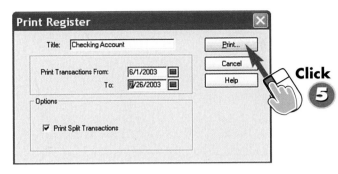

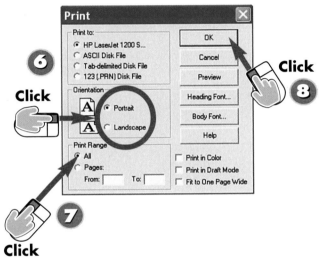

5 Click the **Print** button.

6 The Print dialog box opens. Click the **Portrait** or **Landscape** orientation option button.

7 To print all the pages, leave the All option selected. To print selected pages only, click **Pages** and enter the first and last page in the **From** and **To** boxes.

8 Choose any other print options that apply and click **OK** to print the register.

Is It a Report?
Printing the register is not the same as printing a Quicken report. See the next task to learn how to view a register report.

Control the Printout
You can use the **Heading Font** and **Body Font** buttons to display dialog boxes in which you can change the fonts used for your printout. You can click the **Preview** button to view what your printout looks like before printing.

Creating a Register Report

Start

IFCU Checking	**Register**	**Overview**		

Date ▽	Num	Payee/Category/Memo		Balance
7/25/2003	7808	Euro Motorworks Auto:Service Oil Change		1,681 70
7/25/2003	7809	Marsh Groceries	59 72	1,621 98
7/26/2003	7810	AAA Extermin... Home ...nator	75 00	1,546 98
7/26/2003	7811	Willia... House...	27 02	1,519 96
7/27/2003	Num	Payee Catego...	Payment	Deposit

Report▼ Options▼ How Do I?

Register Report
Expense Summary Graph

Enter   Edit   Split

Ending Balance: 1,519.96

Click ①

Download Transactions | Scheduled
Set Up Download | Make an Online ...

Register Report

Delete Co... Sort▼

Preferences How Do I?

③ Forward Print Date Range: Include all dates ▼   Save Report Customize

Report History:
Register Report - As of

✓ Include all da...
Current Month
Current Quarter
Current Y...
Month to ...
Quarter to date
Year to date
Earliest to date
Last Month
Last Qtr
Last Year
Last 30 Days
Last 12 Months
Custom Date...

eport - As of
...7/27/2003

...ription Memo Category Clr

Date				
BALANCE ...				
1/31/200...		...pening B...	[IFCU ...	R
2/1/2000		Grammy C...	Gift Re...	
3/5/2001		Unknown	Misc	
5/11/200...			Kell... Office ...	
5/31/200...		Greg's Pa... Kell...	Office ...	
4/20/200...		Originally ... Ang...	Office ...	
1/1/2003		Retailers ... Tar...	Credit ...	R
1/1/2003		Menard's	Home ...	R
1/1/2003		Marsh	Groceries	R
1/2/2003		Cinergy PSI	Utilities...	R
1/2/2003		WFNNB Ar... Chair	Misc	R
1/2/2003	IFCU Check... 7372	Jala Wyant Mar...	Misc	R
1/3/2003	IFCU Check... 7367	Vectren E...	Utilities...	R
1/3/2003	IFCU Check... DEP	JDS Pugh'...	Salary ...	R
1/3/2003	IFCU Check... DEP	Pearson Roy...	Royalty	R
1/3/2003	IFCU Check... 7373	Marsh	Groceries	R

② **Click**

Click ④

1. Display the register window you want to create a report for; then click the **Report** button and choose **Register Report**.

2. Quicken opens the Register Report window. Select the date or range for the report.

3. To change the transaction order, you can click the **Sort** button and choose a sort.

4. To customize the report, click the **Customize** button.

INTRODUCTION

Quicken reports are a great way to analyze your register transactions. You can control the range of transaction dates listed in the report, as well as how the transactions are sorted. You can also customize the report to show just the categories you want or view transactions from multiple accounts.

TIP

Print a Report
To print the register report, click the **Print** button to open the Print dialog box, select any additional options, and click **OK** to print.

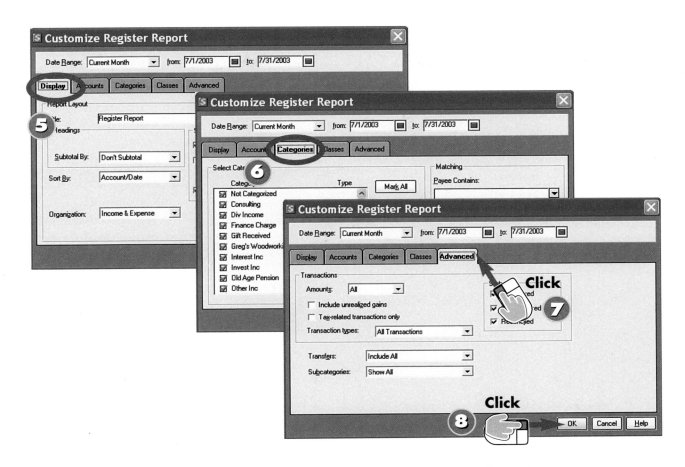

5 The Customize dialog box for the report type opens. Use the **Display** tab options to control how report items appear.

6 Click the **Categories** tab to choose which categories to include in the report.

7 Click the **Advanced** tab to set options for how transactions are used in the report.

8 Click **OK** to view the customized report.

End

Save It
You can save any report's settings you customized to view the report again later. After creating the customized report, click the **Save Report** button. In the Save Report dialog box, type a name for the report, select a center to associate with the report, and click **OK**.

Reopen a Saved Report
To reopen a report you previously saved, open the **Reports & Graphs** window, click the **Saved Reports** tab, and double-click the report you want to view.

Viewing Transactions in the Calendar

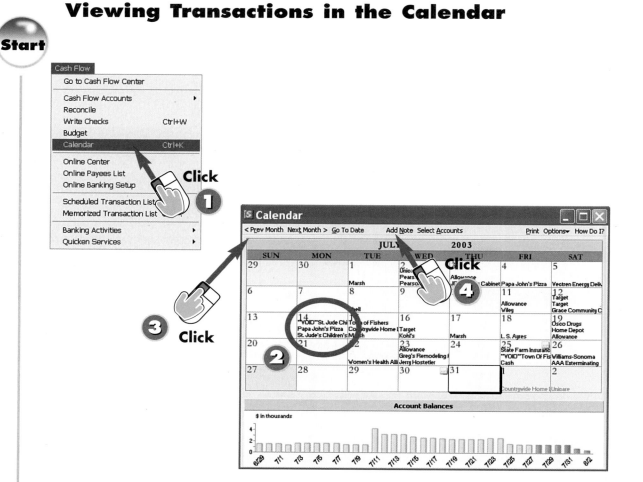

1 Click **Cash Flow**, **Calendar**.

2 Quicken opens the Calendar window. Transactions are displayed on the date in which they were recorded.

3 You can click the **Prev Month** and **Next Month** buttons to scroll back and forth in the Calendar view.

4 To add a note to the calendar, select the date on the calendar and then click the **Add Note** button.

The Quicken Calendar keeps track of all your transactions and lists them in a monthly calendar display. You can use the Calendar window to view transactions, including those you previously recorded as well as future transactions you scheduled. You can even add a reminder note to the Calendar window to remind you about an important transaction or financial matter.

Go To Date

To view a specific date in the Calendar window, click the **Go to Date** button, type the date, and click **OK**.

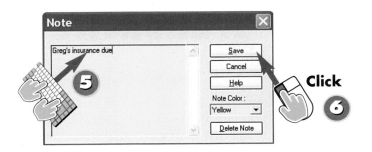

5 Quicken opens the Note dialog box. Enter your note text.

6 Click the **Save** button.

7 To view the note, move the mouse pointer over the Note icon or click the note to open the Note dialog box. Click the **Close** button to close the Calendar.

End

Remove a Note
To delete a note from the Calendar window, select the date containing the note, open the Note dialog box, and click **Delete Note**.

Select Accounts
To control which account transactions appear, click the **Select Accounts** button. In the Calendar Accounts dialog box, specify which accounts to view and click **OK**. The Calendar displays only the selected account's transactions.

Speeding Up Transaction Entries

You might be thinking that using Quicken causes you to swap tedious hours of hand-writing checks for tedious hours of typing transactions at your computer. Not so! This part introduces you to features and tricks you can use to streamline transaction entries in Quicken. After you take a little time to set things up, Quicken rewards you by doing even more of your work.

Quicken includes a variety of features to help you automate the task of entering transactions into your cash flow accounts, such as the checking account register. For example, Quicken is automatically set up to memorize your transactions. This means that Quicken keeps track of your payee names and details about the transactions, including any category you assign to a transaction. When you attempt to type in that same payee name again, Quicken automatically tries to fill in the payee name for you. This feature, called QuickFill, can save you the time of typing in the same name over and over. If the check amount to the payee is the same each time, you can quickly press the Enter key and record the transaction without filling out all the other details again. Quicken "remembers" the details from the previous time you entered the transaction.

Using QuickFill is just one way to speed up your work. This part of the book introduces you to other features, such as scheduled transactions, alerts, and paycheck setup.

The Memorized Transaction List Window

You can use these buttons to make changes to the transactions listed.

A list of memorized transactions appears in alphabetical order.

Description	Amount	Type	Memo	Category	Lock	Show on Calendar
Cash In	50.00	Dep		Other Inc		
Cellular One	-9.40	Pmt		Utilities:Telephone	🔒	
Check	85.69	Dep		Other Inc		
Christy Nasby	-120.00	Pmt	Pescio Project/Finishing & Staining	Office Expense		
Cinergy PSI	-71.09	Pmt		Utilities:Electric		
Countrywide Home Loans	-698.37	Pmt		Mortgage		
Countrywide Home Loans	-698.37	Loan	Mortgage	[House Loan]	🔒	
Countrywide Home Loans	-126.64	Loan		[My Home Equity Loan]	🔒	
Cynthia's Hallmark	-9.38	Pmt		Misc		
Discover Platinum Card	-98.73	Pmt				
Escrow Check	1,722.76	Dep	Escrow Check	Other Inc		
Euro Motorworks	-51.53	Pmt	Oil Change	Auto:Service		
F&L Bath & Interiors	-28.57	Pmt		Misc		
Fishers Do It Center	-60.65	Pmt		Misc		
Gallery 116	-10.60	Pmt	Charms	Misc		
Galyan's	-63.57	Pmt		Misc		
Grace Community Church	-70.00	Pmt	Tithe	Charity		
Greg's Remodeling for Taxes	-375.00	Pmt	Money for Taxes	[IFCU Savings]		
Home Depot	-39.14	Pmt		Home Repair:Landscaping		
Indiana Newspapers, Inc.	-20.00	Pmt	Newspaper Subscription	Subscriptions		
Indianapolis Monthly	-27.00	Pmt		Subscriptions:Magazine		
Indianapolis Water Company	-22.31	Chk		Utilities:Water		
Insight Communications	-49.79	Pmt		Utilities:Cable TV		
JDS Pugh's Cabinets	394.34	Dep		Salary Spouse		
Jeremy Hamilton	-300.00	Pmt	Pescio Project/Side Contractor/Ins...	Office Expense		
Kinkoph Designs	250.00	Dep	Payment for Materials	Other Inc		
Kohl's	-179.42	Pmt		Credit Cards:Kohl's		
Kroger	-42.81	Pmt		Groceries		

You can lock transactions to prevent any changes to the transaction details.

Using Pop-Up Calendars

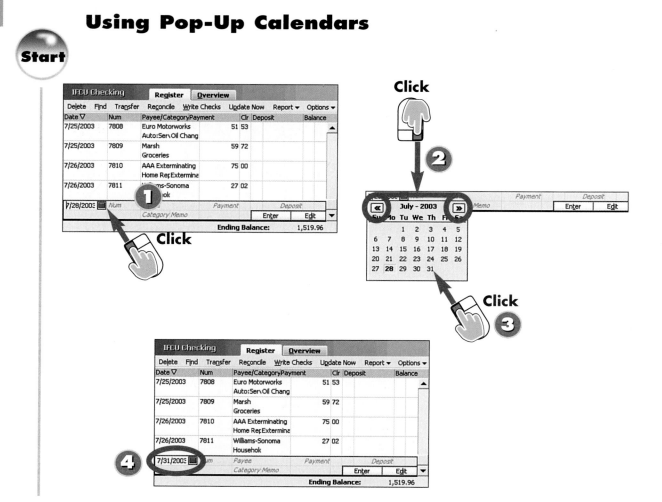

 1 Anytime that you encounter a date field in Quicken, a Calendar icon appears next to the field. Click the **Calendar** icon to activate the feature.

2 You can click the scroll arrow buttons to move back and forth a month at a time in the monthly display.

3 To select a date, click the date.

4 Quicken immediately inserts the full date into the field.

View a Full Calendar
You can view a full calendar of transactions and scheduled transactions. Click **Tools**, **Calendar** to view the feature. The Calendar window differs from the pop-up calendars you use to assign dates.

Using Pop-Up Calculators

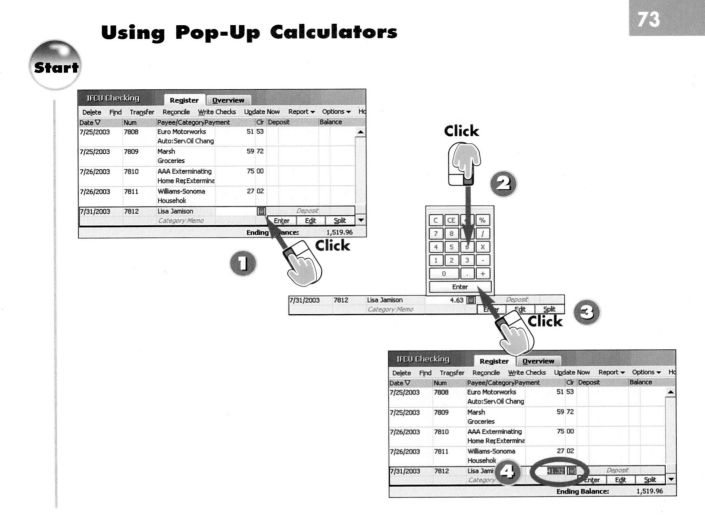

Start

Click

Click

Click

1. Anytime that you encounter an amount field in Quicken, a Calculator icon appears next to the field. Click the **Calculator** icon to activate the feature.

2. Click the numbers you want to add, subtract, multiply, or divide, along with the appropriate operator.

3. Click the **Enter** button to calculate the results.

4. Quicken immediately inserts the results into the field.

End

INTRODUCTION

Another useful tool you can use to speed up your work in Quicken is the pop-up calculator. Calculator icons are located near any field in which an amount is required. When you activate the Calculator icon, Quicken displays a minicalculator you can use to quickly add, subtract, multiply, or divide.

TIP

Larger Please
Click **Tools, Calculator** to open a larger version of Quicken's Calculator, which includes a few more features. To move any results you calculate with the larger calculator, click in the field where you want them to appear and then click the **Paste** button on the Calculator. Click the **Close** button to close the feature.

Using QuickFill with New Transactions

Start

| IFCU Checking | Register | Overview |
| Delete | Find | Transfer | Reconcile | Write Checks | Update Now | Report ▾ | Options ▾ | How Do |

Date ▽	Num	Payee/Category Payment		Clr Deposit	Balance
7/25/2003	7808	Euro Motorworks Auto:Ser\Oil Chang	51 53		1,68 ▲
7/25/2003	7809	Marsh Groceries	59 72		1,62
7/26/2003	7810	AAA Exterminating Home Rep Extermina	75 00		1,54(
7/26/2003	7811	Williams-Sonor Househol	27 02		1,51'
7/31/2003	7812		Payment	Deposit	
		Categ Memo	Enter	Edit	Split ▾

Ending Balance: 1,519.96

| IFCU Checking | Register | Overview |
| Delete | Find | Transfer | Reconcile | Write Checks | Update Now | Report ▾ | Options ▾ | How Do I? |

Date ▽	Num	Payee/Category/Memo	Payment	Clr Deposit	Balance
7/25/2003	7808	Euro Motorworks Auto:Service Oil Change	51 53		1,681 70 ▲
7/25/2003	7809	Marsh Groceries	59 72		1,621 98
7/26/2003	7810	AAA Exterminating Home Repair Exterminator	75 00		1,546 98
7/26/2003	7811	Willia... Gallery 116	-10.60 Misc	Charms	1,51..96
7/31/2003	7812		Payment		
		Category Memo	Enter	Edit	Split ▾

Ending Balance: 1,519.96

1. Fill in the date and check number for the transaction.

2. Click in the **Payee** field and start typing the payee name.

3. If Quicken recognizes the payee as a memorized transaction, it automatically displays the payee name for you.

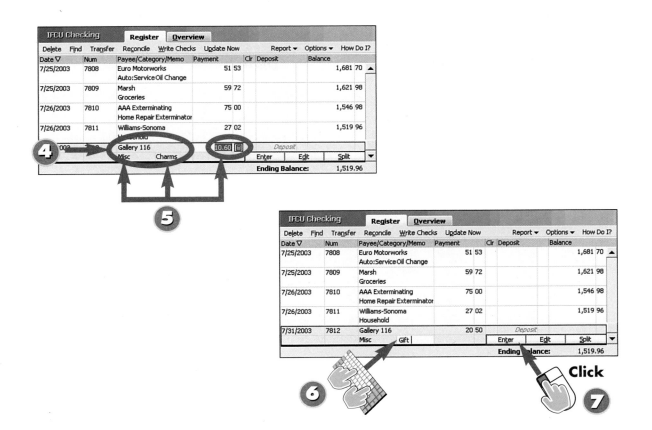

4 Press the **Tab** key to accept the memorized payee name and Quicken adds it to the field.

5 The QuickFill feature also fills in the remaining transaction fields based on the previous details of the same transaction.

6 You can edit the fields, as needed, by typing directly into each field.

7 Click **Enter** to record the new transaction.

End

Turn It Off

If you write checks to the same payees over and over, you may prefer to turn the QuickFill feature off. Click **Edit**, **Preferences**, **Quicken Program**, select the **QuickFill** preference type and deselect the options you want to turn off.

Look Carefully!

If the QuickFill transaction corresponds with a monthly bill, be sure to check the amount due against your new billing statement. The amount might vary by a few cents, or the payee might have made an increase or added a fee.

Viewing Memorized Transactions

Start

Cash Flow

Cash Flow Center	
Cash Flow Accounts	▶
Reconcile	
Write Checks	Ctrl+W
Budget	
Calendar	Ctrl+K
Online Center	
Online Payees List	
Online Banking Setup	
Scheduled Transaction List	Ctrl+J
Memorized Transaction List	Ctrl+T
Banking Activities	
Quicken Services	

1 Click

Click

Click

Memorized Transaction List

New Edit Delete   Use   Report Options▾ Print How Do I?

Description	Amount	Type	Memo		Show on Calendar
			✔ Sort by Description		
			Sort by Amount		
			Sort by Type		
			Sort by Memo		
			Sort by Category		
			View Locked Items Only		
AAA Exterminating	-75.00	Pmt	Exterminator		
Allisonville Nursery	-89.52	Pmt	Sod		
Allowance	-100.00	Pmt			
AT&T	-32.03	Pmt			
AT&T	-29.95	Pmt	Long distance plan		
AT&T	-28.51	Pmt			
AT&T Universal Card	-18.46	Pmt	previously Universal ...	Misc	
AT&T Wireless	-25.23	Chk	Cell Phone	Utilities:Telephone	
BCRS	-10.00	Pmt	Pescio Project	Office Expense	
Bill Bratton	-70.00	Pmt	Pescio Project/Delivery	Office Expense	
Borders Books	-65.69	Pmt		Office Expense	
Brighton Collectibles	3.18	Dep	Return	Gifts	
Build-A-Bear	-29.68	Pmt	Gifts	Misc	
Bureau Of Motor Vehicles	-133.50	Pmt	Plate renewals	Auto	
Cabinet Hardware Designs	-60.67	Pmt	Pescio Project/Hardw...	Office Expense	
Campus Crusade For Christ	-10.00	Pmt		Charity	
Cash	-25.00	Pmt	Dinner cash	Cash	
Cash In	50.00	Dep		Other Inc	
Cellular One	-9.40	Pmt		Utilities:Telephone 🔒	
Check	85.69	Dep		Other Inc	

2 **3** Click

1 Click **Cash Flow**, **Memorized Transaction List**.

2 Quicken opens the Memorized Transaction List window, showing transactions sorted by description. To sort another way, click **Options** and choose a new sort order.

3 Click the **Close** button to close the list window.

End

Quicken memorizes a payee and the accompanying transaction information and places that information on your Memorized Transaction List. You can open the Memorized Transaction List to view and make changes to it. After you've opened the transaction list, you can sort it to list the transactions in a different order so that the one you enter most often will be the one Quicken uses to fill in your transaction data.

TIP

Using a Transaction
Click a transaction in the Memorized Transaction List and then click the **Use** button on the toolbar to insert a copy of that transaction in the currently open account register. You can also double-click the transaction to use it.

Editing the Memorized Transaction List

Start

Click

Description	Amount	Type	Memo	Category	Lock	Show on Calendar
Spencer's You Pick	-8.97	Pmt	Strawberries	Misc		
St. Jude Childrens Resear...	-5.00	Pmt		Charity		
Staple	-18.44	Pmt	Office supplies	Office Expense		
State Farm Insurance	-120.27	Pmt		Insurance		
Super...ibuting	-175.39	Pmt	Pescio Project	Office Expense		
Talb	-14.84	Pmt		Misc		
Ta	-65.69	Pmt		Misc		
Ta	-68.49	Pmt		Household		
TJ Maxx	-37.08	Pmt		Household		
Tow... Fishers	-26.00	Onln	002074-000	Utilities:Sewer		
Tracy Fox	45.00	Dep	Check for Beth Moore...	Other Inc		
Trade Secret	-59.10	Pmt	Hair care products	Misc		
Trader Joe's	-35.59	Pmt		Groceries		
Transfer Money	-500.00	Pmt		[IFCU Savings]		
Twigs Too	-10.60	Pmt		Misc		
U.S. Postmaster	-28.50	Pmt				
Unic	-226.00	Pmt				
VCA Animal Hospital	-59.94	Pmt	Ralph's Vet Bill: rabies...	Misc		
Vectren Energy Delivery	-20.63	Pmt		Utilities:Gas		
VOID	0.00	Dep		Misc		

S Memorized Tran...List — New Edit Delete — Report Options▾ Print How Do I?

Click

Click

Edit Memorized Transaction

Type of Transaction:
Payment

Twigs Two   Address...   Amount: 10.60

Misc   Split...

Memo:

☐ Cleared

OK   Cancel   Help

Click

1. Open the Memorized Transaction List and select the transition you want to edit.

2. To delete a transaction you no longer need, click **Delete** on the toolbar.

3. To change transaction details, click **Edit** on the toolbar.

4. Make any changes you want to the transaction information and click **OK**.

End

INTRODUCTION
You can edit a transaction in the Memorized Transaction List. The next time you use QuickFill to use a copy of the memorized transaction, the transaction displays the edited information. You should periodically delete old transactions.

TIP
Use Caution
You cannot undo your changes to a memorized transaction or recall a memorized transaction if you delete it, so be sure you're making the change you want before you begin.

HINT
List Only
Edits to the memorized transactions affect only the new transactions you enter into the register. Existing transactions are not affected by changes you make to the Memorized Transactions List.

Adding a New Memorized Transaction

Start

Memorized Transaction List

New Edit Delete   Use   Report Options▾ Print How Do I?

Description	Amount	Type	Memo	Category	Lock	Show on Calendar
RA Exterminating	-75.00	Pmt	Exterminator	Home Repair		
lisonville Nursery	-89.52	Pmt	Sod	Misc		
lowance	-100.00	Pmt		Allowance		
T&T	-32.03	Pmt		Utilities:Cell Phone		
	-29.95	Pmt	Long distance plan	Utilities:Telephone		
	-28.51	Pmt		Utilities:Telephone		
niversal Card	-18.46	Pmt	previously Universal ...	Misc		
irel	-25.23	Chk	Cell Phone	Utilities:Telephone		
	-10.00	Pmt	Pescio Project	Office Expense		
Bill Bratton	-70.00	Pmt	Pescio Project/Delivery	Office Expense		
Borders Books	-65.69	Pmt		Office Expense		
Brighton Collectibles	3.18	Dep	Return	Gifts		
Build-A-Bear	-29.68	Pmt	Gifts	Misc		
Bureau Of Motor Vehicles	-133.50	Pmt				
Cabinet Hardware Designs	-60.67	Pmt				
Campus Crusade For Christ	-10.00	Pmt				
Cash	-25.00	Pmt				
Cash In	50.00	Dep				
Cellular One		Pmt				
Check		ep				

Click

2

3

Create Memorized Transaction

Type of Transaction:
Payment

Payee:
Regency Insurance   Address...   Amount: 175.25

Category:
Insurance   Split...

Memo:

☐ Cleared

OK
Cancel
Help

4

Memorized Transaction List

New Edit Delete   Use   Report Options▾ Print How Do I?

Description	Amount	Type	Memo	Category		Show on Calendar
egency Insurance	-175.25	Pmt		Insurance	🔒	
Republic Waste	49.95	Pmt		Trash Removal		
Retailers National Bank	-372.04	Pmt		[Target Visa Card]		
Rockler	-79.48	Pmt	Pescio Project	Office Expense		
Sam's Club	-25.00	Pmt		Misc		
Sarah Mitchell	-8.32	Pmt	Tastefully Simple order	Misc		
SBC	-27.04	Pmt	Telephone Bill	Utilities:Telephone		

1 Open the Memorized Transaction List window. You can press **Ctrl+T** on the keyboard or click **Cash Flow**, **Memorized Transaction List**.

2 Click the **New** button.

3 Fill in the information for each field and click **OK**.

4 Quicken adds the new transaction to the list and locks the information from any changes.

End

INTRODUCTION

You can add new memorized transactions to the Memorized Transaction List window to use later. For example, you might want to create a memorized transaction for a new insurance agency you will start paying soon. After creating the memorized transaction, you can use it the next time you enter checks into your register.

Locking and Unlocking Memorized Transactions

Start

Click

Memorized Transaction List

New Edit Delete | Use | Report Options▾ Print How Do I?

Description	Amount	Type	Memo	Category	Lock	Show on Calendar
Regency Insurance	-175.25	Pmt		Insurance	🔒	🖥
Republic Waste Services ...	-40.95	Pmt		Trash Removal	🔒	🖥
Retailers National Bank	-372.04	Pmt		[Target Visa Card]		🖥
Rockler	-79.48	Pmt	Pescio Project	Office Expense		🖥
Sam's Club	-25.00	Pmt		Misc		🖥
Sarah Mitchell	-8.32	Pmt	Tastefully Simple order	Misc		🖥
SBC	-27.04	Pmt	Telephone Bill	Utilities:Telephone		🖥
Sparkling Earth Products	-12.05	Pmt		Gifts		🖥
Spencer's You Pick	-8.97	Pmt	Strawberries	Misc		🖥
St. Jude Childrens Resear...	-5.00	Pmt		Charity		🖥
Staples	-18.44	Pmt	Office supplies	Office		
State Farm Insurance	-120.27	Pmt		Insura		
Superior Distributing	-175.39	Pmt	Pescio Project	Office		
Talbots	-14.84	Pmt		Misc		
Tan For Less	-65.69	Pmt		Misc		
Target	-68.49	Pmt		House		
TJ Maxx	-37.08	Pmt		House		
Town Of Fishers	-26.00	Onln	002074-000	Utilitie		
Tracy Cox	45.00	Dep	Check for Beth Moore...	Other		
Trade Secret	-59.10	Pmt	Hair care products	Misc		

Memorized Transaction List

New Edit Delete | Use | Report Options▾ Print How Do I?

Description	Amount	Type	Memo	Category	Lock	Show on Calendar
Regency Insurance	-175.25	Pmt		Insurance		🖥
Republic Waste Servic...	-40.95	Pmt		Trash Removal		🖥
Retailers National Bank	-372.04	Pmt		[Target Visa Card]		🖥
Rockler	-79.48	Pmt	Pescio Project	Office Expense		🖥
Sam's Club	-25.00	Pmt		Misc		🖥
Sarah Mitchell	-8.32	Pmt	Tastefully Simple order	Misc		🖥
SBC	-27.04	Pmt	Telephone Bill	Utilities:Telephone	🔒	🖥
Sparkling Earth Products	-12.05	Pmt		Gifts		🖥
Spencer's You Pick	-8.97	Pmt	Strawberries	Misc		🖥
St. Jude Childrens Resear...	-5.00	Pmt		Charity		🖥
Staples	-18.44	Pmt	Office supplies	Office Expense		🖥
State Farm Insurance	-120.27	Pmt		Insurance		🖥
Superior Distributing	-175.39	Pmt	Pescio Project	Office Expense		🖥
Talbots	-14.84	Pmt		Misc		🖥
Tan For Less	-65.69	Pmt		Misc		🖥
Target	-68.49	Pmt		Household		🖥
TJ Maxx	-37.08	Pmt		Household		🖥
Town Of Fishers	-26.00	Onln	002074-000	Utilities:Sewer		🖥
Tracy Cox	45.00	Dep	Check for Beth Moore...	Other Inc		🖥
Trade Secret	-59.10	Pmt	Hair care products	Misc		🖥

① Open the Memorized Transaction List window. You can press **Ctrl+T** on the keyboard or click **Cash Flow**, **Memorized Transaction List**.

② Select the transaction you want to lock, and then click the **Lock** column for the transaction row.

③ Quicken adds a lock icon to the transaction.

④ To unlock a transaction, click the **Lock** icon in the Lock column for the transaction row.

End

INTRODUCTION

If you use QuickFill but make a slight change to the transaction, such as changing the payment amount, Quicken also makes that change to the memorized transaction. To prevent any changes to a memorized transaction, you can lock the transaction in the Memorized Transaction List. Later you can unlock the transaction if you do need to change it.

List Shortcut
You can press **Ctrl+T** on the keyboard to quickly open the Memorized Transaction List window.

Scheduling a Transaction

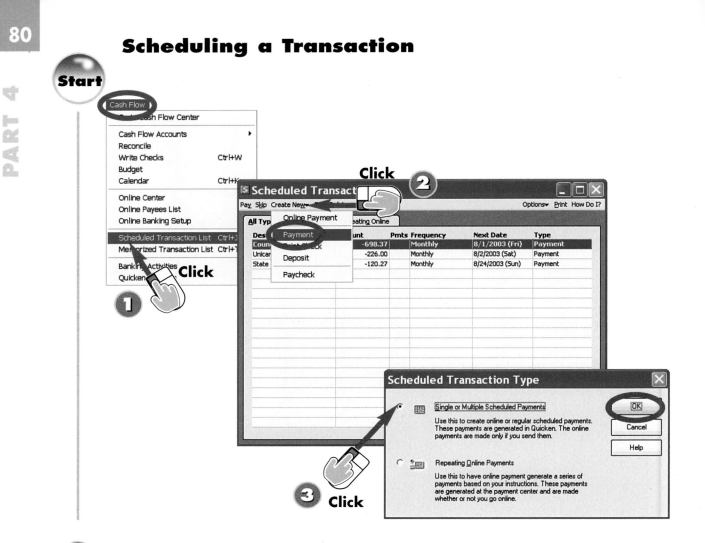

1. Choose **Cash Flow**, **Scheduled Transaction List**.

2. Quicken opens the Scheduled Transaction List window. Click the **Create New** button and select the type of transaction you want to schedule.

3. The Scheduled Transaction Type dialog box opens. Select a payment type and click **OK**.

INTRODUCTION

You use the Scheduled Transaction List to create and manage scheduled transactions. You can create a scheduled transaction for a bill, such as your mortgage, or a deposit, such as your pay deposit. Quicken reminds you of each scheduled transaction and can even enter the transaction for you, if you tell it to.

HINT

Scheduled Transaction Tab
You can also click the **Scheduled Transaction** tab at the bottom of the register and click the **Add a Transaction** button to start a new transaction.

Create Scheduled Transaction

Type of Transaction:
Payment

Account to use:
IFCU Checking
- IFCU Checking
- IFCU Savings
- House
- Target Visa Card
- House Loan
- My Home Equity Loan

Payee:

Category:

Memo:

Amount
- ● Always $
- ○ Estimate from last 2 payment(s).
- ○ Use full credit card balance.

Schedule
- ○ Once on 7/28/2003
- ● Repeat Monthly From 7/28/2003
  - ● Indefinitely
  - ○ 999 time(s).

Action
- ● Prompt me to enter in register 3 day(s) before due date.
- ○ Enter in register without prompting 3 day(s) before due date.

☑ Show as a bill.

OK   Cancel   Help

Click 4

Create Scheduled Transaction

Type of Transaction:
Payment

Account to use:
IFCU Checking

Payee:
Indiana Newspapers, Inc.   Address...

Category:
	9.14	Home Repair...
Indiana Newsp...	-20.00	Subscriptions
Indianapolis M...	-27.00	Subscriptions...
Indianapolis W...	-22.31	Utilities:Water
Insight Commu...	-49.79	Utilities:Cable...
JDS Pugh's Ca...	394.34	Salary Spouse
Jeremy Hamilton	-300.00	Office Expense
Kinkoph Designs	250.00	Other Inc

Memo:

Amount
- ● Always $
- ○ Estimate from last payment(s).
- ○ Use full credit card balance.

Schedule
- Repeat Monthly From 7/28/2003
  - ● Indefinitely
  - ○ 999 time(s).

Action
- ● Prompt me to enter in register 3 day(s) before due date.
- ○ Enter in register without prompting 3 day(s) before due date.

☑ Show as a bill.

Group

OK   Cancel   Help

Click 5

4 The Create Scheduled Transaction dialog box opens. Click the **Account to Use** drop-down arrow and specify which account to associate the transaction to.

5 Enter a payee for the transaction. You can click the **Payee** drop-down arrow and select from your list of memorized transactions.

See next page

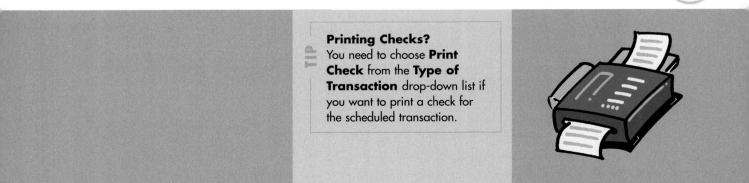

Printing Checks?
You need to choose **Print Check** from the **Type of Transaction** drop-down list if you want to print a check for the scheduled transaction.

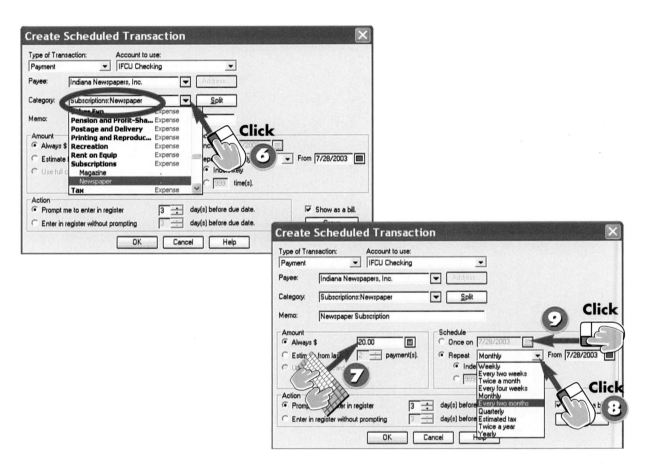

 Click the **Category** drop-down arrow, assign a category to the transaction, and then enter any memo text you want to include.

 Enter an amount for the payment.

8 Specify a schedule for the payment. For repeat payments, select the **Repeat** option and specify how often.

9 For single payments, click the **Once On** option and specify a date.

INTRODUCTION

After you create a scheduled transaction, Quicken lists it when it is due in both the Quicken Home page and in the Cash Flow Center window.

TIP

Allow Enough Time
For payments scheduled on the actual bill due date, increase the **Record This Many Days in Advance** setting to at least seven. Now you can print and mail the check a week before, avoiding a late payment.

Create Scheduled Transaction

Type of Transaction: Payment

Account to use: IFCU Checking

Click

Payee: Indiana Newspapers, Inc.   Address...

Category: Subscriptions:Newspaper   Split

Newspaper Subscription

Amount
- Always $ 20.00
- Estimate from last 2 payment(s).
- Use credit card balance.

10

Schedule
- Once on 7/28/2003
- Repeat Every two months From 7/28/2003
  - Indefinitely
  - 999 time(s).

Action
- Prompt me to enter in register 3 day(s) before due date.
- Enter in register without prompting 3 day(s) before due date.

OK   Cancel

Click 12

11

Click

Click

13

Scheduled Transaction List

Pay Skip Create New▾ Edit Delete   Options▾ Print How Do I?

All Types Scheduled Repeating Online

Description	Amount	Pmts	Frequency	Next Date	Type
Indiana Newspapers, I...	-20.00		Every two months	7/28/2003 (Mon)	Payment
Nationwide Home Loan	-698.37		Monthly	8/1/2003 (Fri)	Payment
Unicare	-226.00		Monthly	8/2/2003 (Sat)	Payment
State Farm Insurance	-120.27		Monthly	8/24/2003 (Sun)	Payment

10 If you want Quicken to prompt you to record the transaction, select this option and specify how far in advance you want to be reminded.

11 If you want Quicken to record the transaction for you, select this option and specify how far in advance to record the transaction.

12 Click **OK**.

13 Quicken adds the transaction to the list. Click the **Close** button to exit the window. Quicken lists any scheduled transactions on the Quicken Home page window.

End

Scheduled Deposits
If you receive a paycheck every two weeks, make sure you choose **Two Weeks** from the **Repeat** drop-down list.

Don't Forget to Write the Check!
Quicken can help you remember to enter a scheduled transaction, but it doesn't remind you to print the checks for these transactions. This burden falls on your shoulders.

Viewing the Scheduled Transaction List

Start

[Screenshot: Quicken 2004 Premier - QDATA - [Cash Flow Center]]

Click

4

2

Scheduled Transaction List

3

Click

1

Click

1 Click the **Cash Flow Center** link and scroll to the bottom of the page to view scheduled transactions; then click the **Show Full List** button.

2 Quicken opens the Scheduled Transaction List window. Each transaction is listed along with the amounts, scheduled frequency, and date.

3 To make any changes to a scheduled transaction, select it and click the **Edit** button.

4 Click the **Close** button to close the window.

End

After you set up one or more scheduled transactions, you can use the Scheduled Transaction List window to view all your scheduled transactions. The Scheduled Transaction List window includes options for editing your scheduled transactions.

TIP

Another Way to the Window
If the Cash Flow Center is displayed, you can click the **Show Full** List button that appears under the Bills and Scheduled Transactions heading to open the Scheduled Transactions List window.

Applying a Scheduled Transaction

Start

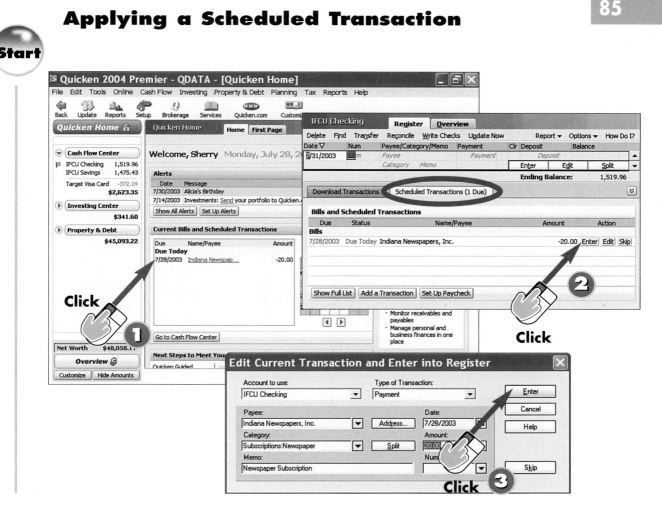

Click 1

Click 2

Click 3

1. When you start Quicken, scroll down to check for due transactions on the Quicken Home page, and then click the scheduled transaction you want to record.

2. Quicken opens the associated account register. Click the **Scheduled Transactions** tab, and then click the **Enter** button.

3. The Edit Current Transaction and Enter into Register dialog box appears. Click **Enter** and the transaction is recorded.

End

INTRODUCTION

When you open Quicken, upcoming scheduled transactions are listed on the Quicken Home page as well as in the Cash Flow Center window. You should get in the habit of checking this list to make sure you enter any scheduled transaction. You can use the Scheduled Transaction List to select and enter the next instance of the scheduled transaction into the register.

TIP

Entered Automatically
You should especially check the home page for scheduled transactions Quicken enters automatically, to be sure you remember to print checks for these transactions.

Editing a Scheduled Transaction

Start

Scheduled Transaction List

Pay Skip Create New▾ Edit Delete   Options▾ Print How Do I?

| All Types | Scheduled | Repeating Online |

Description	A...	Pmts Frequency	Next Date	Type
Indiana Newspapers, I...	.00	Every two months	7/28/2003 (Mon)	Payment
Countrywide Home Loans	37	Monthly	8/1/2003 (Fri)	Payment
Unicare	0	Monthly	8/2/2003 (Sat)	Payment
State Farm Insurance	20.27	Monthly		Payment

Click 1

Scheduled Transaction List

Pay Skip Create New▾ Edit Delete   Options▾ Print How Do I?

| All Types | Scheduled | Repeating Online |

Description	Amount	Pmts Frequency	Next Date	Type
Indiana Newspapers, I...		Every two months	7/28/2003 (Mon)	Payment
		Monthly	8/1/2003 (Fri)	Payment
Unicare		Monthly	8/2/2003 (Sat)	Payment
State Farm Insurance		Monthly	8/24/2003 (Sun)	Payment

Click 3

Edit All Future Transactions

Type of Transaction: Account to use:
Payment   ▼   IFCU Checking

Payee: Indiana Newspapers, Inc.   ▼   Address

Category: Subscriptions:Newspaper   ▼   Split

Memo: Newspaper Subscription

Amount
○ Always $ 15.00   ▦
○ Estim. from la...   2 ⬍ payment(s)
○ ...card t...

Schedule
○ Once on
● Repeat
  ● Indef...
  ○ 999...

Action
● Prompt... enter in register   3 ⬍ day(s) before due date.
○ Enter in register without prompting 3 ⬍ day(s) before due date.

☑ Show as a bill.
Group

OK   Cancel   Help

 2

1. Open the Scheduled Transaction List window, select the scheduled transaction you want to change, and click the **Edit** button.

2. Make the necessary changes to the transaction details and click **OK**.

3. To remove a transaction entirely, select it and click the **Delete** button. Click **OK** in the prompt box that appears.

 End

You can make changes to a scheduled transaction through the Scheduled Transaction List window. For example, you may want to change the frequency or date, or you may want to remove the scheduled transaction entirely.

Windows Shortcut
You can press **Ctrl+J** on the keyboard to quickly open the Scheduled Transaction List window.

Skip It
You can skip a scheduled transaction by clicking the **Skip** button in the Scheduled Transaction List window. A confirmation box appears; click **Yes** to skip the transaction.

Using Alerts

Start

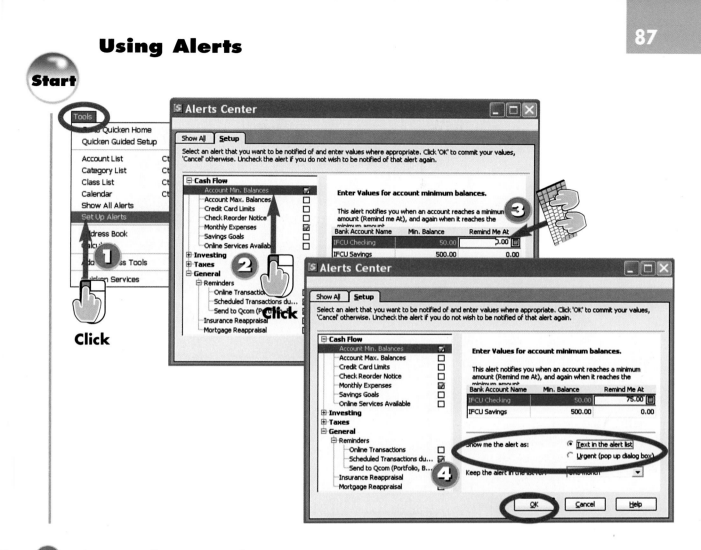

1. Choose **Tools**, **Set Up Alerts**.

2. The Alerts Center window opens. Click the **Cash Flow** alerts to expand the category and click the type of alert you want to create.

3. Select the item to which you want to assign a value and type in the value.

4. Select how you want the alert to appear and click **OK**. Quicken activates the alert and if you meet the criteria, a warning prompt box appears.

End

INTRODUCTION

Alerts remind you about maximum balances, check reorders, scheduled transactions, and more. For example, you can set up an alert that tells you if you drop below your minimum required checking account balance for the month. If you do meet the alert criteria, Quicken displays a prompt box warning you of the problem or lists the alert on the Quicken Home page.

TIP

List Them
To view a list of your alerts, click **Tools, Show All Alerts**. To remove an alert, select it and click the **Delete** button in the Alerts Center window.

Using Paycheck Setup

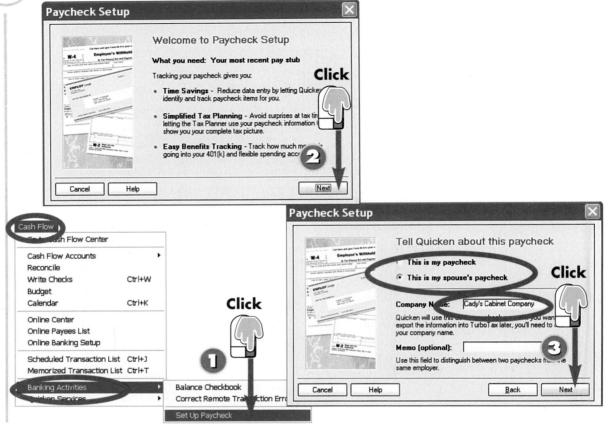

1. Choose **Cash Flow, Banking Activities, Set Up Paycheck**.

2. Review the information in the first dialog box and then click **Next**.

3. Fill in information about the paycheck, as directed, and then click **Next**.

Paycheck Setup automates how you record your paycheck into your account register and tells Quicken how to enter each pay and tax component of your paycheck on payday. This feature is especially useful if your paycheck is the same amount each time. If you want Quicken to prepare tax information for you, it needs to know each tax amount withheld from the paycheck.

Not Taxing?

HINT

If you don't plan to use Quicken for tax planning or to track information for tax time, you can simply enter a transaction for the net pay, the amount after taxes, each time you receive a paycheck.

Edit Future Paychecks (series)

Company Name: Cady's Cabinet Company   Date: 7/28/2   [Done]

Memo (optional):   [Cancel]

How often: Every two weeks   ○ Prompt me to enter in regis   [Help]
    ○ Enter without prompting

Account: IFCU Checking   **Click** ⑤

Earnings

Name	Category	Amount		
Salary	Salary Spouse	567.00	Edit	Delete

Add Earning ▼

Pre-Tax Deductions

What are your pre-tax deductions?
Click the Add Pre-Tax Deduction button below to enter your pre-tax deductions.

Add Pre-Tax Deduction ▼

Taxes

Name	Category	Amount		
Federal Tax	Tax Spouse:Fed	46.25	Edit	Delete
State Tax	Tax Spouse:State	18.62	Edit	Delete
Social Security (FICA)	Tax Spouse:Soc Sec	35.15	Edit	Delete
Medicare Tax	Tax Spouse:Medicare	8.22	Edit	Delete

Paycheck Setup

How much of y⬚
want to track?

○ I want to track all earnings, taxes, and deductions
Choose this if you w⬚

• Track your tax withholdings and help you minimize your tax bill
• Simplify tax preparation by exporting your tax information into TurboTax
• Track deposits to your company benefit plans, such as your 401(k) plan and flexible spending accounts

○ I want to track net deposits only.   **Click** ④

[Cancel]   [Help]   [Next]

Enter Year-to-Date Information

Do you want to enter the year-to-date amounts for this paycheck?
Quicken will use the year-to-date amounts in the Tax Planner to show your complete tax picture and help with tax planning.

○ I want to enter the year-to-date information

● I do not want to enter this information

[OK]   ⑥

Click

④ Specify how you want Quicken to track the paycheck and click **Next** to continue.

⑤ Fill out all the paycheck details, making sure to scroll through to see all the fields. Then click **Done**.

⑥ Quicken prompts you to record year-to-date information. Click the negative option and click **OK**. Quicken records the paycheck as a scheduled transaction.

End

Going Back
You can click the **Back** button while using Paycheck Setup to return to a previous dialog box and change your entries or choices.

Edit the Paycheck Details
You can return to Paycheck Setup and edit the check details. Click the **Setup Paycheck** button on the **Scheduled Transactions** tab, select the paycheck, and click the **Edit** button.

Balancing Accounts

To keep all your bank account information current, you must reconcile your accounts. Reconciling an account is the process of checking your paper bank statement against your account register to make sure the balance matches. It is a good practice to reconcile your Quicken bank accounts each month when you receive a paper statement.

When your bank or financial institution executes a transaction, such as paying a check or depositing interest, that transaction has cleared. Correspondingly, you must mark these cleared transactions from your paper statement as cleared in Quicken.

The goal in reconciling an account is to reach a zero balance when comparing the paper statement to your Quicken account. However, errors do occur and you must take steps to correct any mistakes. After investigating why the balance does not equal zero, you may need to edit some transactions or add missing transactions, which can be done within the reconciliation process.

At the end of the reconciliation process, you can generate a report and view an account summary.

The tasks in this part of the book teach you how to handle each phase of the reconciliation. Although the tasks in this section of the book focus on reconciling your checking or savings accounts, you can also apply these same techniques to reconcile other types of accounts in Quicken.

Statement Summary Window

Use these buttons to edit your transactions.

Check each deposit marked as cleared in your bank statement.

Check each payment marked as cleared in your bank statement.

Quicken keeps a running total of the difference between your Quicken account and your bank statement.

When you finish balancing your account, click the Finished button.

Statement Summary: Checking

New   Edit   Delete   Back to Statement Summary   View ▾   How Do I?

Payments and Checks

Clr	Date	Chk #	Payee	Amount
✓	5/29/2...	7635	Target	-137.67
✓	5/22/2...	7636	Walz Craft	-643.63
✓	5/27/2...	7637	BCRS	-20.00
✓	5/30/2...	7638	BCRS	-10.00
✓	6/1/2003	7639	Wal-Mart	-7.81
✓	6/3/2003	7640	Marsh	-3.51
✓	6/7/2003	7641	Lowe's	-37.05
✓	6/18/2...	7642	JDS Pugh's C...	-490.33
✓	5/26/2...	7685	Marsh	-18.87
✓	5/28/2...	7687	Home Depot	-10.58
✓	5/29/2...	7689	Sarah Mitchell	-19.77
✓	6/1/2003	7691	Countrywide ...	-698.37
✓	6/1/2003	7692	Retailers Nat...	-167.52
✓	5/31/2...	7693	Bureau Of M...	-133.50
✓	6/1/2003	7694	Vectren Ener...	-59.12
✓	6/1/2003	7695	Cinergy PSI	-51.76
✓	6/1/2003	7696	AAA Extermi...	-75.00
✓	5/30/2...	7697	Fishers Do It ...	-53.70

82 checks, debits   -5,502.46

Deposits

C	Date	Chk #	Payee	Amount
✓	6/4/2003	DEP		409.77
✓	6/6/2003	DEP		274.23
✓	6/13/2...	DEP		330.84
✓	6/20/2...	DEP		317.43
✓	6/27/2...	DEP		234.12
	7/2/2003	DEP		310.42
	7/11/2003	DEP		3,000.00

5 deposits, credits   1,566.39

Cleared Balance:	4,244.14
Statement Ending Balance:	3,956.21
Difference:	287.93

Mark All   Cancel   Finish Later   Finished

PART 5

Start

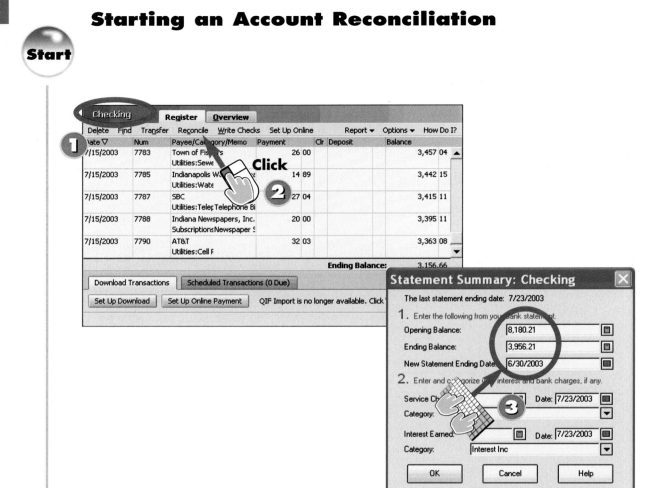

Click

1 Open the account register that you want to balance.

2 Click the **Reconcile** button on the account register window tool bar.

3 The Statement Summary dialog box opens. Verify the opening balance, type the ending balance from your paper statement, and specify a statement ending date.

INTRODUCTION

When you balance a paper checkbook, you *reconcile* your check register to make sure the balance matches the balance on the statement from your bank. Similarly, each time you receive a paper statement for a bank account, you need to reconcile the corresponding Quicken account.

Online Reconciliation

Online banking makes it easier to enter and reconcile your account. If you click the **Reconcile** button for an online account, the Reconcile Online Account dialog box opens instead, and you can reconcile your register to your bank statement or to the balance last downloaded for the account. See Part 6, "Using Online Banking Features," to learn more about downloading bank account information.

Statement Summary: Checking

The last statement ending date: 7/23/2003

1. Enter the following from your bank statement.

Opening Balance: 8,180.21

Ending Balance: 3,956.21

New Statement Ending Date: 6/30/2003

2. Enter and categorize your interest and bank charges, if any.

Service Charge: 27.90　Date: 6/18/2003

Category: Bank Charge:Check Printing

Interest Earned:　Date: 7/23/2003

Category: st Inc

Cancel　Help

4

Statement Summary: Checking

The last statement ending date: 6/30/2003

1. Enter the following from your bank statement.

Opening Balance: 8,180.21

Ending Balance: 3,956.21

New Statement Ending Date: 6/30/2003

2. Enter and categorize your interest and bank charges, if any.

Service Charge: 27.90　Date: 6/18/2003

Category: Bank Charge:Check Printing

Interest Earned: 2.25　Date: 6/30/2003

Category: Interest Inc

OK　Cancel　Help

Click

6

5

4 Enter any service charges, the date that they accrued, and choose a category for the charges.

5 Enter any interest earned on the account and the date it was added to your account.

6 Click **OK** and move to the next task—clearing a transaction.

End

HINT

Service Charges and Interest

Enter any monthly service charge for your account during this first reconciliation stage, but not ATM fees or bounced check charges. Also, enter any interest earned at this time.

TIP

Statement Changes

If you made an error when entering information in the opening dialog box, click the **Back to Statement Summary** button at the top of the reconciling window, make the changes, and click **OK**.

Clearing a Transaction

Start

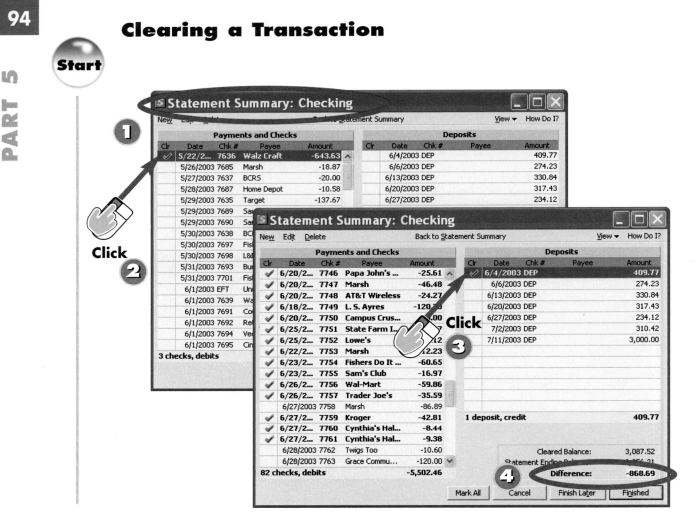

Click

Click

1. For the next step in the reconciliation process, Quicken displays the Statement Summary window.

2. Compare your paper statement to the items listed and click in the **Clr** column of the Payments and Checks list to check each cleared transaction.

3. In the Deposits list, click in the **Clr** column to check each cleared deposit transaction.

4. As you continue marking cleared transactions, the **Difference** amount between the statement and your Quicken account adjusts automatically.

End

Transactions your bank or financial institution has paid are considered cleared. After starting an account reconciliation, you must mark these cleared transactions from your paper statement as cleared in your Quicken account. As you clear transactions, the Difference amount in the Statement Summary window decreases, bringing you closer to a reconciled account.

TIP

Transaction Mismatch
If your statement shows a different amount for a transaction, you need to adjust the transaction in Quicken, as demonstrated in the next task. If your statement lists a transaction that Quicken doesn't, you'll need to add a transaction.

Adjusting a Transaction

Start

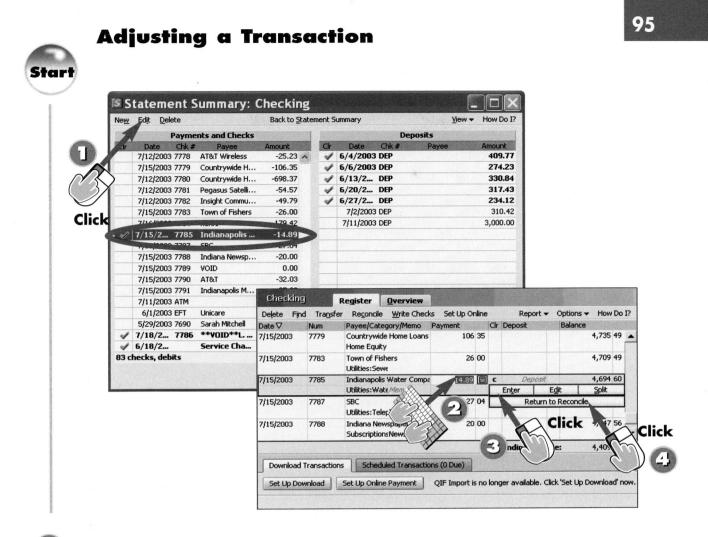

1. Select the transaction you want to adjust and click the **Edit** button.

2. Quicken displays the account register. Edit the transaction Payment or Deposit amount and any other information, as needed.

3. Click the **Enter** button to record your changes.

4. Click **Return to Reconcile** to return to the Statement Summary window.

End

INTRODUCTION

If the transaction you entered into Quicken does not match what is shown on your paper statement, you might need to edit the Quicken transaction so that your account will balance. You can edit transactions in the middle of the reconciliation process and return to the reconciling window to continue balancing your account.

HINT

Don't Let It Go
Accurate records keep you out of trouble down the line, so it's important to fix transaction amounts when you encounter them.

Entering a Missing Transaction

Start

Statement Summary: Checking

New Edit Delete   Back to Statement Summary   View ▼ How Do I?

Payments and Checks

Clr	Date	Chk #	Payee	Amount
✓	5/2...	7635	Target	-137.67
✓	5/22...	7636	Wela Craft	-643.63
✓	5/27...	7		-20.00
✓	5/30/2...	7638	L	-10.00
✓	6/1/2003	7639	Wal-Mart	-7.81
	6/3/2003	7640	Marsh	-3.51
	6/7/2003	7641	Lowe's	-37.05
✓	6/18/2...	7642	JDS Pugh's C...	-490.33
✓	5/26/2...	7685	Marsh	-18.87
✓	5/28/2...	7687	Home Depot	-10.58
✓	5/29/2...	7689	Sarah Mitchell	-19.77
✓	6/1/2003	7691	Countrywide ...	-698.37
✓	6/1/2003	7692	Retailers Nat...	-167.52
✓	5/31/2...	7693	Bureau Of M...	-1...
✓	6/1/2003	7694	Vectren Ener...	-...
✓	6/1/2003	7695	Cinergy PSI	-...
✓	6/1/2003	7696	AAA Extermi...	-...
✓	5/30/2...	7697	Fishers Do It ...	-...
82 checks, debits				**-5,5...**

Deposits

Clr	Date	Chk #	Payee	Amount
✓	6/4/2003	DEP		409.77
✓	6/6/2003	DEP		274.23
✓	6/13/2...	DEP		330.84
✓	6/20/2...	DEP		317.43
✓	6/27/2...	DEP		234.12
	7/2/2003	DEP		310.42
	7/11/2003	DEP		3,000.00

Click

1

Checking   **Register**   **Overview**

Delete Find Transfer Reconcile Write Checks Set Up Online   Report▼ Options▼ How Do I?

Date ▽	Num	Payee/Category/Memo	Payment		Clr	Deposit	Balance	
7/15/2003	7791	Indianapolis Monthly	27	00			4,603	42
		Subscriptions						
7/15/2003	7785	Indianapolis Water Compa	14	89			4,588	53
		Utilities:Wate						
7/16/2003	7784	Kohl's	179	42			4,409	11
		Credit Cards						
7/18/2003	7786	**VOID**L. S. Ayres			c		4,409	11
		Credit Cards						
6/27/2003	7688	Telephony, Inc.	287	93		*Deposit*		
		Office Expen						

Enter   Edit   Split

Return to Reconcile

2

Download Transactions   Scheduled Transactions (0 Due)

Set Up Download   Set Up Online Payment   QIF Import is no longer available. C... n Dow...d' now.

Click

3

1 Click the **New** button in the Statement Summary window.

2 Quicken returns you to the account register. Enter all the transaction information for the missing transaction.

3 Click **Enter** to record the new transaction in the register.

Suppose you've marked all the cleared transactions and adjusted some transactions, but you still have a difference greater than $0. At this point, you need to check for transactions on your paper account statement for which you haven't entered a corresponding transaction in Quicken. Examples include charges for insufficient funds and ATM use.

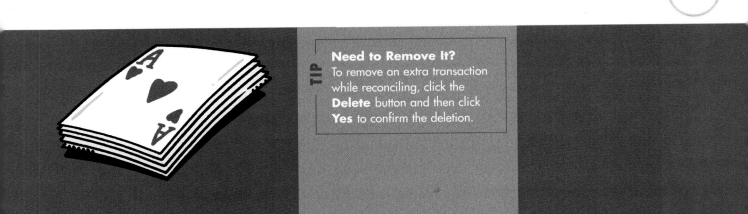

Quicken 2004 Premier - MY FINANCES - [Checking]

File Edit Tools Online Cash Flow Investing Property & Debt Planning Tax Reports Help
Beta

Back   Update   Reports   Setup   Brokerage   Services   Quicken.com   Customize

Checking   **Register**   **Overview**

Delete Find Transfer Reconcile Write Checks Set Up Online   Report▾ Options▾ How Do I?

Date ▽	Num	Payee/Category/Memo	Payment		Clr	Deposit		Balance	
7/15/2003	7791	Indianapolis Monthly Subscriptions	27	00				4,315	49
7/15/2003	7785	Indianapolis Water Compa Utilities:Wate	14	89				4,300	60
7/16/2003	7784	Kohl's Credit Cards	179	42				4,121	18
7/18/2003	7786	**VOID**L. S. Ayres Credit Cards			c			4,121	18
5/27/2003	Num	Payee Category Memo	Payment			Deposit			

Enter   Edit   Split
Return to Reconcile

Download Transactions | Scheduled Transactions (0 Due)

Set Up Download   Set Up Online Payment   QIF Import is no longer available. Click 'Set Up Download'

Statement Su...   Receive free Quicken newsletters for financial tips

---

ent Summary   View▾ How Do I?

Deposits

Clr	Date	Chk #	Payee	Amount
✓	6/4/2003 DEP			409.77
✓	6/6/2003 DEP			274.23
✓	6/13/2... DEP			330.84
✓	6/20/2... DEP			317.43
✓	6/27/2... DEP			234.12
	7/2/2003 DEP			310.42
	7/11/2003 DEP			3,000.00

5 deposits, credits   1,566.39

Click   4

	7/15/2003 7791	Indianapolis M...	-27.00
	7/11/2003 ATM		-140.00
	6/1/2003 EFT	Unicare	-226.00
✓	6/27/2... 7688	Telephony, I...	-287.93
	5/29/2003 7690	Sarah Mitchell	-71.53
	7/15/2003 7785	Indianapolis W...	-14.89
✓	7/18/2... 7786	**VOID**L. ...	0.00

83 checks, debits   -5,790.39

Cleared Balance:	3,956.21
Statement Ending Balance:	3,956.21
Difference:	**0.00**

Mark All   Cancel   Finish Later   Finished

Click

Click   5

---

④ Click the **Return to Reconcile** button.

⑤ Quicken returns you to the Statement Summary window. You can now mark the item as cleared.

End

TIP

Need to Remove It?
To remove an extra transaction while reconciling, click the **Delete** button and then click **Yes** to confirm the deletion.

Finishing the Reconciliation

Start

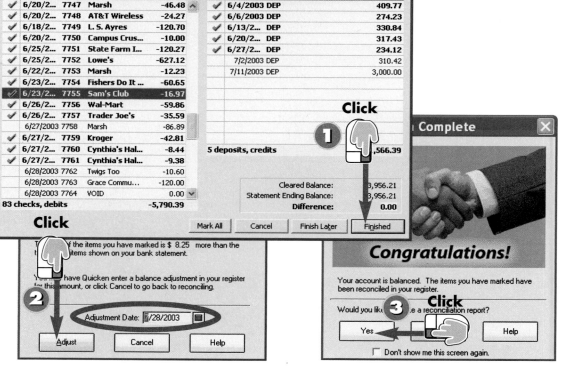

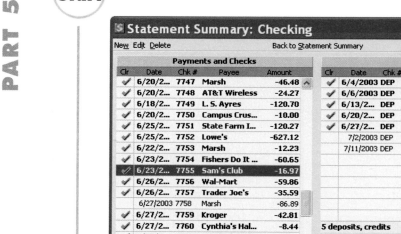

Click

Click

1. Click the **Finished** button at the bottom of the Statement Summary window.

2. If you did not balance the account, an Adjust Balance dialog box appears. Specify an Adjustment Date and then click **Adjust**.

3. If your reconciliation did balance, click **Yes** to have Quicken generate a report about the reconciliation activity and continue to the next task.

End

TIP

Cleared
The next time you view the register, any reconciled transactions appear marked with an R to indicate they are cleared.

Printing the Reconciliation Report

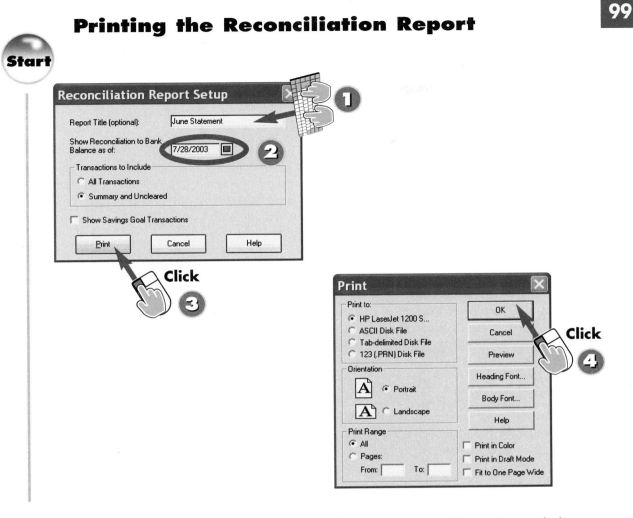

1. If you chose to print a reconciliation report, the Reconciliation Report Setup dialog box appears. Enter a title for the report.

2. Change the **Show Reconciliation to Bank Balance As of** date, if needed.

3. Select which transactions you want to include, and then click **Print**.

4. The Print dialog box appears. Click **OK** to print the report using the default settings.

End

You can print a report that details the reconciliation. By default, the report prints the reconciled transactions in your account. You can also print a report showing all the transactions to see details for every transaction in addition to summary information.

TIP

Savings Goals
The Reconciliation Report Setup dialog box also offers an option for including any reconciled transactions relating to savings goal contributions. This feature is available only in Quicken Deluxe, Premier, and Premier Home and Business.

Using Online Banking Features

This part introduces you to a variety of online banking features offered by Quicken, such as paying bills online. Paying bills online can save you the trouble of remembering to write out a check, place it in an addressed envelope, add postage, and mail the bill. As you can already guess, online activities can really speed up the way in which you handle your banking transactions.

In addition to bill paying, you can also update your account information, store your PIN numbers in one convenient location, and email your bank—all from within the Quicken program window. If your Quicken program isn't handy, you can also record your transactions from the Quicken.com Web site and then download them into your Quicken file at a later time. To use all these online features, you must have an Internet connection. You can connect to the Internet using a modem or a network.

If your financial institution offers online banking services, you can sign up and make online payments directly from your checking account.

If it turns out your bank is not one of Quicken's financial partners, you can still pay your bills online using Bill Pay. Bill Pay is a payment service that lets you write checks from your checking account for online payments.

Quicken's Online Center

You can choose which financial institution to pay.

You can specify which account to use to pay the online payment.

When you're ready to send your online payments, click the **Update/ Send** button.

Online Center

Delete Payees Repeating Contact Info   PIN Vault   Print Options▾

Financial Institution: *Quicken*   Update/Send...
Quicken Bill Pay   **bill pay**

Payments   E-mail   NEW FEATURES

Account: IFCU Checking

Processing Date [   ]   Delivery Date   7/30/2003

Payee   Town Of Fishers   ± 26.00

Account # 002

Category   Utilities:Sewer ±   Split   Memo [   ]   Enter

Status   Process   Delivery   Num   Payee   Amount

Update Status

You can write an online check here the same as you enter transactions in the register.

Setting Up Quicken's Internet Connection

Start

Internet Connection Setup ☒

How do you want to connect to the Internet?

○ Use the following connection:
  🌐 Broadband Connectio...
  🌐 Other Int...   **2** **Click**

● ...se my computer's Internet connection settings to estab...
  ...plication accesses the Internet.

○ ...do not have a way to connect to the Internet. Please ...
  ...up an Internet account.

Click

3 Next >

Internet Connection Setup ☒

Connection Settings

💻 Your computer is configured to use a direct connection to the Internet.

- Click Done to use these settings whenever an online feature of this product is accessed.

─ Advanced ──────────────
- Click Advanced Connection Settings if you want to view or change your preferences.

  Please note that changing these settings may
  affect how other programs connect to the
  Internet, including Internet Explorer.   Advanced Connection Settings...

  4 **Click**

  < Back   Done   ...   Help

Edit
  Cut
  Copy
  Paste   Shift+Ins
  Find & Replace   ▶
  Customize Account Bar
  Customize Tool Bar
  Preferences   ▶   Quicken Program
                                 Customize Online Updates
  1 **Click**   Internet Connection Setup

1 Click **Edit**, **Preferences**, **Internet Connection Setup**.

2 Quicken opens the Internet Connection Setup dialog box. Choose how you want to connect to the Internet.

3 Click **Next** to continue.

4 Quicken evaluates your selection and offers additional information, if needed. Click **Done**.

Before you attempt to use any of Quicken's online features, take a moment to make sure that Quicken can work with your Internet connection. You can connect to the Internet using a dial-up connection or a network. After setting up your connection, you can test it by accessing the Quicken.com Web site. Quicken includes an integrated browser for viewing Web pages.

TIP

Online Account Setup
When you created your first Quicken account, you may have chosen to use your bank's online features. If so, Quicken is already set up to use your Internet connection and you do not have to perform this task again.

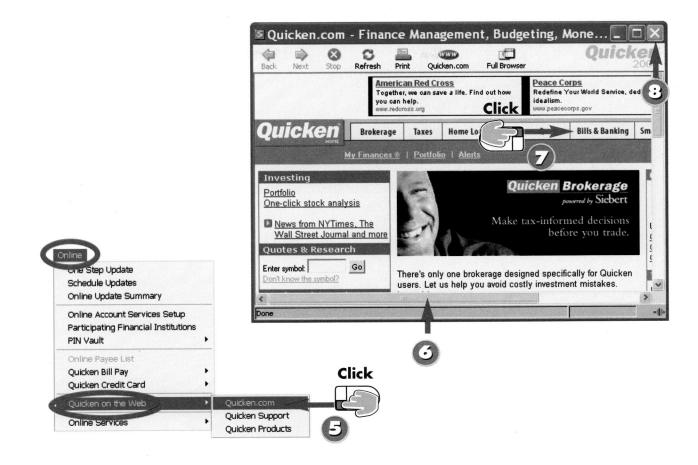

5 To test the connection, click **Online**, **Quicken on the Web**, **Quicken.com**.

6 Depending on your type of Internet connection, you may need to log on first; an integrated browser window is opened and displays the Quicken.com home page.

7 You can click a link to view other pages on the Web site.

8 Click the **Close** button to close the browser window.

Other Windows Appear
Other windows may open in addition to the Quicken.com Web page. You can close the windows by clicking the **Close** button located in the upper-right corner of each window.

Disconnect
If you logged on to the Quicken.com Web page using your modem, you must disconnect to log off. Click **File**, **Disconnect** to log off the connection from within Quicken.

Finding a Participating Institution

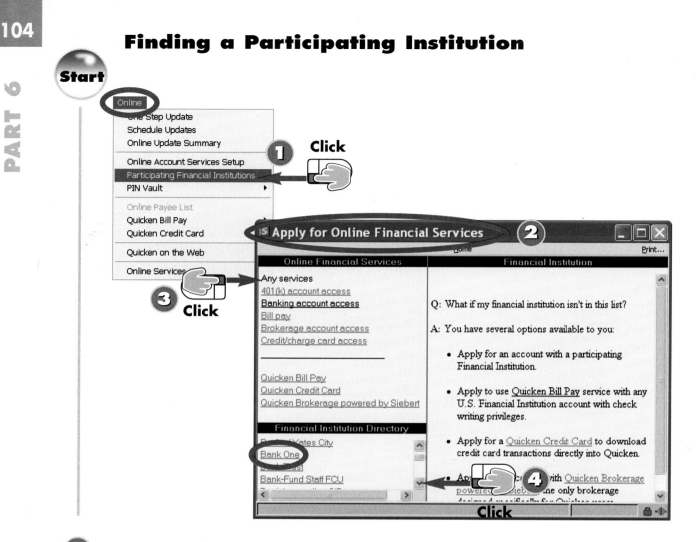

Start

1 Click

3 Click

4 Click

 1 Click **Online**, **Participating Financial Institutions**.

 2 Quicken opens the Apply for Online Financial Services dialog box.

3 Click the **Any Services** link if it is not already selected.

4 Scroll through the list of institutions to locate the one you want to use, and then click the bank name.

INTRODUCTION

If you plan to track your banking accounts online, you must first determine whether your bank is a Quicken financial partner. If your bank is a participating institution, you can apply for online financial services. Many banks offer online features, some of which are available for a small fee.

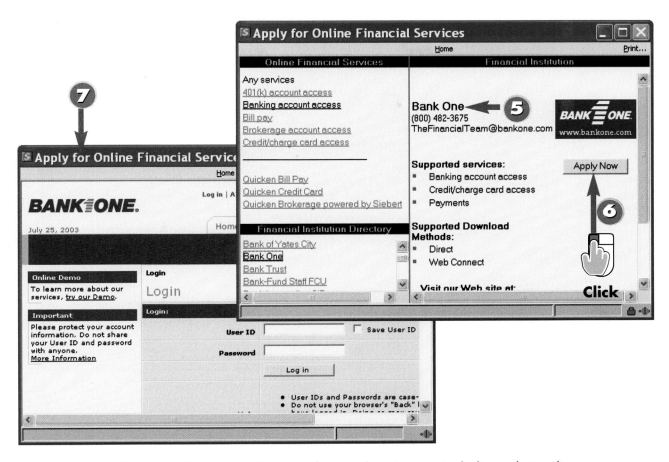

5 Quicken displays information about the financial institution, including what online services it supports.

6 Click the **Apply Now** button.

7 Another window detailing how to sign up for the services appears. Locate the link for sign-up directions and follow the procedure to complete the sign-up process.

End

It's Updating!

Quicken takes a moment to update the list whenever you open or exit the Apply for Online Financial Services dialog box and displays a prompt box showing the update status. After a moment or two, the update is complete.

Quicken Bill Pay

If your bank is not a Quicken partner, that does not mean you cannot pursue online bill paying. You can use Quicken's Bill Pay feature to pay your bills online. Learn more about this feature in the next task.

Setting Up Quicken Bill Pay

Start

1 Click **Online**, **Quicken Bill Pay**, **Set Up Quicken Bill Pay Account**.

2 Quicken opens the Quicken Account Setup dialog box. Click the **Sign Up Now** button.

3 Quicken opens the browser window. Click the **Enroll Now** link.

INTRODUCTION

You can sign up for Quicken Bill Pay, for a fee, and pay your bills online. Quicken Bill Pay is an online payment service. Online payment is available for any financial institution in the United States where you have a check-writing account. Even if your bank does not offer online services, you can still use Bill Pay to pay your bills online.

What Does It Cost?

As of this writing, Quicken offers Bill Pay for $9.95 per month, and the first month is free when you sign up.

TIP

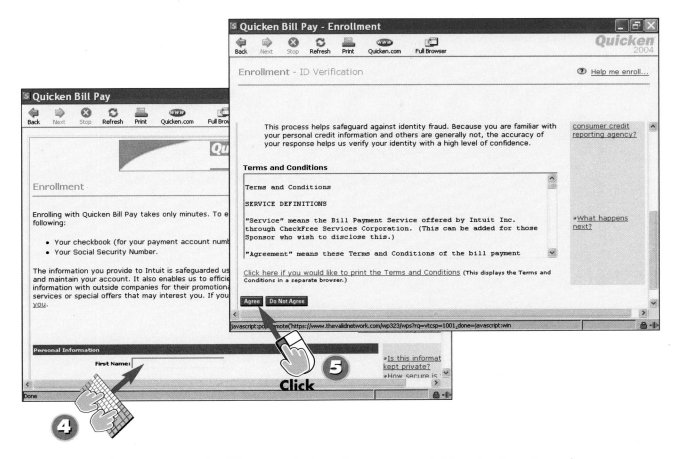

4 Follow the instructions for filling out the Enrollment form, clicking the **Continue** button at the bottom of the page to move on.

5 Read the agreement page and click the **Agree** button to continue.

See next page

HINT
What's Required?
To sign up for Bill Pay, have your checkbook handy as well as your Social Security number.

TIP
Scroll Away
The forms you fill out to enroll in Bill Pay require you to scroll down to view all the information on a page. Buttons for continuing the process also appear at the bottom of the Web page.

Setting Up Quicken Bill Pay Continued

Quicken Bill Pay - Enrollment

Back Next Stop Refresh Print Quicken.com Full Browser

Quicken 2004

Enrollment - ID Verification

⑦ Help me enroll...

Please answer the following questions about your current credit information. To protect against identity fraud, these questions might not always apply to you. If these questions do not apply to you, select NONE OF THE ABOVE as your answer.

1. Your credit file inc
around February 200
from the following op
   ⃝ ACCUBANC MO
   ⃝ COUNTRYWIDE
   ⃝ FIRST REPUBLIC
   ⃝ SOUTHTRUST M
   ⃝ NONE OF THE A

2. Please choose the
previously reference
your lender's statem

Done

Quicken Bill Pay - Enrollment

Back Next Stop Refresh Print Quicken.com Full Browser

Quicken 2004

Enrollment - ID Verification

⑦ Help me enroll...

We are processing your information...

We have completed the verification process. Please click **Continue**.

Continue

Click ⑦

Copyright © 2001 CheckFree. All rights reserved.

⑥ The next page of the form asks you to verify some credit information. Complete the questions and click **Continue**.

⑦ Another page appears, indicating that Intuit is processing your information. When processing is complete, click **Continue**.

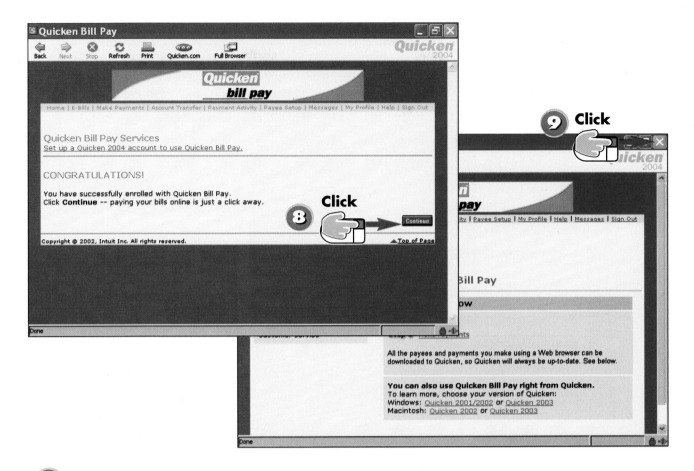

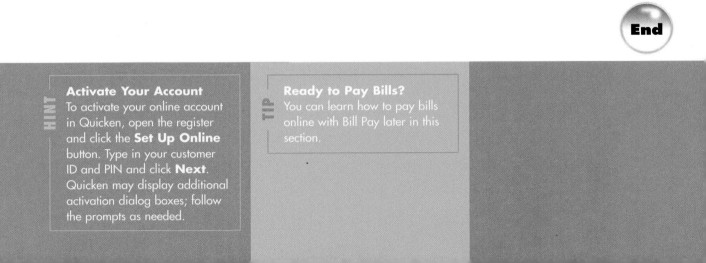

8 A congratulations page appears. Click **Continue** again.

9 A welcome page appears. You can start paying bills now or click the **Close** button to close the window and close your online connection.

End

Setting Up an Online Payee

Start

Online Payee List

New Edit Delete   Use   Report Print How Do I?

Financial Institution: [Quicken Bill Pay ▼]   Quicken bill pay

Lead Time   Account Number

Click

Online
One Step Update
Schedule Updates
Online Update Summary
Online Account Services
Participating Financial
PIN Vault
Online Center
Online Payee List
Quicken Bill Pay   ▶
Quicken Credit Card   ▶
Quicken on the Web   ▶
Online Services   ▶

Set Up Online Payee

Name and Address
Name: [Town Of Fishers ▼]   OK
Description (optional)   Staples   Cancel
                                 State Farm Insurance
                                 Superior Distributing
                                 Talbots
                                 Tan For Less
                                 Target
City: TJ Maxx
State: Town of Fishers
                                 Trade Secret
Payee Number Trader Joe's
Account #: [_____]
Phone: [_____]

Click

1. Click **Online**, **Online Payee List**.

2. Quicken opens the Online Payee List window. Click the **New** button.

3. The Set Up Online Payee dialog box appears. Type in the payee name or click the drop-down arrow and choose from the memorized transaction list.

INTRODUCTION

For your bank or Quicken's Bill Pay service to send a payment, you must record information about the payee. For example, you need to tell Quicken the payee name and address. You can create an Online Payee list that keeps track of all the people you pay through your online account access.

TIP

Just Read Your Statement
You'll find all the information about a payee on your billing statement.

Set Up Online Payee

Name and Address

Name: Town Of Fishers

Description: (Optional)

Street: 1 Municipal Dr.

City: Fishers

State: IN   Zip: 46038

Payee Numbers

Account #: 555555

Phone: 555-555-5555

OK

Cancel

Help

Click 5

4

Confirm Online Payee Information

Here is the payee information you entered. This information must be accurate in order for payments to arrive on time. Please take a moment to recheck it for errors.

Name and Address
Name: Town Of Fishers
Street: 1 Municipal Dr.

City: Fishers
State: IN   Zip: 46038

Payee Numbers
Account #: 555555
Phone: 555-555-5555

Accept

Cancel

Click

6

Online Payee List

New Edit Delete   Use   Report Print H? Do I?

Financial Institution: Quicken Bill Pay

Quicken bill

Payee	Lead Time	Account Number
Town Of Fishers	4	555555

7

Click

(4) Fill out the payee's address and account number, and include the payee's phone number in case something goes wrong.

(5) Click **OK**.

(6) Verify the information, check for any mistakes, and then click **Accept**.

(7) Quicken adds the payee to the Online Payee List window. You can now use the payee in a transaction online. Add more payees or click **Close** to exit the window.

End

TIP

Delete It
To remove a payee you no longer need, select the payee in the Online Payee List window and click the **Delete** button.

Paying a Bill Online

Start

```
Online
  One Step Update
  Schedule Updates
  Online Update Summary

  Online Account Services Setup
  Participating Financial Institutions
  PIN Vault                              ▶

  Online Center
  Online Payee List
  Quicken Bill Pay                       ▶
  Quicken Credit Car

  Quicken on the We

  Online Services                        ▶
```

1 **Click**

Online Center

Delete Payees Repeating Contact Info   PIN Vault   Print Options▾

Financial Institution:
Quicken Bill Pay ▾   **2**   **Quicken** *bill pay*   Update/Send...

Payments E-mail NEW FEATURES

Account: IFCU Checking ▾   **3**   ter Balance: 706.45

                        Processing Date [   ]   Delivery Date 7/30/2003 📅

Payee   Town Of Fishers   ± $ 0.00

           Town Of Fishers   <Online Payee>
Category   Vectren Energy Delivery   <Online Payee>   Enter

Status   Cancel Payment

                                                                        Update Status

4

Click

1 Click **Online**, **Online Center**.

2 Quicken opens the Online Center window. Select the bank or payment service you want to use to pay the bill.

3 Select the account from which funds should be drawn and enter a delivery date.

4 Click the **Payee** drop-down arrow and choose a payee. Quicken automatically adds the account number.

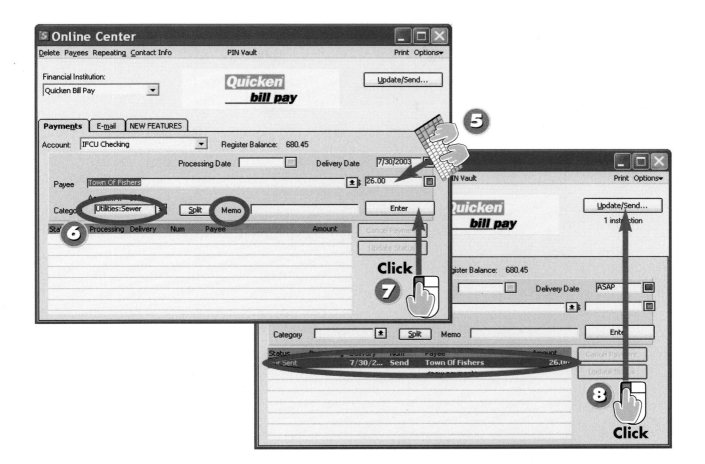

5 Fill in a payment amount for the check.

6 Select a category for the payment. You can also record memo information for the payment if needed.

7 Click the **Enter** button.

8 The payment is added to the list. You can add more payments to the list and then click the **Update/Send** button when you are ready to send.

See next page

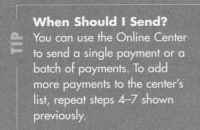

When Should I Send?
You can use the Online Center to send a single payment or a batch of payments. To add more payments to the center's list, repeat steps 4–7 shown previously.

Paying a Bill Online Continued

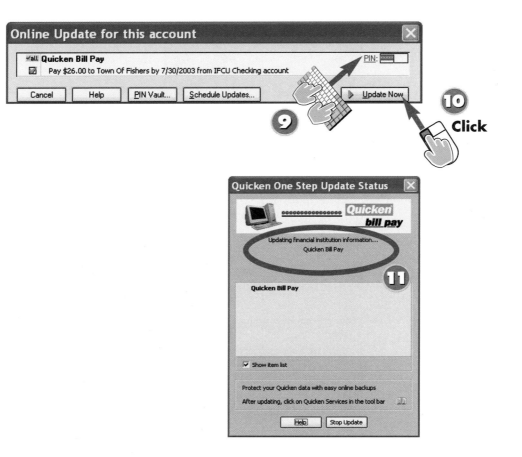

 The Online Update for this Account dialog box appears. Type in your PIN.

10 Click the **Update Now** button.

11 The Quicken One Step Update Status dialog box opens and updates the account information, sending your payment to the banking institution or payment service.

After recording the details about the payment, you can log on to your banking institution or Bill Pay and send the payment.

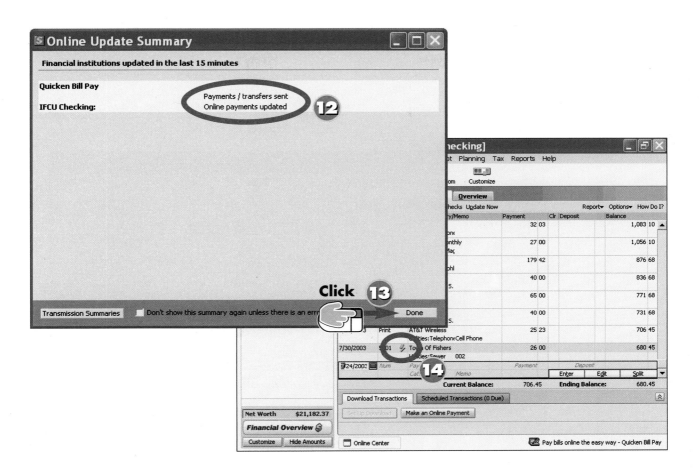

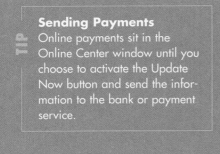 When the download is complete, the Online Update Summary window appears, listing your payment summary.

 Click **Done**.

 Returning to the account register, you can see the online payment identified in the register with a lightning bolt icon.

End

Sending Payments
Online payments sit in the Online Center window until you choose to activate the Update Now button and send the information to the bank or payment service.

Canceling an Online Payment

Start

Online
~~One~~ Step Update
Schedule Updates
Online Update Summary

Online Account Services Setup
Participating Financial Institutions
PIN Vault ▸

Online Center
Online Payee List
Quicken Bill Pay
Quicken Credit Card

Quicken on the Web

Online Services

1 **Click**

Quicken 2004 for Windows

? Cancel payment for $26.00 to "Town Of Fishers" dated 7/30/2003?

4 **Click** → Yes   No   Help

S Online Center

Delete Payees Repeating Contact Info   PIN Vault   Print Options▾

Financial Institution: **Quicken**   Update/Send...
Quicken Bill Pay ▾   **bill pay**

Click
3

Payments E-mail NEW FEATURES

Account: IFCU Checking ▾   Register Balance: 680.45

Processing Date ASAP   Delivery Date P

Payee   ±$

Category   ±   Split   Memo   ▾ Enter

Status   Processing Delivery Num   Payee   Amount   Cancel Payment
Sent   7/30/2... 5001   Town Of Fishers   26.00
          <new payment>   Update Status

2

---

1 Click **Online**, **Online Center**.

2 Quicken opens the Online Center window. Select the payment you want to stop.

3 Click the **Cancel Payment** button.

4 Quicken asks you if you want to cancel the payment. Click **Yes**.

Online Center

Delete Payees Repeating Contact Info   PIN Vault   Print Options▾

Financial Institution:
Quicken Bill Pay   *Quicken*   Update/Send...
                                    bill pay   1 instruction

Payments E-mail NEW FEATURES

Account: IFCU Checking   Register Balance: 680.45

Processing Date

Payee

Category   ±   Split   Memo

Cancel   Processing Delivery Num   Payee
                    7/30/2... 5001   Town Of Fishe
                                      <new payment>

Click 5

Online Update Summary

Financial institutions updated in the last 15 minutes

Quicken Bill Pay
                                   Payments / transfers sent
IFCU Checking: Online payments updated

Online Update for this account

☑all **Quicken Bill Pay**
 ☑   Cancel 7/30/2003 payment to Town Of Fishers for $26.00 from IFCU Checking a PIN: ✻✻✻✻✻

Cancel   Help   PIN Vault...   Schedule Updates...   6   ▷ Update Now

Click

Click 7

Transmission Summaries   ☐ Don't show this summary again unless there is an err   Done

5 Quicken changes the status of the payment in the Online Center. Click the **Update/Send** button.

6 Type in your PIN and click the **Update Now** button. Log on to your Internet connection, if needed, and Quicken sends the cancellation instruction.

7 The Online Update Summary window displays the summary of the payment. Click **Done** to exit the window, and the canceled payment is marked Void.

End

Transferring Funds
If you have more than one online banking account, you can transfer funds from one account to another. Click the **Transfers** tab in the Online Center and specify the source, destination, and amount of transfer. After entering the transaction into the list window, click the **Update/Send** button to finish the process.

Updating Account Information

Start

Click **1**

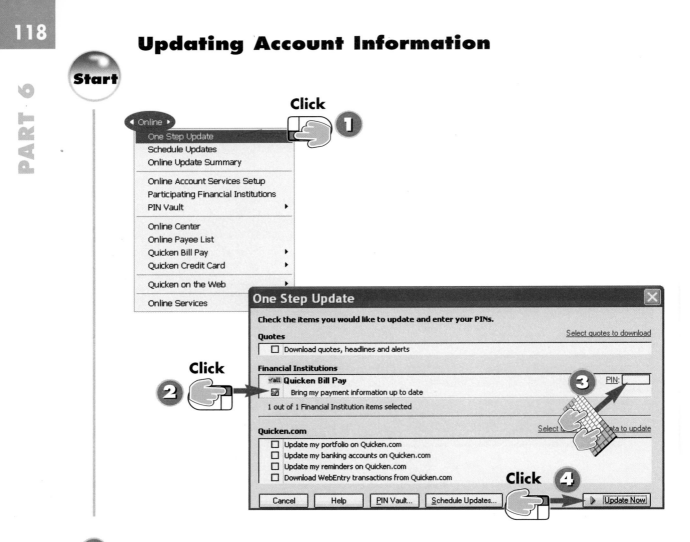

Click **2**

Click **4**

1 Click **Online**, **One Step Update**.

2 Quicken opens the One Step Update dialog box. Select the items you want to update.

3 Type your PIN.

4 Click the **Update Now** button.

Periodically, you need to go to the Online Center window and download information to update your account. For example, you might want to download your bank account information monthly, transfer transactions to the register, as needed, and then reconcile the account.

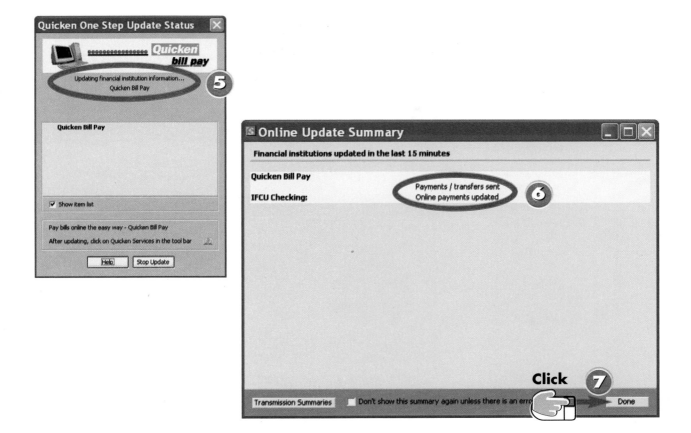

5. Log on to your Internet connection, if needed, and Quicken updates your financial information.

6. The Online Update Summary window displays the download summary.

7. Click **Done** to close the Summary window.

End

Schedule Your Updates
You can schedule automatic updates. Click **Online**, **Schedule Updates**. From the Schedule Updates dialog box, select the items to place on an update schedule. Then specify which days and times for the updates and click **OK**.

HINT

Using the PIN Vault

Start

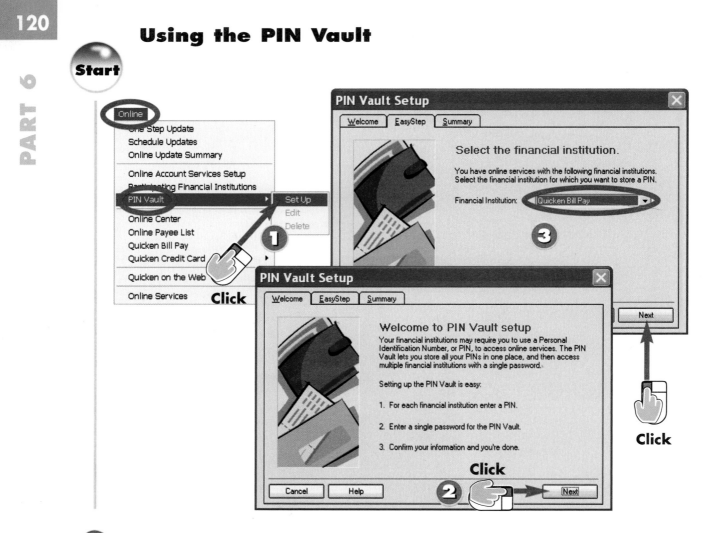

---

1 Click **Online**, **PIN Vault**, **Setup**.

2 Quicken opens the PIN Vault Setup dialog box. Click **Next** to continue.

3 Choose the financial institution or payment service for which you want to store a PIN and click **Next**.

TIP

Vault Password
Part of storing PINs is creating a password for the PIN Vault feature. This ensures that other users can't open your Quicken file and access your account PINs.

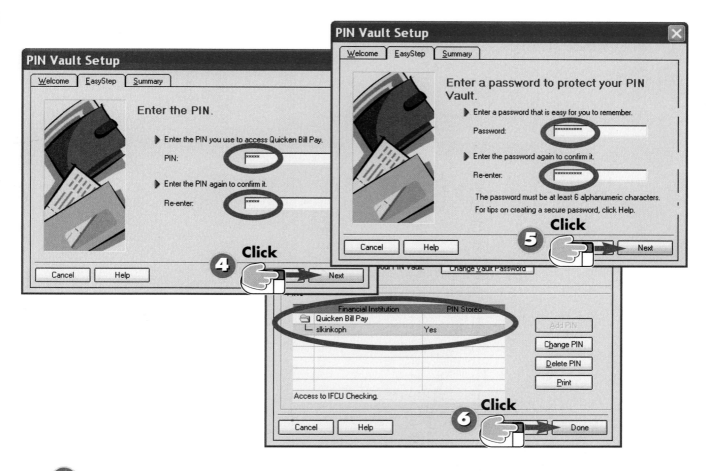

4 Type the PIN, retype it again to confirm it, and then click **Next**.

5 Type a password for the PIN Vault, retype to confirm the password, and then click **Next**.

6 The Summary tab displays the PIN record. Click **Done**. Quicken automatically fills in the PIN in your online activities for you.

End

TIP
Changing PINs
To change a pin for an account, click **Online**, **PIN Vault**, **Edit**. In the **Summary** tab, select the account you want to change and click the **Change PIN** button. Enter your new PIN data and click **Change**.

Emailing Your Financial Institution

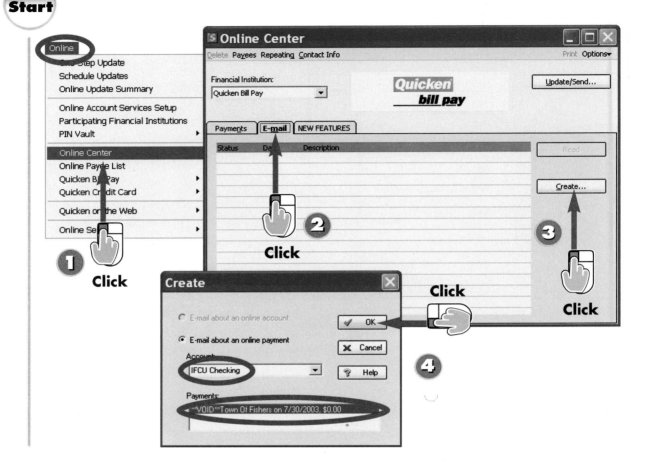

1. Click **Online**, **Online Center**.

2. The Online Center window opens. Click the **E-mail** tab.

3. Click the **Create** button.

4. If the message concerns an online payment, select the account and payment and then click **OK**.

TIP

Your Own Post Office
You can use the E-mail tab in the Online Center window a post office box. When you perform a One Step Update, Quicken downloads emails you receive from your financial institution and displays them in the E-mail tab.

Click

E-mail About an Online Payment

Check number:	5001
Payee:	**VOID**Town Of Fishers
Amount:	0.00
Status:	Canceled on 7/24/2003

OK

Cancel

Help

Message:

Can you please verify that this payment was, indeed, cancelled? Thank you very much.

Sincerely, Sherry

Quicken
bill pay

Print Options▾

Update/Send...

1 instruction

Payments | E-mail | NEW FEATURES

Status | Date | Description | Read
Not Sent | 7/24/2... | To: Customer Service, **VOID**Town Of Fishers 0.00 on 7... |

Create...

5 A message dialog box opens. Type your message text.

6 Type your name into the **Sincerely** field and click **OK**.

7 The email message is added to the E-mail tab. The next time you pay bills online, you can send the message with the payments.

End

Send It Now
To send an email message as soon as it appears in the Online Center, click the **Update/Send** button.

TIP

Using WebEntry to Enter Transactions

Start

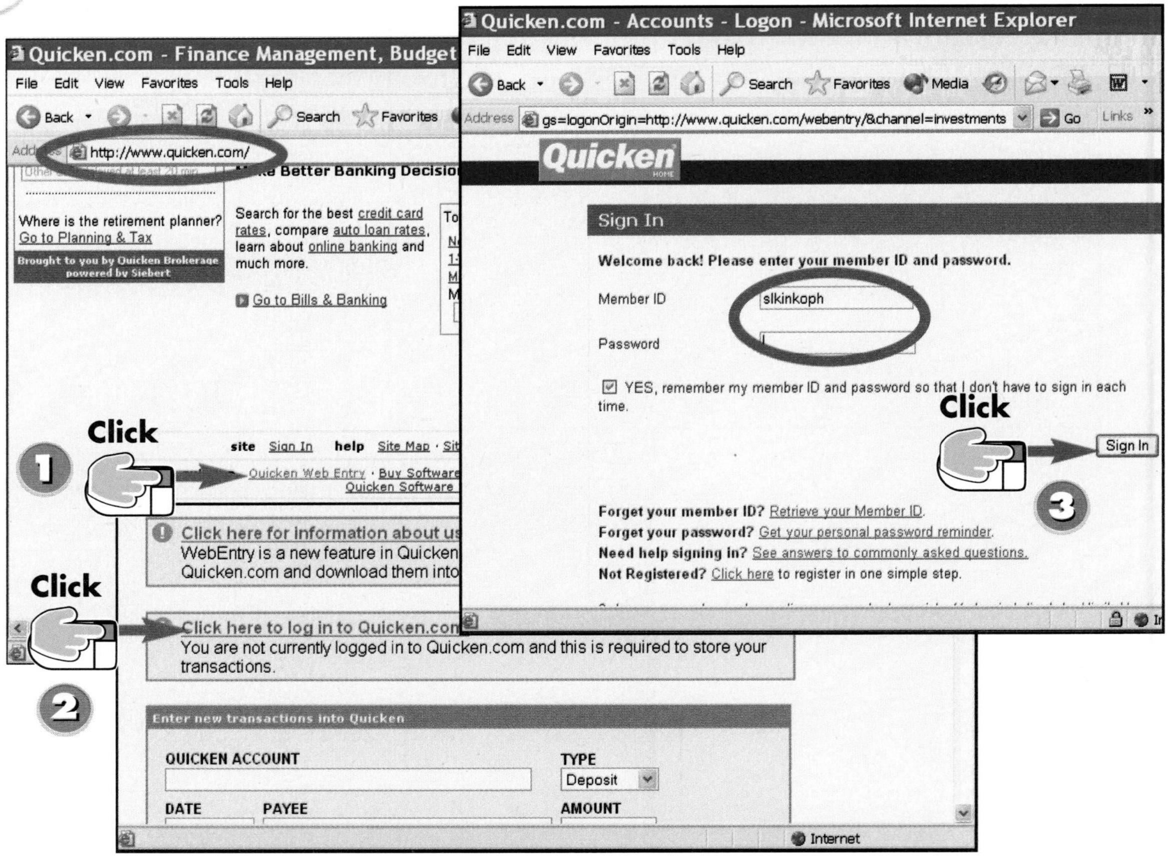

1. Open a Web browser to the Quicken.com Web site, scroll down the page, and click the **Quicken Web Entry** link.

2. Click the log in link.

3. Enter your member ID and password and click the **Sign In** button.

PART 6

INTRODUCTION

If you travel often and need to enter transactions into Quicken but do not have the program available, you can use the WebEntry feature. WebEntry allows you to enter transactions to your home Quicken program using the Quicken Web site. When you're back home with your Quicken program in front of you, you can download any transactions you recorded on the Web site.

Register First
To use WebEntry, you must first register as a Quicken.com user. If this is your first visit to the feature, create a member name and password.

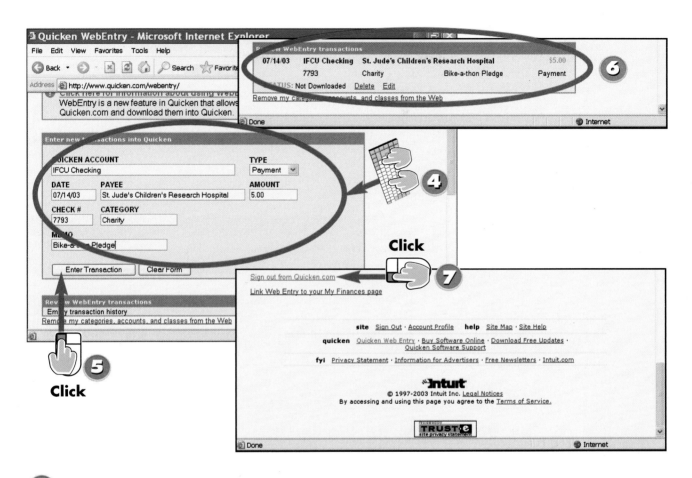

4 Type your transaction data into the check form.

5 Click **Enter Transaction**.

6 Quicken.com keeps a list of your recorded transactions. You can continue entering transactions.

7 When you finish, scroll to the bottom of the page and click the **Sign Out** link. You can log off your Internet connection.

Tab It
You can press the **Tab** key to move from form field to form field on the Web page.

Downloading WebEntry Transactions

Start

Click **1**

> Online
>
> One Step Update
> Schedule Updates
> Online Update Summary
>
> Online Account Services Setup
> Participating Financial Institutions
> PIN Vault ▶
>
> Online Center
> Online Payee List
> Quicken Bill Pay ▶
> Quicken Credit Card ▶
>
> Quicken on the Web ▶
>
> Online Services ▶

One Step Update

Check the items you would like to update and enter your PINs.

Quotes   Select quotes to download

☐ Download quotes, headlines and alerts

Financial Institutions

✓all **Quicken Bill Pay**   PIN: *****

☑ Bring my payment information up to date

1 out of 1 Financial Institution items selected

Quicken.com   Select Quicken.com data to update

☐ Update my portfolio on Quicken.com
☐ Update my banking accounts on Quicken.com
☐ Update my reminders on Quicken.com
☑ Download WebEntry transactions from Quicken.com

Click 2

Click 3

[Cancel] [Help] [PIN Vault...] [Schedule Updates...] [▶ Update Now]

1 To download your Quicken.com transactions, click **Online**, **One Step Update**.

2 In the One Step Update dialog box, click the **Download WebEntry Transactions from Quicken.com** item.

3 Click the **Update Now** button. You may need to log on to your Internet connection to continue.

When you return home to your Quicken program, you can use the One Step Update feature to download your WebEntry transactions and then add them to your account register.

TIP

Click a Button Instead You can also start a One Step Update by clicking the **One Step Update** button on the Quicken Home page in your Quicken program window.

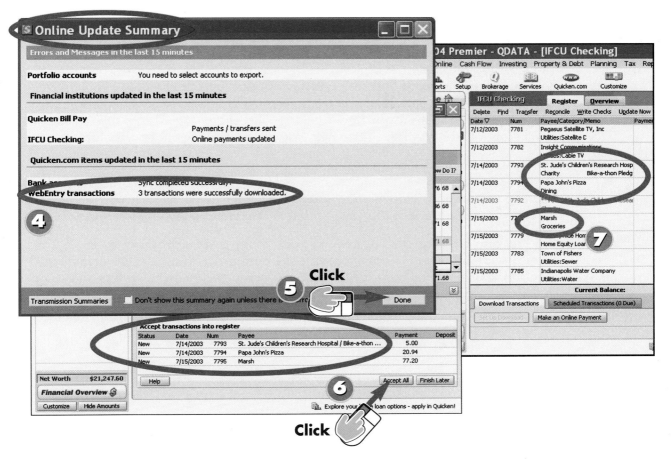

4 Quicken downloads the transactions and opens the Online Summary Update window. WebEntry transactions are listed here.

5 Click **Done**.

6 Downloaded transactions are listed in the tab at the bottom of the register. To transfer all the transactions into your register, click the **Accept All** button.

7 Quicken records the transactions for you.

End

Next Time
The next time you log on to Quicken.com to use WebEntry, the account and category fields now include drop-down lists you can select from. This will speed up your transaction entries.

Tracking Your Cash Flow

The Cash Flow Center is a centralized window for viewing a snapshot of your cash flow accounts, including checking and savings accounts. In the previous chapters, you learned how to enter and edit transactions and balance your accounts, all of which are based in the Cash Flow Center. In this chapter, you learn more about the Cash Flow Center and how it can help you keep track of your financial status.

You can create alerts that appear in the Cash Flow Center to let you know if you exceed a set amount or are under a target figure for any of your cash flow accounts. You can view reports that let you visually see what's going on with your finances and create customized reports to show just the information you want to analyze.

You can also create a cash account to track your pocket money. For example, if you have a small business, you might keep petty cash on hand to pay for incidentals. Tracking your personal cash is also a great way to find out what you're spending money on and analyze ways to save more money.

The Cash Flow Center

The Expenses report shows a pie chart of your monthly spending.

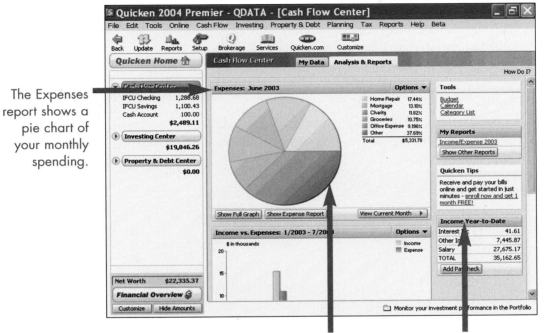

The Income vs. Expenses report compares how much you bring home and how much you spend.

The Income Year-to-Date area shows your cumulative financial data.

Viewing the Cash Flow Center

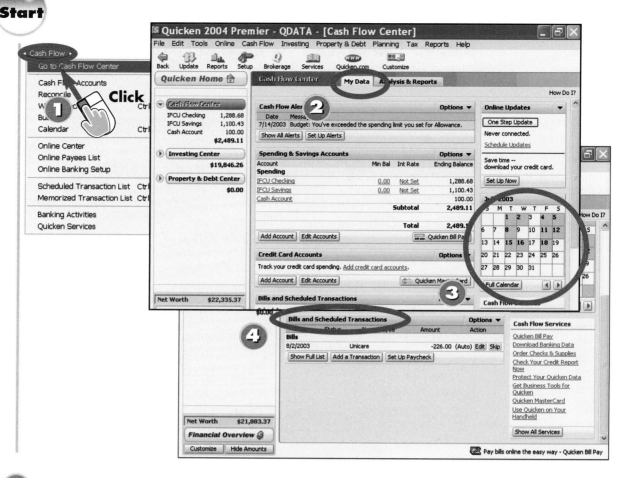

1. Choose **Cash Flow, Go To Cash Flow Center**.

2. Quicken opens the Cash Flow Center window and displays the My Data tab by default; it lists alerts, spending and savings accounts, and credit card accounts.

3. The calendar highlights days in which transactions were made or scheduled.

4. View bills that are due in the Bills and Scheduled Transactions area.

INTRODUCTION

Use Quicken's Cash Flow Center for a visual picture of your financial status. The Cash Flow Center window includes the My Data tab, which shows information about your cash flow accounts, and the Analysis & Reports tab, which includes graphs and reports based on your cash flow accounts.

Opening the Cash Flow Center
Another way to open the Cash Flow Center is to click the **Cash Flow Center** link at the top of the Account bar.

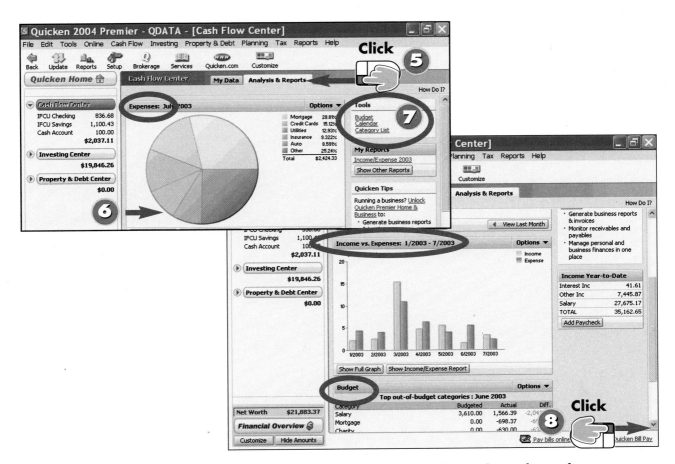

5 Click the **Analysis & Reports** tab to view summaries and snapshots of your financial status presented in graphs and charts.

6 The Expenses pie chart shows your expenses for the current month.

7 The Tools area gives you quick access to cash flow tools, such as setting up a budget and editing the category list.

8 View a snapshot comparing income and expenses in the Income vs. Expenses area.

End

Create a Budget

TIP

See Part 11, "Setting Up a Budget," to learn how to use Quicken's budgeting tools to set up a budget.

Need a Report?

TIP

You can generate all kinds of reports about your financial data in Quicken. See the tasks "Viewing Cash Flow Reports" and "Creating a Customized Report" later in this section to learn more.

Setting Up Cash Flow Alerts

Start

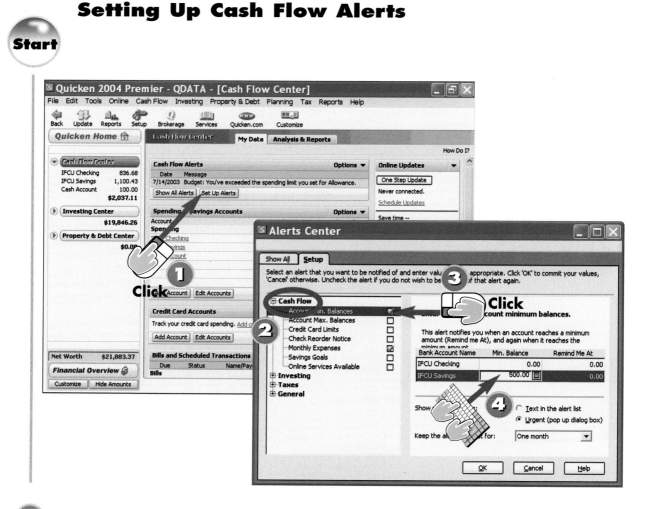

1 From the Cash Flow Center, click the **Set Up Alerts** button.

2 Quicken opens the Alerts Center window and displays the Cash Flow alerts.

3 Click the check box next to the item to which you want to assign an alert. Quicken displays options related to the item you selected.

4 Click the value you want to change and type a new value.

Alerts warn if you go over or under a specified figure in an account. With your cash flow accounts, you might use an alert to let you know if you drop below your checking account's minimum balance. Alerts appear at the top of the Cash Flow Center window so you can easily spot them when they occur.

TIP

Finding the Center
To quickly access the Cash Flow Center, click the **Cash Flow Center** link at the top of the Account bar. You can also click **Tools**, **Set Up Alerts** to display the Alerts Center window.

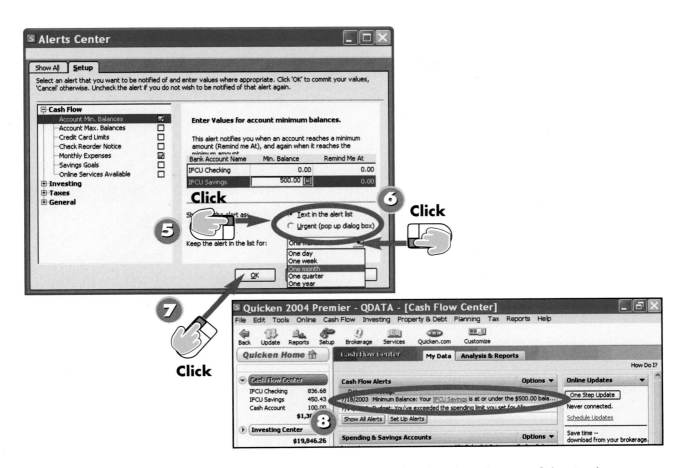

5 Select an option for displaying the alert. To see the alert listed at the top of the Cash Flow Center window, select **Text in the Alert List** option.

6 To display the alert for a set amount of time, set the time using the **Keep the Alert in the List For** option.

7 Click **OK** to save your settings and close the window.

8 When circumstances occur that meet the alert criteria, the alert appears in the Cash Flow Center.

End

Alert Prompt Box
If you'd rather set a more obvious alert, choose the Urgent option in the Alerts Center window. With this option activated, the alert appears as a prompt box. Click **OK** to close the box and continue working with Quicken.

Remove an Alert
To remove an alert you no longer want, reopen the Alerts Center window and deselect the check box beside the item to which an alert is assigned.

Viewing Cash Flow Reports

Start

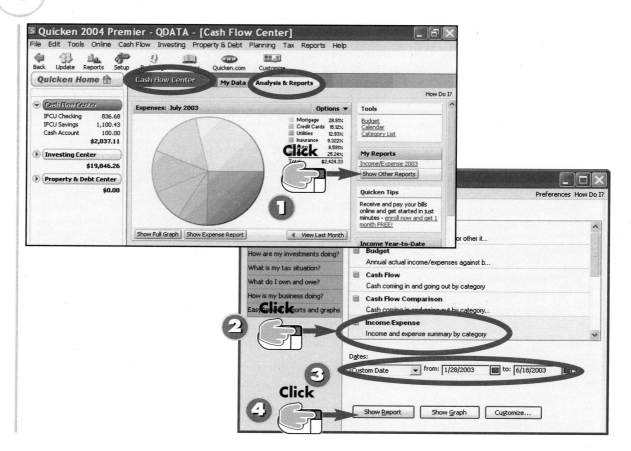

1 From the Cash Flow Center, click the **Analysis & Reports** tab, and then click the **Show Other Reports** button.

2 Quicken opens the Reports and Graphs window. Select the report type you want to view.

3 Select the date or range for the report.

4 Click the **Show Report** button.

Quicken reports are a great way to analyze your financial data. Cash flow reports can help you analyze your spending habits and find ways to improve your financial situation. Quicken installs with numerous predefined reports and graphs. The Cash Flow Center includes reports such as Banking Summary, Income/Expense, Itemized Categories, and Spending, to name just a few.

Another Route
You can also get to the Reports and Graphs window by clicking the **Reports** menu and choosing **Reports and Graphs**.

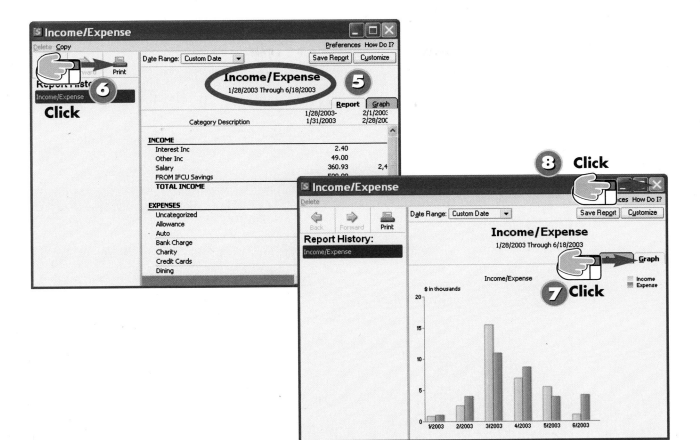

5 Quicken opens the report window and displays the report.

6 To print the report, click the **Print** button.

7 To view a graph of the report, click the **Graph** tab.

8 Click the **Close** button to close the report.

Customize It
You can create a customized report of your cash flow information. See the next task to learn how.

EasyAnswer Reports
Quicken's EasyAnswer reports answer specific questions, such as "How much did I spend on...?" Select the **EasyAnswer Reports and Graphs** tab in the Reports and Graphs window, and then click the question and view a report.

Creating a Customized Report

Start

1. From the Cash Flow Center, click the **Analysis & Reports** tab, and then click the **Show Other Reports** button.

2. Choose the report type you want to view, select a date or range, and then click the **Customize** button.

3. The Customize dialog box for the report type opens. Use the **Display** tab options to control how report items appear.

INTRODUCTION

Customized reports show only the data you want and can be saved to use again. For example, you might create a cash flow report of your expenses, but choose to chart your checking account only. The Customize dialog box offers you a variety of customizing features, from setting the report title to controlling which categories and classes are used in the report.

TIP

Before or After
You can customize a report before or after you generate the report. To customize the report after creating the report, click the **Customize** button in the Report window.

Customize Cash Flow Comparison

Compare Custom Date ▾ from: 1/1/2003 to: 6/1/2003
to Custom Date ▾ from: 1/1/2003 to: 6/1/2003

Click

Accounts | Categories | Classes | Category Groups | Advanced

④

count Group | Account | Type
ending
ow | ☑ IFCU Checking | Bank | Mark All
Investing | ☐ IFCU Savings | Bank |
All Accounts | ☐ Cash Account | Cash | Clear All

Customize Cash Flow Comparison

Compare Custom Date ▾ from: 1/1/2003 to: 6/1/2003
to Custom Date ▾ from: 1/1/2003 to: 6/1/2003

Display | Accounts | **Categories** | Classes | Category Groups | Advanced

Select Categories

Category | Type | Match
 | | Payee

⑤

Click

Customize Cash Flow Comparison

Compare Custom Date ▾ from: 1/1/2003 to: 6/1/2003
to Custom Date ▾ from: 1/1/2003 to: 6/1/2003

Display | Accounts | Categories | Classes | Category Groups | **Advanced**

Transactions

Amounts: All ▾
☐ Include unrealized gains
☐ Tax-related transactions only
Transaction types: All Transactions ▾

Transfers: Exclude Internal ▾
Subcategories: Show All ▾

Status
☑ Not cleared
☑ Newly cleared
☑ Reconciled

⑥

Click

⑦ **Click**

Show Report | Cancel | Help

④ Click the **Accounts** tab and click which accounts to include in the report.

⑤ Click the **Categories** tab to click which categories to include in the report.

⑥ Click the **Advanced** tab to set options for how transactions are used in the report.

⑦ After setting any customizing options, click the **Show Report** button to view the finished report.

End

INFO

Save It
After you customize a report, you can save the settings and view the report again. Click the **Save Report** button, and in the Save Report dialog box, type a name for the report, select a center to associate with the report, and click **OK**.

Reopen a Saved Report
To reopen a report you previously saved, open the Reports and Graphs window, click the **Saved Reports** tab and double-click the report you want to view.

Tracking Your Pocket Cash

Start

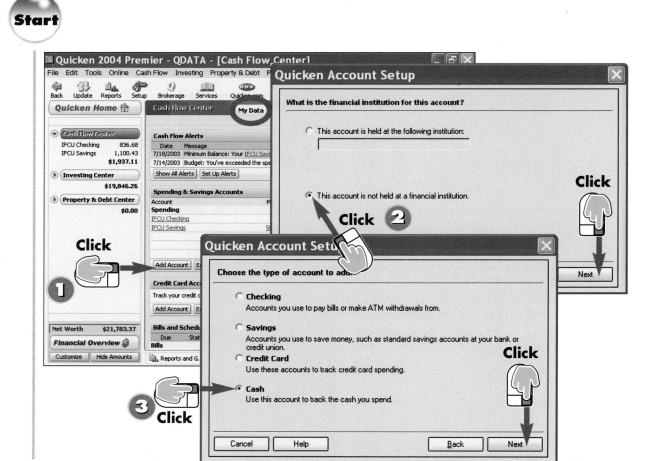

1. From the Cash Flow Center, click the **Add Account** button on the My Data tab.

2. The Quicken Account Setup dialog box opens. Click the **This Account Is Not Held at a Financial Institution** option and click **Next**.

3. Click the **Cash** option and click **Next**.

You can create a special account to track your pocket cash, or in the case of a business, petty cash. Like your account registers for checking and savings, a cash account allows you to manage where your pocket money goes and lets you keep track of your spending.

More Accounts

You can create all kinds of accounts in Quicken. See Part 2, "Setting Up Accounts," to learn more about setting up additional types of Quicken accounts.

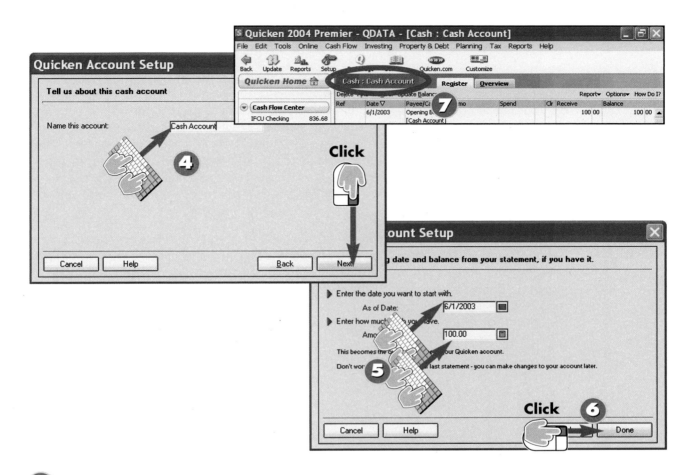

4️⃣ Type a name for the account or use the default name, and then click **Next**.

5️⃣ Type a start date for the account and a start balance.

6️⃣ Click **Done**.

7️⃣ Quicken creates and opens the account register. You can record your spending by entering transactions the same as in a checking account.

End

Delete It
You can easily delete a cash account you no longer want to track. Open the Account List window, select the account, and click **Delete**. Type **Yes** and click **OK** to permanently remove the account and all of its transactions.

Tracking Credit Card Debt

Whether you use one credit card or a dozen, Quicken can help you manage your credit card debt. Credit card debt is a serious problem these days, so keeping tabs on your credit card spending is increasingly important to good financial health. You can use credit card accounts in Quicken to track purchases and payments on all your major credit cards. This enables you to see immediately where you are accumulating debt and take steps to keep it in check. Tracking your credit card spending in separate accounts takes a bit of discipline, especially if you use multiple cards. However, a little bit of monthly effort pays off in the long run if it helps you to manage and pay off your credit card debt.

A credit card account works similarly to your other cash flow accounts, such as your checking and savings accounts. Like checking account transactions, you can assign categories to your credit card transactions so that you can clearly see where your money is going. This chapter shows you how to set up a credit card account and record various card-related transactions. You also learn how to view a spending report and graph to see where and how much you are charging to your credit card.

Account Register

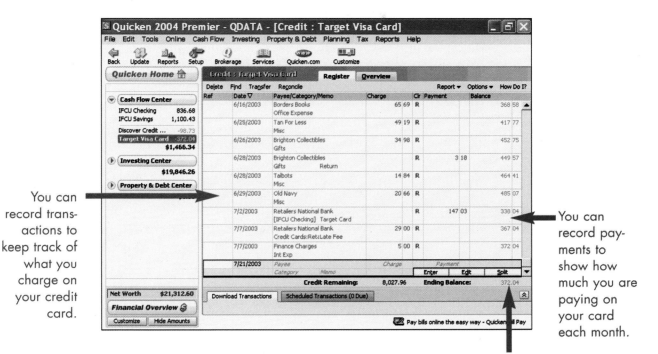

You can record transactions to keep track of what you charge on your credit card.

You can record payments to show how much you are paying on your card each month.

The balance always appears in red because it indicates amounts you owe.

Creating a Credit Card Account

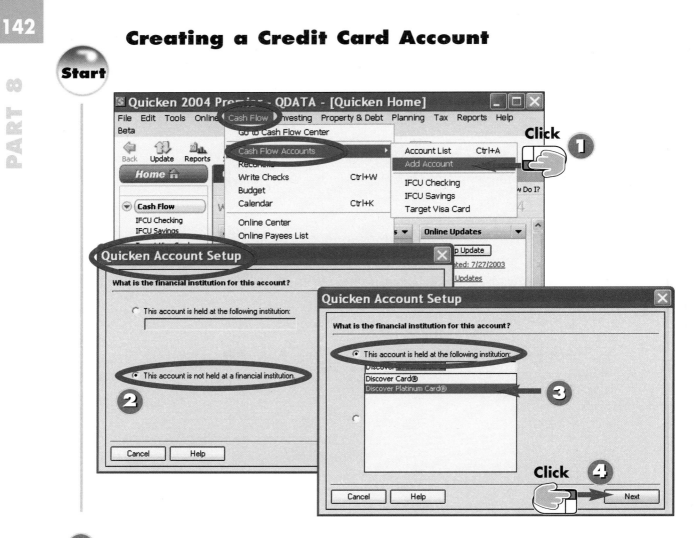

1. Click **Cash Flow**, **Cash Flow Accounts**, and then click **Add Account**.

2. The Quicken Account Setup dialog box opens. If your card is not associated with a financial institution, choose this option.

3. If the card is associated with a bank, click this option and type the name of the bank or select it from the pop-up list that appears.

4. Click the **Next** button to continue.

Use the Cash Flow Center
You can also start a new account from the Cash Flow Center. Click the **Add Account** button on the My Data tab to open the Quicken Account Setup dialog box.

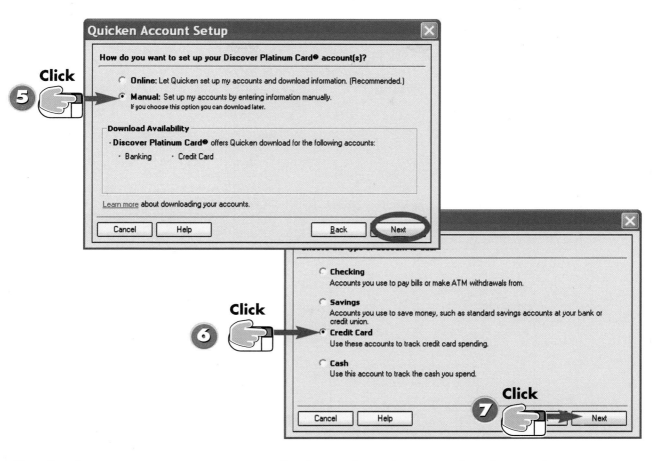

5 Quicken may prompt you to sign up for the credit card company's online services. Click **Manual** for now and activate online features later. Click **Next** to continue.

6 Click the **Credit Card** option to specify the type of account you want to create.

7 Click **Next** to continue.

See next page

Bank Not Listed?
If you enter a bank not listed on Quicken's financial institutions list, another dialog box may appear asking you to match the bank with one on the list. If your bank is listed, select it; if not, click **None of These**.

When to Create a Credit Card Account
If you carry a balance each month, a credit card account can help you see where you are accumulating debt.

Quicken Account Setup

Tell us about this credit card account

Name this account: `Discover Credit Card`

8

Click 9

Cancel | Help | Next

Setup

Enter the ending date and balance from your statement, if you have it.

▶ Enter the ending date on the statement.

Statement Date: `6/23/2003`

▶ Enter the ending ... nce ... he statement.

Endi... `0.00`

This becomes the op... ... of ... icken account.

Don't worry if you do... ... last ... t - you can make changes to your account later.

10

Cancel | Help | Back | Next

---

8 Type a name for the account or use the default name.

9 Click **Next** to continue.

10 Locate your latest credit card statement and then type a start date for the account. You can use the ending date of your latest statement as the start date.

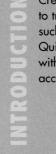

INTRODUCTION

Credit card accounts are designed to track money that you owe. As such, they are organized under Quicken's Cash Flow Center along with your checking and savings accounts.

TIP

Online Services
If your credit card's banking institution offers online services, you can download your online statements. Display the account register for the credit card and then click the **Set Up Now** button and follow the onscreen prompts.

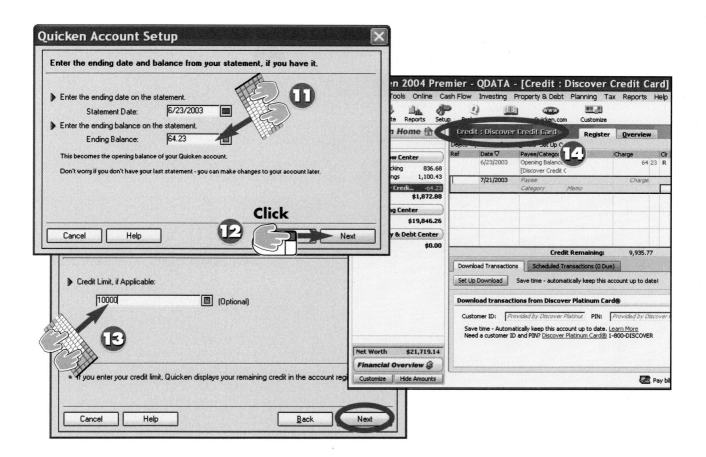

 Type in the balance owed at the end of the last billing period as the account's opening balance.

 Click **Next** to continue.

 Type in the amount of your credit card limit and click **Next**.

 Quicken creates and opens the account register.

Delete It

You can easily delete a credit card account you no longer want to track. Open the Account List window, select the account, and click the **Delete** button. Type **Yes** into the confirmation box and click **OK** to permanently remove the account and its transactions.

Entering Credit Card Charges

Start

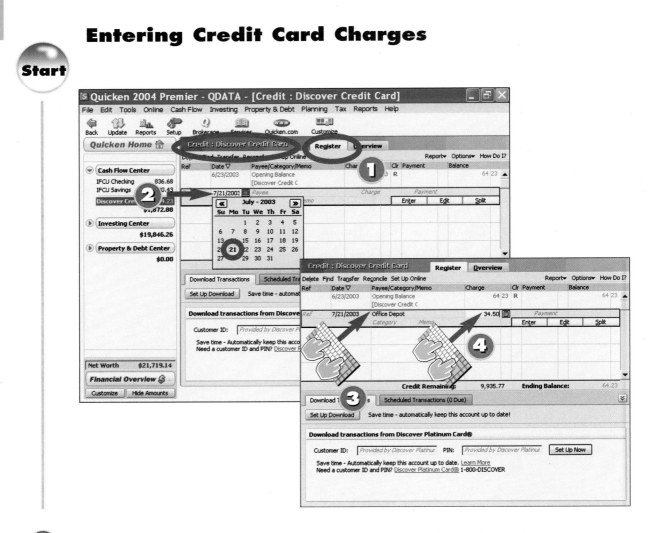

1. Click the credit card account in the Account bar to open the credit card register.

2. Type the charge date for the item you need to record. You can also click the Calendar icon and select a date.

3. Type in the name of the business or store from which you made the purchase.

4. Type in the amount of the purchase.

INTRODUCTION

You can record two types of transactions in a credit card account: charges and payments. Charges include any purchases you make with the credit card. Charges also include late fees, finance charges, and membership dues. Charges can also be negative, such as for an item you returned; the price is credited back to your account.

TIP

Do I Need a Ref?
You can leave the Ref field empty in your credit card register when recording transactions.

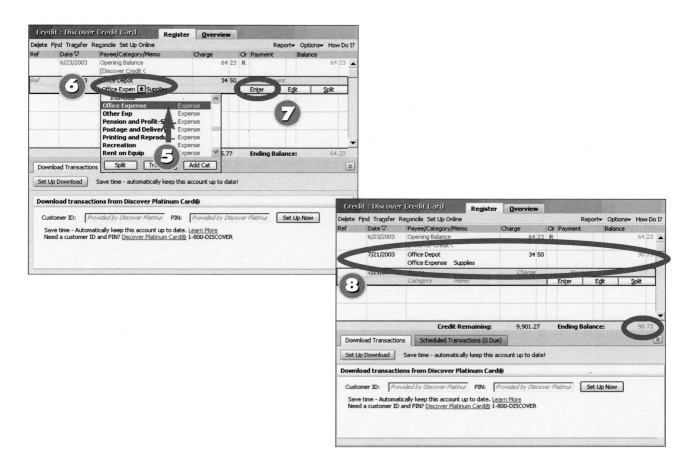

5 Assign a category to the transaction. Categories are crucial to track the way in which you use your charge card.

6 Optionally, you can record details about the purchase in the **Memo** field.

7 Click the **Enter** button.

8 Quicken records the transaction and displays the new account balance.

End

My Balance Is Red!
Because credit card charges represent money that you owe to the card issuer, the balance Quicken displays is color coded in red. The color red always denotes a negative balance in Quicken.

Category Help
To make the best use of Quicken's tracking features, be sure to assign categories to your credit card transactions. You can then view a report that shows you in what areas you are going into debt.

Paying Credit Card Bills

Start

Click

1 Open the checking account register.

2 Enter the transaction showing your payment to the credit card company.

3 nstead of selecting a category, choose a transfer to the credit card account. You can scroll to the bottom of the category list to find transfer listings.

INTRODUCTION

When it comes time to record a payment on your credit card, you can record the payment in your checking account register, but treat the payment as a transfer to the credit card account. Quicken automatically adds the transaction to your credit card account and updates the balance for you.

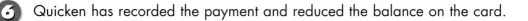

 Click the **Enter** button to finish recording the transaction.

Open the credit card account register.

Quicken has recorded the payment and reduced the balance on the card.

End

Reconciling a Credit Card Account

Start

Quicken 2004 Premier - QDATA - [Credit : Target Visa Card]

File   Edit   Tools   Online   Cash Flow   Investing   Property & Debt   Planning   Tax   Reports   Help

Back   Update   Reports   Setup   Brokerage   Services   Quicken.com   Customize

Quicken Home   Credit : Target Visa Card   **Register**   **1**

Delete   Find   Transfer   Reconcile

Ref	Date ▽	Payee/Category/Memo	Charge		Clr	Payment	Balance
	6/7/2003	TJ Maxx Household	37 08				290 84
	6/11/2003	S...rth... G...	12 05				302 89
	6/16/2003	Borders Books Office Expense	65 69				368 58
	6/25/2003	Tan For Less Misc	49 19				417 77
	6/26/2003	Brighton Collectibles Gifts	34 98				452 75
	6/28/2003	Brighton Collectibles Gifts Return			3 18		449 57
	6/28/2003	Talbots Misc	14 84				
	6/29/2003	Old Navy Misc	20 66				
	7/2/2003	Retailers National Bank [IFCU Checking] Target Card					
	6/28/2003	Payee Category Memo	Charge				

Cash Flow Center
IFCU Checking   836.68
IFCU Savings   1,100.43
Discover Credit ...   -98.73
Target Visa Card   -338.04
$1,500.34

Investing Center
$19,846.26

Property & Debt Center
$0.00

Net Worth $21,346.60

Financial Overview

Customize   Hide Amounts

Report ▾   Options ▾   How Do I?

Click

Credit Remaining: 8,061.96   End...

Download Transactions   Scheduled Transactions (0 Due)

Download quotes, news

Statement Summary: Target   **3**

The last statement ending date: N/A

1. Enter the following from your statement.

Charges, Cash Advances: 341.22
(other than finance ch...)

Payments, Credits: **4**   150.21

Ending Balance:

New Statement...:   7/21/2003

2. Enter and categ... interest charges, if any.

Finance Charges: Date: 7/21/2003
Category: Int Exp

OK   Cancel   Help

1 With your monthly credit card statement on hand, open the credit card account register.

2 Click the **Reconcile** button.

3 The Statement Summary dialog box opens. Type in the amount of charges as shown on the monthly statement.

4 Enter the amount of payments and credits as shown on the statement.

When you receive your monthly credit card statement, take a moment to reconcile the account. Reconciling a credit card account is similar to reconciling a checking or savings account, with just a few differences.

TIP

Speedy Opening
The quickest way to open your credit card account register is to click the account name listed in the Account bar.

Statement Summary: Target Visa ...

The last statement ending date: N/A

1. Enter the following from your statement.

Charges, Cash Advances: `341.22`
(other than finance charges)

Payments, Credits: `150.21`

Ending Balance: `372.04`

New Statement Ending Date: `7/7/2003`

«	July - 2003	»
Su Mo Tu We Th Fr Sa
1 2 3 4 5
6 7 8 9 10 11 12
14 15 16 17 18 19
21 23 24 25 26
27 30 31

2. Enter and categorize your interest charges, if any.

Finance Charges:

Category: `Int Exp`

OK

Click

Statement Summary: Target Visa ...

The last statement ending date: N/A

1. Enter the following from your statement.

Charges, Cash Advances: `341.22`
(other than finance charges)

Payments, Credits: `150.21`

Ending Balance: `372.04`

New Statement Ending Date: `7/7/2003`

2. Enter and categorize your interest charges, if any.

Finance Charges: `5.00`   Date `7/7/2003`

Categ: `Int Exp`   Cancel

July - 2003	»
Su Mo Tu We Th Fr Sa
1 2 3 4 5
6 7 8 9 10 11 12
13 14 15 16 17 18 19
20 21 22 23 24 25 26
27 28 29 30 31

⑤ Enter the new balance displayed on the statement.

⑥ Click the Calendar icon and select the statement ending date.

⑦ Enter the finance charges applied during the month and using the Calendar icon, enter the date on which they were applied.

See next page

Tab It
You can press the **Tab** key to quickly move from one field in the Statement Summary dialog box to the next.

Reconciling a Credit Card Account Continued

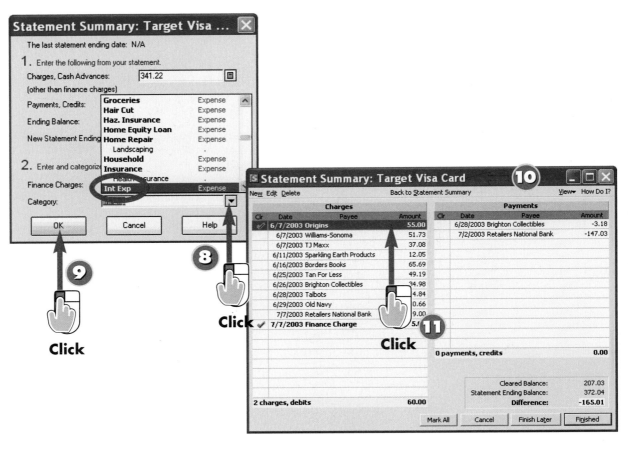

Click

Click

Click

 Use the **Category** drop-down list to categorize the finance charges as an interest expense by choosing **Int Exp** from the list.

9 Click **OK**.

10 Quicken opens the Statement Summary window for the account.

11 Locate the first charge listed on the actual statement and click the charge in the Statement Summary window to mark the charge as cleared.

If you are tracking multiple credit cards using Quicken, you'll need to use these same steps to reconcile each account every month.

TIP

Missing Charges
If you missed recording any charges, you can do so during reconciliation. Click the **Edit** button at the top of the Summary window and enter the transaction. Click the **Return to Reconcile** button to view the Summary window again.

Statement Summary: Target Visa Card

New Edit Delete — Back to Statement Summary — View▾ How Do I?

Cir	Date	Charges — Payee	Amount
✓	6/7/2003	Origins	55.00
✓	6/7/2003	Williams-Sonoma	51.73
✓	6/7/2003	TJ Maxx	37.08
✓	6/11/2...	Sparkling Earth Products	12.05
✓	6/16/2...	Borders Books	65.69
✓	6/25/2...	Tan For Less	49.19
✓	6/26/2...	Brighton Collectibles	34.98
✓	6/28/2...	Talbots	14.84
✓	6/29/2...	Old Navy	20.66
✓	7/7/2003	Retailers National Bank	29.00
✓	7/7/2003	Finance	

Cir	Date	Payments — Payee	Amount
✓	6/28/2...	Brighton Collectibles	-3.18
	7/2/2003	Retailers National Bank	-147.03

12 — 11 charges, debits

Statement Summary: Target Visa Card

New Edit Delete — Back to Statement Summary — View▾ How...

Cir	Date	Charges — Payee	Amount
✓	6/7/2003	Origins	55.00
✓	6/7/2003	Williams-Sonoma	51.73
✓	6/7/2003	TJ Maxx	37.08
✓	6/11/2...	Sparkling Earth Products	12.05
✓	6/16/2...	Borders Books	65.69
✓	6/25/2...	Tan For Less	49.19
✓	6/26/2...	Brighton Collectibles	34.98
✓	6/28/2...	Talbots	14.84
✓	6/29/2...	Old Navy	20.66
✓	7/7/2003	Retailers National Bank	29.00
✓	7/7/2003	Finance Charge	5.00

Cir	Date	Payments — Payee	Amo...
✓	6/28/2...	Brighton Collectibles	-...
✓	7/2/2003	Retailers National Bank	-14...

2 payments, credits — -150.21

11 charges, debits — 375.22

Cleared Balance:	372.04
Statement Ending Balance:	372.04
Difference:	0.00

Mark All — Cancel — Finish Later — **Finished**

14 Click

Make Credit Card Payment

Do you want to make a payment now?
You have an outstanding balance of $372.04

If you would like to pay some or all of this amount, select a bank account below and click Yes.

Bank Account: IFCU Checking ▾

Payment Method
● Printed Check
○ Hand Written Check

Click

Yes — No

☐ Don't show me this screen again.

15

---

12 Repeat step 11 to mark the remaining charges found on the statement.

13 Next, locate any payments listed on the account statement and click to mark the payments as cleared in the Statement Summary window.

14 Continue marking off each item on the charge card statement, and then click **Finished** when the balance is zero.

15 The Make Credit Card Payment dialog box opens if you still have an outstanding balance on the account. Click **No** to close the dialog box and make a payment later.

End

No Payment Required
HINT
If, after reconciling the account, your balance is zero, a prompt box appears telling you that no payment is required. Click **OK**.

Make a Payment
TIP
To pay on your account from the Make Credit Card Payment dialog box, choose a payment method. If you choose **Hand Written Check**, Quicken creates a transaction in your account, but it's up to you to write the check.

Creating a Register Report

Start

Click ①

Click ④

Screenshot: Quicken 2004 Premier - QDATA - [Credit : Target Visa Card]

File Edit Tools Online Cash Flow Investing Property & Debt Planning Tax Reports Help

Back Update Reports Setup Brok... Quicken.com Customize

Quicken Home   Credit : Target Visa Card   Register Overview

Report ▾   ions ▾

Delete Reconcile

Ref	Date ▽	Payee/Category/Memo				Balance
	6/16/2003	Borders Books / Office Expense			Register Report / Expense Summary Graph	
	6/25/2003	Tan For Less / Misc	49 19	R		417 77
	6/26/2003	Brighton Collectibles / Gifts	34 98	R		452 75
	6/28/2003	Brighton Collectibles / Gifts Return		R	3 18	449 57
	6/28/2003	Talbots / Misc	14 84	R		464 41
	6/29/2003	Old Navy / Misc	20 66	R		485 07
	7/2/2003	Retailers National Bank		R	147 03	338 04

Cash Flow Center
IFCU Checking   836.68
IFCU Savings   1,100.43
Discover Credit ...   -98.73
Target Visa Card   -372.04
                    $1,466.34

Investing Center
                   $19,846.26

Property & Debt Center
                        $0.00

Net Worth $21,312.60

Financial Overview
Customize Hide Amounts

Register Report

Preferences How Do I?

Click Copy Sort ▾

Print

History:
Register Report - As of

③

Date Range: Include all dates ▾   Subtotal By: Don't subtotal ▾   Save Report Customize

②

Register Report - As of
1/31/2000 Through 7/21/2003

Date	Account	Num	Description	Memo	Category	Clr	Amount
BALANCE 1/30/2000							**0.00**
6/7/2003	Target Visa...		Opening Balance		[Target Visa Card]	R	-147.03
6/7/2003	Target Visa...		Origins		Household	R	-55.00
6/7/2003	Target Visa...		Williams-Sonoma		Household	R	-51.73
6/7/2003	Target Visa...		TJ Maxx		Household	R	-37.08
6/11/2003	Target Visa...		Sparkling Earth Pro...		Gifts	R	-12.05
6/16/2003	Target Visa...		Borders Books		Office Expense	R	-65.69
6/25/2003	Target Visa...		Tan For Less		Misc	R	-49.19
6/26/2003	Target Visa...		Brighton Collectibles		Gifts	R	-34.98
6/28/2003	Target Visa...		Talbots		Misc	R	-14.84
6/28/2003	Target Visa...		Brighton Collectibles Return		Gifts	R	3.18
6/29/2003	Target Visa...		Old Navy		Misc	R	-20.66
7/2/2003	Target Visa...		Retailers National ...	Target Card	[IFCU Checking]	R	147.03
7/7/2003	Target Visa...		Retailers National ...	Late Fee	Credit Cards:R...	R	-29.00
7/7/2003	Target Visa...		Finance Charges		Int Exp	R	-5.00
TOTAL 1/31/2000 - 7/21/2003							**-372.04**

① Open the credit card account register, click the **Report** drop-down arrow and click **Register Report**.

② Quicken opens the Report window and displays a summary of your credit card charges and payments.

③ Click **Print** to generate a printout of the report.

④ Click the **Close** button to close the Report window.

End

You can view a register report that summarizes your credit card account transactions, showing how much you are spending and how much you are paying on the account. Quicken reports are a great way to view your financial data in detail, and in the case of credit card reports, you can easily keep an eye on what you are charging to your credit card.

TIP

Need a Customized Report?
The Report window offers plenty of ways to create a custom report. To learn more about making a customized report, see the task "Creating a Customized Report" in Part 7, "Tracking Your Cash Flow."

Viewing an Expense Summary Graph

Start

Quicken 2004 Premier - QDATA - [Credit : Target Visa Card]

File   Edit   Tools   Online   Cash Flow   Investing   Property & Debt   Planning   Tax   Reports   Help

Back   Update   Reports   Setup   Broker...   Quicken.com   Customize

Quicken Home 🏠   Credit : Target Visa Card   **Register**   **Overview**

Report ▾   Options ▾   How Do I?   **Click**   ①

Ref	Date ▽	Payee/Category/Memo			Balance
	6/16/2003	Borders Books	Register Report		3
		Office Expense	Expense Summary Graph		
	6/25/2003	Tan For Less	49 19	R	417 77
		Misc			
	6/26/2003	Brighton Collectibles	34 98	R	452 75
		Gifts			
	6/28/2003	Brighton Collectibles		R 3 18	449 57
		Gifts Return			
	6/28/2003	Talbots	14 84	R	464 41
		Misc			
	6/29/2003	Old Navy	20 66	R	485 07
		Misc			
	7/2/2003	Retailers National Bank			
		[IFCU Checking] Target Card			
	7/7/2003	Retailers National Bank			
		Credit Cards:Ret Late Fee			
	7/7/2003	Finance Charges			
		Int Exp			
	7/25/2003	*Payee*			
		Category *Memo*			

Cash Flow Center
IFCU Checking   836.68
IFCU Savings   1,100.43
Discover Credit ...   -98.73
Target Visa Card -372.04
$1,466.34

Investing Center
$19,846.26

Property & Debt Center
$0.00

Credit Remaini...

Net Worth $21,312.60
Financial Overview 🔍
Customize   Hide Amounts

Download Transactions   Scheduled Transactions (

Expense Summary

1/1/2003 - 7/21/2003

②

Household	38.65%
Misc	22.76%
Office Expense	17.66%
Gifts	11.79%
Credit Cards	7.795%
Other	1.344%
Total	$372.04

These are the categories where you have spent the most money so far.

Click   ③

OK

End

① From the credit card account register, click the **Report** button and click **Expense Summary Graph**.

② Quicken displays the Expense Summary dialog box showing a graph of categorized spending for your credit card.

③ Click **OK** to return to the credit card account register.

INTRODUCTION

Graphs can speak volumes when it comes to examining where your money goes. The Expense Summary Graph for your credit card account shows you which categories you charge to when you use your charge card. To use this graph, you must faithfully assign categories to the credit card transactions you record.

TIP

Use Those Categories!
Categories are an important part of tracking your spending habits. You can learn more about using Quicken categories in Part 2, including how to edit and add new categories.

Tracking Loans

When you borrow money from a person or financial institution, you usually take out a loan—a formal agreement to pay the lender back. That loan debt is a *liability*. In Quicken, setting up a loan simultaneously sets up a liability account to track your payment progress. For example, for most people, owning a house also involves paying a mortgage; owning a car includes making car payments. When you create an account to track an asset such as a house or car, Quicken also walks you through steps for setting up a liability account for tracking loan payments. To create a liability account for your loan, you'll need to know how much you owe on the loan, how many loan payments you owe, and what the interest rate is.

In addition to helping you track loans, Quicken also includes several calculator tools you can use to project loan costs and payments, college costs, and more. This section of the book introduces you to several of the calculator tools that can help you with existing and future loans.

The View Loans Window

View Loans: House Loan

New Delete   Choose Loan (x)▾   Print How Do I?

| Loan Summary | Payment Schedule | ✓ House Loan |

Opening Date: 9/1/1992

Loan Amount: 98,000.00

Payment Amount: 698.37

Current Interest Rate: 5.0%

Original Length: 30 Years

Payment Frequency: Monthly

Compounding Period: Daily

Edit Loan...

Edit Payment...

Make Payment...

Rate Changes...

Payee: Countrywide...
Current Balance: 80,000.00
Remaining Pmts: 157
Final Pmt Date: 8/1/2016

Loan details appear here.

You can edit loan details by clicking the Edit Loan button.

You can edit your loan payment by clicking the Edit Payment button.

You can instruct Quicken to make a payment on the loan for you and specify which account to use.

If your loan's interest rate changes, you can record the new rate using this button.

Tracking a House Loan

Start

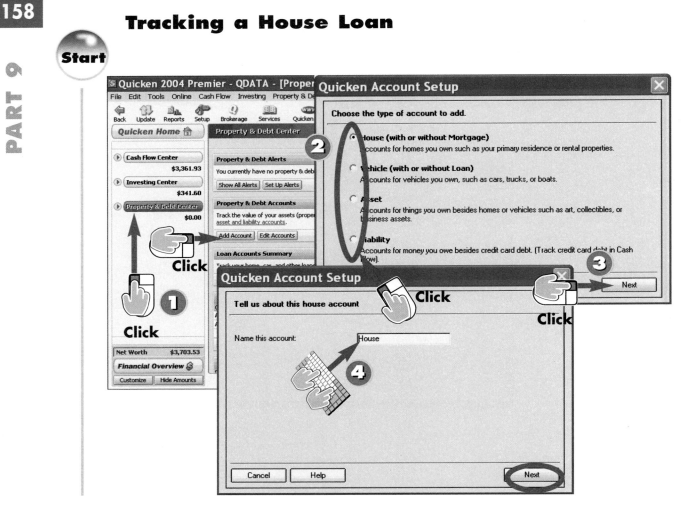

1. Click the **Property & Debt Center** in the Account bar, and then click the **Add Account** button.

2. Quicken displays the Quicken Account Setup dialog box. Select a loan type.

3. Click **Next** to continue.

4. Type a name for the loan and click **Next**.

INTRODUCTION

You can create a loan account to track the progress of your loan payments. For example, you might set up a loan account for your house or car. In Quicken, setting up a loan simultaneously sets up a liability account to track your payment progress. Although this task focuses on tracking a home loan, you can also use these steps to track a car loan.

TIP

Other Types of Loan Accounts
You can also select the Asset account to track the value of other assets you own, such as personal property, or select a Liability account to track money that you owe to others.

Quicken Account Setup ☒

Enter the starting point information.

When did you acquire this property? 9/1/1992

Purchase price: 104,000.00

Estimate its current value: 145,000.00

- It's okay to enter appr____ ___es. You will be able to change them later.

5

Cancel   Help

6 **Click**   Next

7 **Click**

...count Setup ☒

Is there a mortgage on this property?

⦿ Yes, create a liability account for me.

○ There is a mortgage, and I'm already tracking it in Quicken.

Account: [▾]

○ The house is paid for, so I don't need a liability account.

8 **Click**

Cancel   Help   Done

5 Enter the purchase date, price, and the current value. You can estimate and change details later.

6 Click the **Next** button to continue.

7 To create a liability account for the mortgage on the home, leave the **Yes, Create a Liability Account for Me** option selected.

8 Click **Done**.

See next page

TIP

Asset or Liability
If you choose to create an asset or liability account for something other than a house, your steps will differ from the ones shown in this task. You're prompted to enter a starting date and the value or amount owed.

HINT

Tax Info
To associate a tax form with the loan, you can click the **Tax** button and choose a tax form and line for the account.

Tracking a House Loan Continued

Edit Loan

Loan Information:
Opening Date: 9/1/1992
Original Balance: 98,000.00
Original Length: 30 Years
Compounding Period: Daily

Payment Period
○ Standard Period: Monthly
○ Other Period: Payments per Year

Cancel   Help   Next

9

10 Click

Balloon Information
○ No Balloon Payment
○ Amortized Length: Years
○ Calculate

Current Balance
Current Balance: 80,000.00 as of: 7/27/2003

Payment
○ Payment Amount (P+I): 698.37 due on: 8/1/2003
○ Calculate   Interest Rate: 5.0%

Cancel   Help   Back   Done

11

12

9 The Edit Loan dialog box opens for creating the liability account. Fill in the loan information.

10 Choose a payment period for the loan and then click **Next** to continue.

11 Fill in information about balloon payments, the current balance, and the date for the current balance.

12 Enter your loan payment amount, date due, and interest rate, and then click **Done**.

INTRODUCTION

To create a house loan account, you'll need to know how much you owe, how many loan payments you must make, and what the interest rate is. After you complete the task of filling in each dialog box, Quicken creates the loan and displays the register for the loan account. You can use the register to record future transactions associated with the loan.

TIP

What If I Enter the Wrong Info?
Don't worry if you're not sure about a value for a particular field. You can always edit the loan information later after creating the account. The next task shows you how.

Click

Edit Loan Payment

Payment

Current Interest Rate:	5.0%
Principal and Interest:	698.37
Other amounts in payment:	0.00
Full Payment:	698.37

E_dit..._

Transaction

Type:	Payment
Payee:	
Memo:	
Next Payment Date:	8/1/2003
Category for Interest:	Mortgage Int:Bank

Show __ bill

OK
Cancel
Address...
Pay Now...
Help

A - [Asset : House]

_g_ Property & Debt Planning Tax Reports Help

ervices   Quicken.com   Customize

Register   **Overview**

er Update Balance

Payee/Category/Memo	Decrease	Clr	Increase	Balance
Opening Balance [House]			104,000 00	104,000 00
Balance Adjustment [House]		R	41,000 00	145,000 00
Payee	Decrease		Increase	
Category Memo			Enter Edit Split	

Report▾ Options▾ How Do I?

House	145,000.00
House Loan	-80,000.00
	$65,000.00

Ending Balance: 145,000.00

Net Worth	$68,703.53

Financial Overview 🔄

Customize   Hide Amounts

Scheduled Transactions (0 Due)

↑ See how you can pay lower rates - check your FICO score

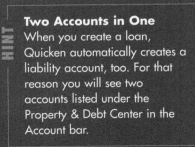

13 Verify the principal and interest payments calculated by Quicken.

14 Fill in details about your loan transactions, including payment type and lender name. Then click **OK**.

15 Quicken opens a register for the loan account. You can now enter future transactions for the loan using the register.

End

Two Accounts in One

When you create a loan, Quicken automatically creates a liability account, too. For that reason you will see two accounts listed under the Property & Debt Center in the Account bar.

Editing Your Loan Information

Start

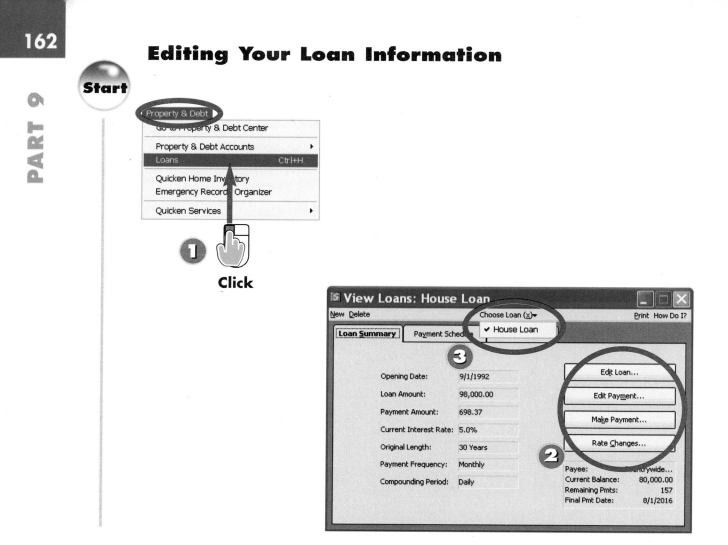

Click

1 Click **Property & Debt**, **Loans**.

2 Quicken opens the View Loans window. Each button opens a dialog box where you can make changes to the loan information.

3 If you have more than one loan account set up, click the **Choose Loan** drop-down arrow and select the loan you want to view.

INTRODUCTION

You can make changes to the information in your loan account using the View Loans window. For example, you may need to correct a wrong figure entered during the loan setup procedure. The View Loans window includes three tabs for viewing details about a loan, as well as buttons you can activate to make changes to the loan information.

TIP

Change the Interest Rate
To change the loan's interest rate, click the **Rate Changes** button in the View Loans window and edit the interest rate information.

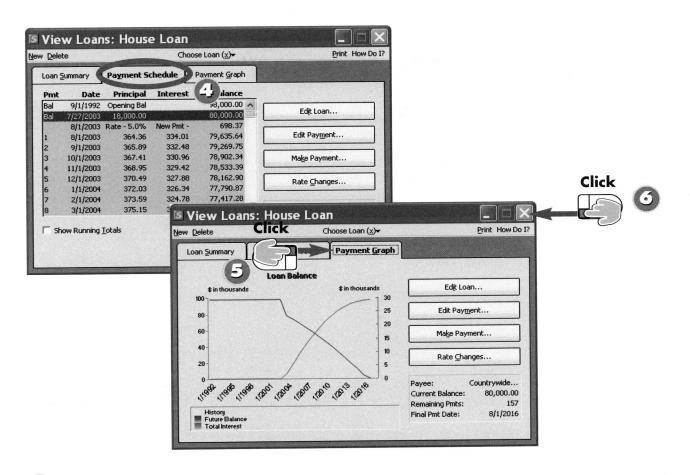

4 Click the **Payment Schedule** tab to view a payment schedule for the loan.

5 Click the **Payment Graph** tab to view a graph of your loan payment over time.

6 Click the **Close** button to exit the View Loans window.

End

Print It

You can print out the information found on any of the tabs in the View Loans window. Click the tab you want to print, and then click the **Print** button.

Recording a Loan Payment

Start

Property & Debt
 Go to Property & Debt Center
 Property & Debt Accounts
 Loans   Ctrl+H
 Quicken Home Inventory
 Emergency Records Organizer
 Quicken Services

Click 1

View Loans: House Loan

New Delete   Choose Loan (x)▼   Print How Do I?

Loan Summary | Payment Schedule | Payment Graph

Opening Date: 9/1/1992
Loan Amount: 98,000.00
Payment Amount: 69?   **Click 2**
Current Interest Rate: 5.0
Original Length: 10 Years
Payment Frequency: Monthly
Compounding Period: Daily

Edit Loan...
Edit Payment...
Make Payment...
Rate Changes...

Payee: Countrywide...
Current Balance: 80,000.00
Remaining Pmts: 0
Final Pmt Date:

Loan Payment

Is this your regularly scheduled payment, or an extra payment to this loan?

Click 3   Regular   Extra   Cancel   Help

1 Click **Property & Debt**, **Loans**.

2 In the View Loans window, select the loan account you want to pay from the **Choose Loan** drop-down menu, if needed. Click the **Make Payment** button.

3 Quicken asks you what type of payment you want to make. Click a payment type.

INTRODUCTION

After you set up your loan account, you can record payment transactions in the account register. You can specify whether you're making a regular payment or an extra payment. Regular payments are the actual payments required by the loan. Extra payments include any amounts over your normal payment.

HINT

Don't Forget to Pay
After recording a payment, don't forget to actually make the payment.

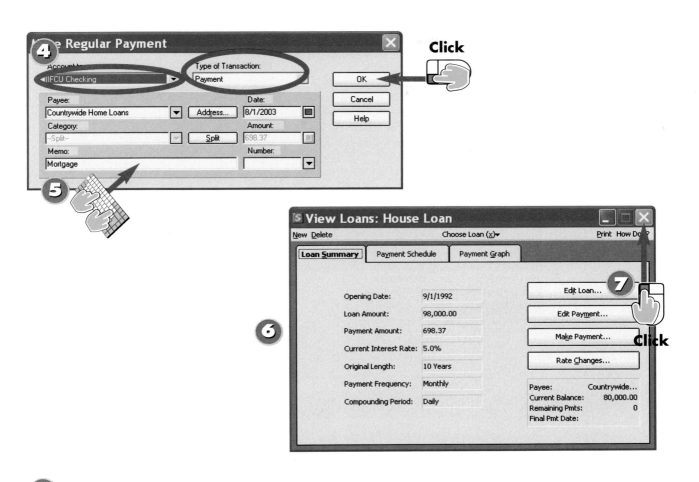

Click

Click

Choose an account to make the payment from and select a payment type.

Fill in the transaction details the same as you would when writing a check and click **OK**.

Quicken records the payment in the account register you selected in step 4 and adjusts the balance in the loan account register.

Click the **Close** button to exit the View Loans window.

End

What About Asset Accounts?
You can record transactions in your asset account just as you do a regular cash flow account. For example, you might sell an asset, thus decreasing the value of the account. Remember, asset accounts can help you track the value of personal property.

Using the Loan Calculator

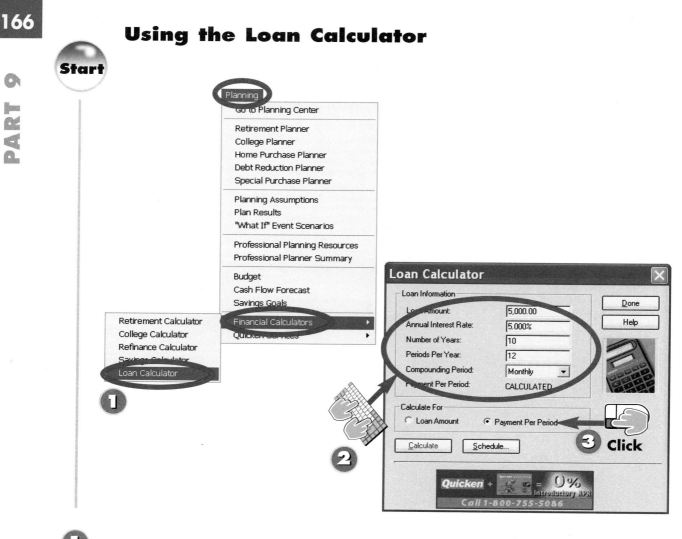

1 Click **Planning**, **Financial Calculators**, **Loan Calculator**.

2 Type the loan information into the Loan Calculator dialog box.

3 Select whether to calculate for a loan amount or payment per period.

INTRODUCTION

Quicken includes a Loan Calculator tool that you can use to calculate loan payments and balances. You can quickly calculate the principal or periodic payment for a loan.

TIP

Or Click the Link
You can also access Quicken's calculators through the Planning Center window. Simply click the link for the calculator you want to open.

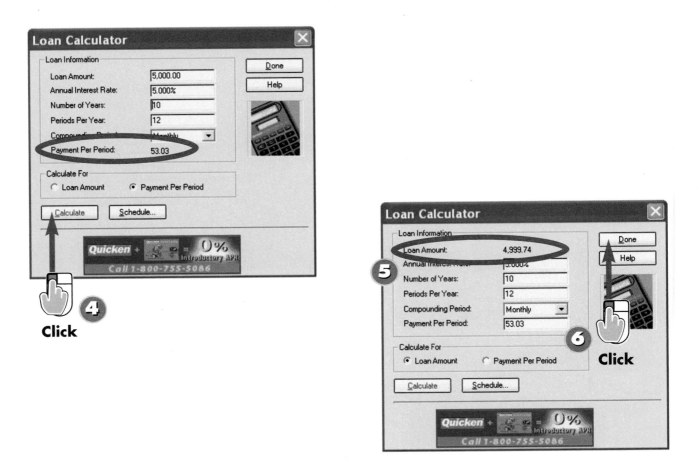

Click

Click

4 Click the **Calculate** button. If you're calculating a payment, Quicken automatically calculates the amount and displays it in the Payment Per Period field.

5 If you're calculating a loan amount, Quicken displays the calculation in the Loan Amount field.

6 When finished calculating loan amounts or payments, click the **Done** button to close the Loan Calculator.

End

Other Calculators

Quicken offers five calculators you can use to make financial calculations: the Retirement Calculator, the College Calculator, the Refinance Calculator, the Savings Calculator, and the Loan Calculator. See Part 10, "Tracking Investments," to learn about the Retirement Calculator.

TIP

Using the College Calculator

Start

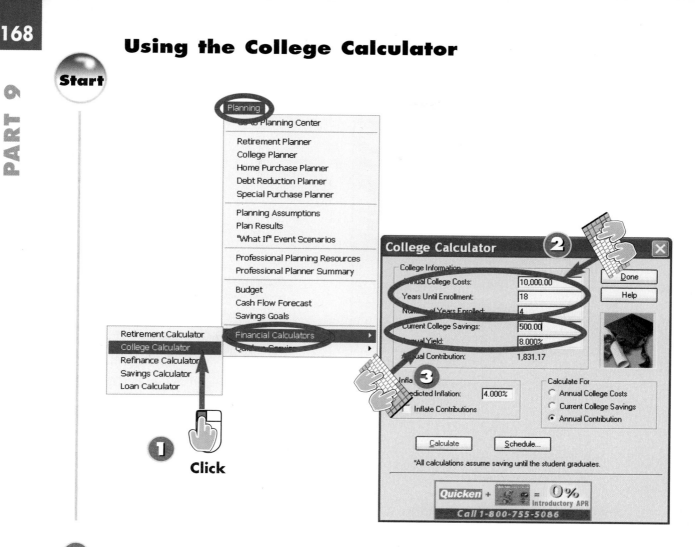

1 Click **Planning**, **Financial Calculators**, **College Calculator**.

2 In the College Calculator dialog box, fill in the information for the tuition, the number of years until enrollment, and the expected number of years enrolled.

3 Type in your current college savings amount and the annual yield.

INTRODUCTION

Another useful tool you can use in Quicken is the College Calculator. If you have a child you plan to send to college, you can use the College Calculator to determine how much you need to save each year to meet the goal.

TIP

Changing Values
Depending on what choice you make in the Calculate For area of the College Calculator, the College Information fields may vary.

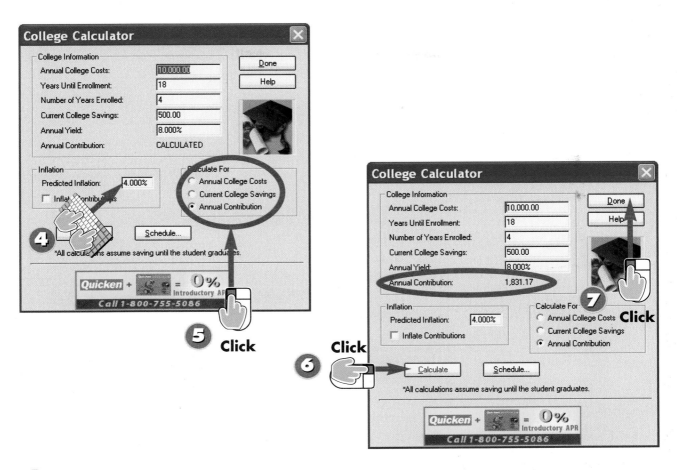

4. Type an inflation rate.

5. Select whether you want to calculate for annual costs, current savings, or annual contribution.

6. Click the **Calculate** button. Quicken calculates the cost.

7. Continue adjusting the data as needed. When finished, click the **Done** button to close the Loan Calculator.

End

See a Schedule
You can click the **Schedule** button to see a printable list of deposits you would need to make to reach your savings goal.

Using the Debt Reduction Planner

Start

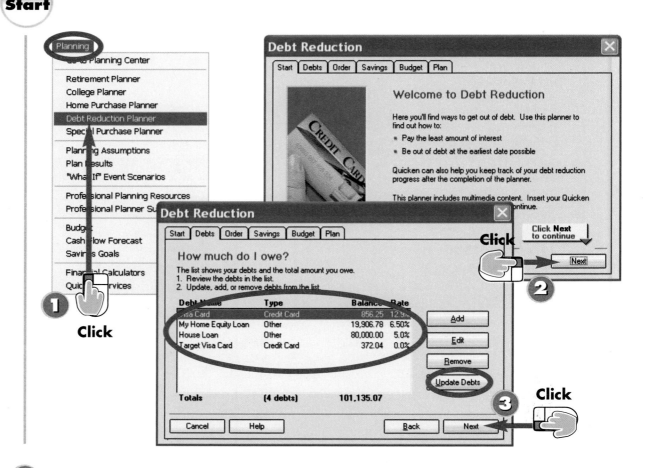

1 Click **Planning**, **Debt Reduction Planner**.

2 Quicken opens the Debt Reduction Wizard. Start by clicking the **Next** button.

3 Quicken lists your current debts. If the list is not current, click the **Update Debts** button. Click **Next** to continue.

INTRODUCTION

The Debt Reduction Planner is used for ways to reduce your debt. If you have your Quicken CD, you can insert it and view some short movies with each step of the planner. This task skips the video portion of the planner. If you decide to view each video, click the Next button to continue to the next phase of the planner.

TIP

Start a New One
If you've previously used the Debt Reduction Planner, Quicken opens the Debt Reduction window. Click the **New Plan** button to create a new plan.

TIP

Edit Debts
You can edit the list of debts. For example, you can click the **Add** button and fill in information for another debt account. Or you can select a debt and click the **Remove** button to keep Quicken from figuring it into the plan.

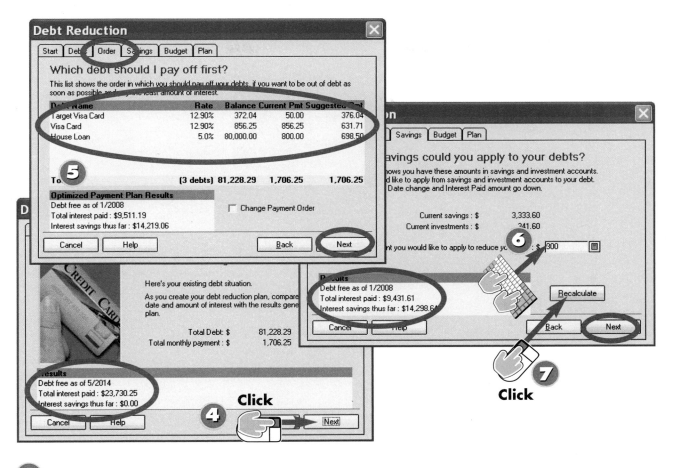

4. The Debts tab lists your current debt status. Click **Next** to continue.

5. The Order tab suggests the order in which you should pay off your debt and the payment amount. Click **Next** to continue.

6. The Savings tab enables you to enter a onetime amount toward paying down the debt.

7. If you entered a onetime payment amount, click the **Recalculate** button to view the results in the lower-left corner. Click **Next** to continue.

See next page

Change Payment Order
On the Order tab, you can change the order in which the Debt Planner lists your debts for paying off. Click the **Change Payment Order** check box and another dialog box appears with controls for rearranging the list items.

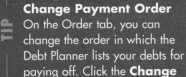

Using the Debt Reduction Planner
Continued

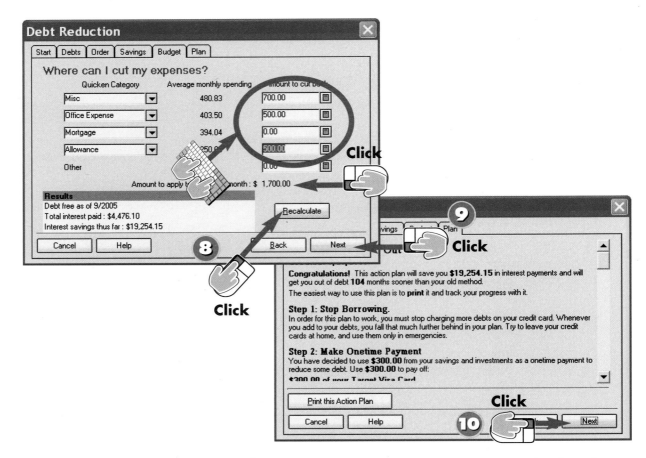

8. The Budget tab lists your top four expenses. Enter an amount you can cut back on for each and click the **Recalculate** button.

9. Quicken recalculates the savings. Click the **Next** button to continue.

10. The Debt Planner displays an Action Plan you can use to help you get out of debt. Click **Next** to continue.

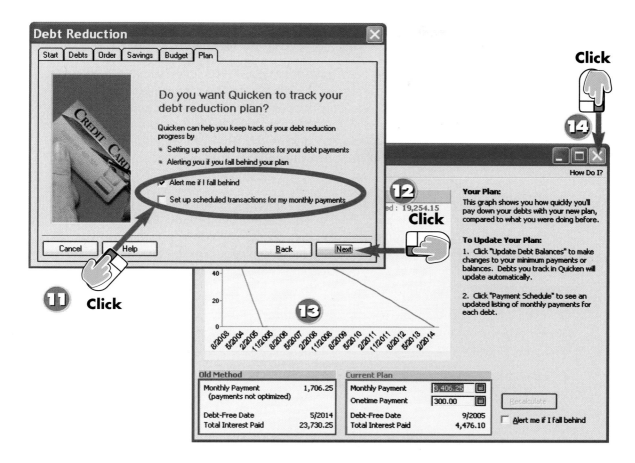

11   The final dialog box prompts you to select how you want Quicken to track your plan.
Select an option.

12   Click **Next**.

13   Quicken displays the Debt Reduction window along with a chart comparing your
present course and the plan you created.

14   Click the **Close** button to close the Debt Reduction window.

View Your Plan
To view your action plan at any
time, click **Planning, Debt
Reduction Planner**. For
example, if you make any sig-
nificant changes to your debt
balances, you can return to the
plan and update the balances.

Tracking Investments

Quicken can help you manage your investment accounts. Investments are any security or asset that you expect to increase in value over time. Investments include CDs, money market funds, stocks, brokerage accounts, employee stock options, treasury bills, 401(k)s, and IRAs, to name a few. You can add an investment account to track all types of investments in Quicken. This part of the book shows you how to use Quicken to manage an account, record transactions, download stock quotes, and more.

You can set up four types of investment accounts: brokerage, IRA or Keogh, 401(k) or 403(b), or single mutual fund. Before you begin, be sure to have your latest account statement handy. Quicken's Account Setup will ask you to fill in a variety of data to describe the investment. If you're lucky and your institution offers online services, you can simply download your account information directly into Quicken and save yourself some typing.

Quicken's Investing Center keeps your investment *portfolio* in one convenient spot. A portfolio is the total of all your investments. From the Investing Center, you can analyze your investments, view their performance, and check their daily values.

This part of the book explains the basics of Quicken's investing features.

Investing Center

You can use the other tabs to view charts and graphs of your investment's performance and current status.

You can use the Watch List to track stocks and other securities.

You can control how items appear listed in the portfolio.

	Quicken 2004 Premier - QDATA - [Investing Center]							

File Edit Tools Online Cash Flow Investing Property & Debt Planning Tax Reports Help

Back Update Reports Setup Brokerage Services Quicken.com Customize

Today's Data Performance Analysis **Portfolio**

Download Quotes   Download Historical Prices   Quicken Brokerage ▼   Options ▼   Glossary   How Do I?

Show: Value   Group by: Accounts   As of: 7/27/2003

Cash Flow Center
$3,263.20

Investing Center
E*Trade Invest...   341.60
Retirement Plan 20,480.18
$20,821.78

Property & Debt Center
$60,000.00

Name	Quote/Price	Day Change	Day Change (%)	Shares	Market Value	Cost Basis
E*Trade Investmen...					387.60	*
⊞ Raytheon	est. 32.30			12	387.60	Enter
Retirement Plan					20,480.18	20,480.18
Cash					20,480.18	20,480.18
Watch List						
Dodge & Cox	est. 66.89					
Eclipse	est. 11.55					
Eclipse Growth Fund	est. 17.72					
Fidelity Magellan Fund	est. 89.57					
Janus Overseas Fund	est. 16.86					
MFS Mid Cap Growt...	est. 7.04					
Pimco	est. 10.78					
Totals:					20,867.78	20,480.18*

*Placeholder Entries for missing data are used in these calculations.

Net Worth	$84,084.98

Financial Overview ⑤

Customize   Hide Amounts

Online quotes by S&P Comstock, delayed at least 20 minutes. Updated 7/26/2003 at 2:53 pm local time. Historical quotes by Iverson.

Receive free Quicken newsletters for financial tips

Setting Up an Investment Account

Start

1 Click the **Investing Center** link on the Account bar and then click the **Add Account** button to open the Quicken Account Setup dialog box.

2 If the account is associated with a brokerage, click this option and type the name of the financial institution or select it from the pop-up list that appears.

3 Click the **Next** button to continue.

INTRODUCTION

In Quicken, you create an *investment account* for each brokerage statement you receive. An investment account tracks mutual funds, stocks, bank CDs, and other investments. You can use it to track changes to the share price or value of each investment, such as a stock or mutual fund. In this task, you learn how to download account information from a brokerage.

No Institution?

TIP If your account is not associated with a financial institution, choose the **This Account Is Not Held at a Financial Institution** option in the first Quicken Account Setup dialog box, and then set up the account manually.

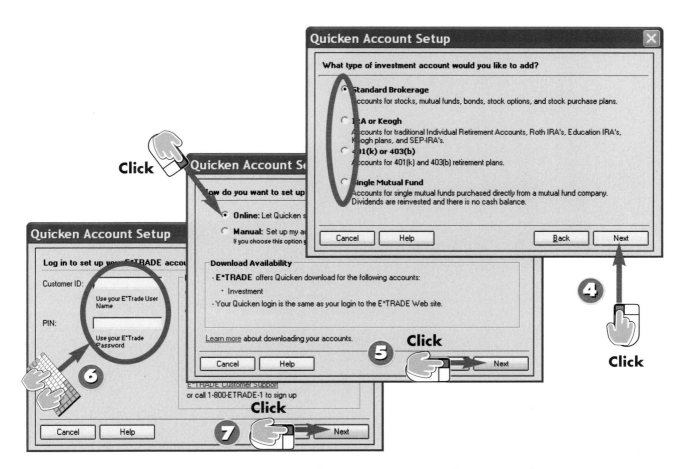

4 Depending on the institution you selected in step 3, you may be prompted to specify a type of an investment account. Select an option and click **Next**.

5 If applicable, Quicken prompts you to sign up for the firm's online services. Click **Online** and click **Next** to continue.

6 Type in your account's Customer ID and PIN.

7 Click **Next** to continue.

See next page

Menu Method
You can also start a new account from the Investing menu. Click Investing, Investment Accounts, Add Account to open the Quicken Account Setup dialog box.

Online Availability
If you specify a financial institution, one of the first Quicken Account Setup dialog boxes you'll encounter describes the firm's download availability options. If your firm is not accessible online, you must choose the **Manual** option and manually record your investment data.

Setting Up an Investment Account
Continued

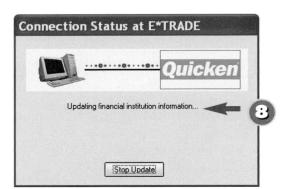

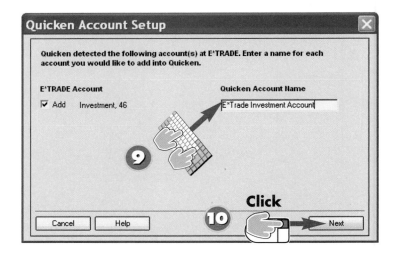

8 Log on to your Internet account, if needed, and Quicken connects to your financial institution and downloads your account data.

9 The Add check box is checked automatically. Type a name for the account.

10 Click **Next** to continue.

TIP

Track a Mutual Fund
To set up an account to track a mutual fund, your steps may vary from the ones shown in this task. You will need to specify whether the account is tax deferred or exempt and then fill in account details as prompted.

Quicken Account Setup

You have successfully set up the following account(s) in Quicken:

E'TRADE Account   **Quicken Account**

Investment (46)  **11**   E*Trade Investment Account

Next Step
Download your holdings and all available historical transactions. Typically, the available
transaction history is 60-180 days.

Click

Cancel   Help   **12**   Next

Quicken One Step Update Status

Quicken

Sending Online Instructions...
E*TRADE   **13**
0%

E*TRADE

☑ Show item list

Learn how to best track your credit card spending
After updating, click on Quicken Services in the tool bar

Help   Stop Update

11 Quicken describes the accounts you have set up. Now it is ready to download your
investment information.

12 Click the **Next** button to continue setting up the account.

13 Quicken downloads your account history.

See
next
page

Creating an IRA Account
TIP
If you are setting up an IRA or
Keogh account, your steps will
differ from those shown in this
task. Different dialog boxes
appear for you to fill in your
account holdings data.

Setting Up an Investment Account
Continued

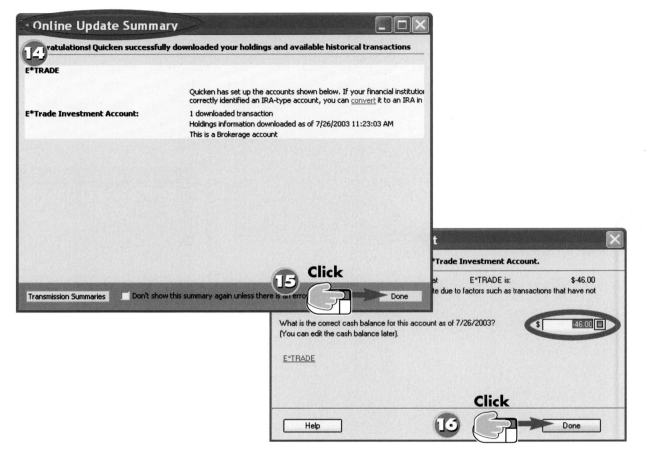

 When the download is complete, the Online Update Summary dialog box appears detailing your holdings.

15 Click **Done** to complete the account setup process.

16 The Cash Balance Adjustment dialog box may appear. Update the balance, if needed, and then click **Done**.

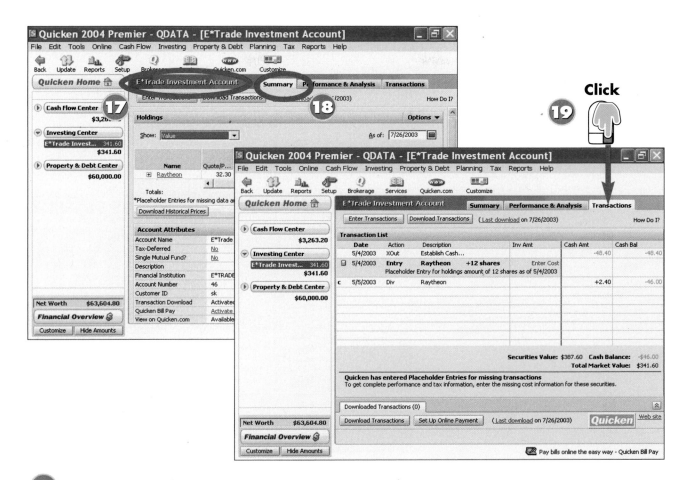

17 Quicken opens the investment account's register in the Investing Center.

18 The Summary tab displays by default and lists a summary of your account.

19 Click the **Transactions** tab to view the register portion of the account. You can enter and edit transactions here.

End

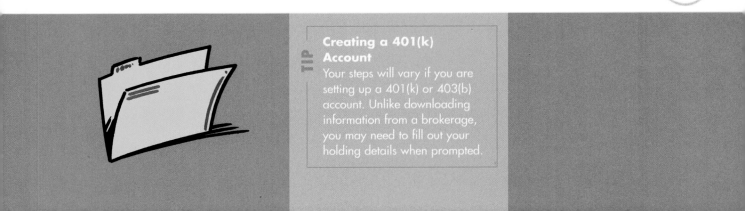

TIP

Creating a 401(k) Account
Your steps will vary if you are setting up a 401(k) or 403(b) account. Unlike downloading information from a brokerage, you may need to fill out your holding details when prompted.

Recording an Investment Transaction

Start

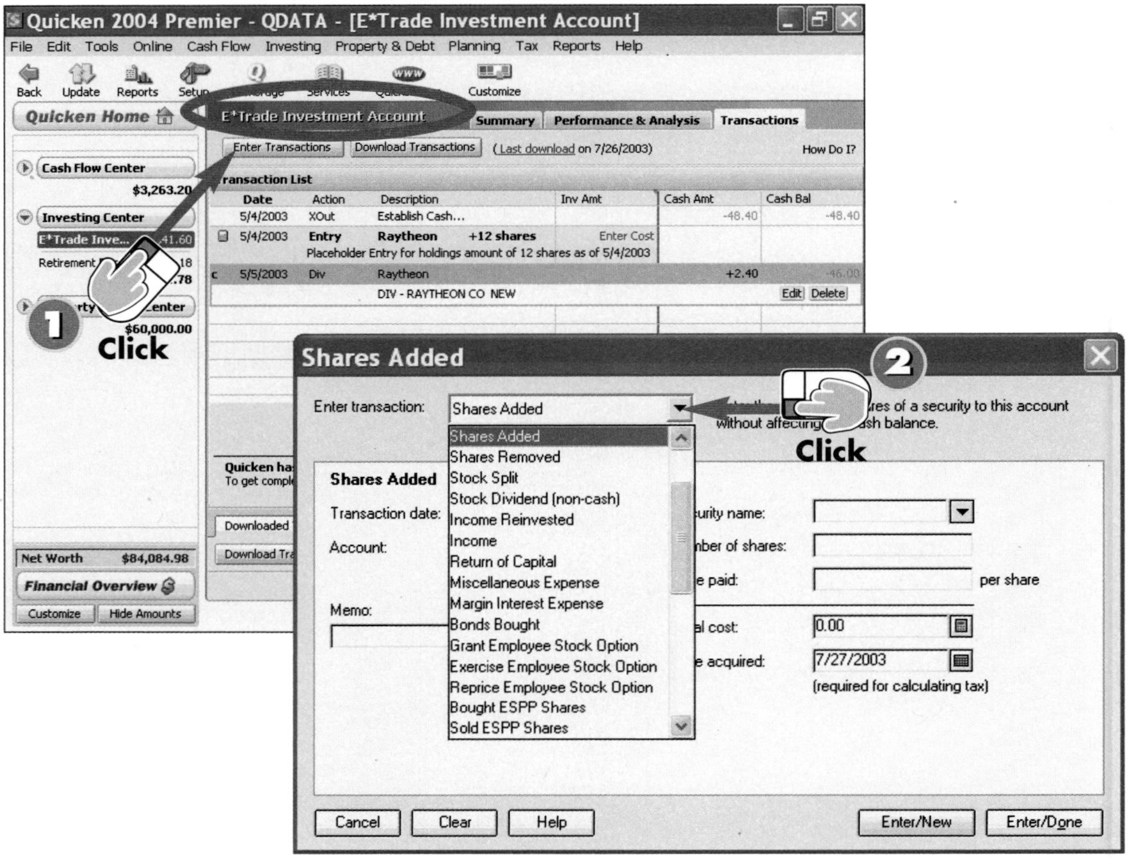

① Click

② Click

① Display the account register for which you want to add transactions and click the **Enter Transactions** button.

② Click the **Enter Transaction** drop-down arrow and select the type of transaction you want to record.

Tailor Made
Depending on the type of transaction you select, the Enter Transaction dialog box displays different data fields for transaction details. If you are buying shares, the dialog box has fields to specify how many, how much, and commission fees.

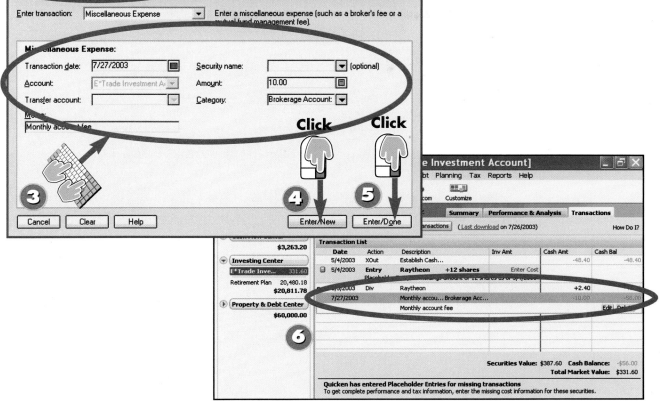

3 Quicken retitles the dialog box to reflect your transaction choice. Fill out the transaction details.

4 Click **Enter/New** to record this transaction and keep the dialog box open to record another transaction.

5 Click **Enter/Done** to record the transaction and exit the dialog box.

6 Quicken records the transaction in the register.

End

Edit the Transaction
To make changes to a transaction you've already recorded, select the transaction in the register and click the **Edit** button.

Viewing Your Portfolio

Start

Click

Click

1. Click the **Investing Center** link on the Account bar.

2. Click the **Portfolio** tab.

3. Quicken lists all your investments.

End

Setting Up an Investment Alert

Start

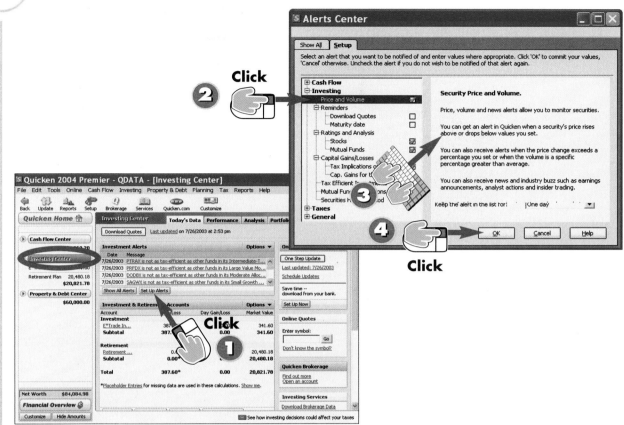

Click ②

Click ③

Click ①

Click ④

End

① Click the Investing Center link, click the **Today's Data** tab, and click the **Set Up Alerts** button.

② Quicken opens the Alerts Center window and displays the Investing alerts. Click the item to which you want to assign an alert.

③ Quicken displays options related to the selected item. Fill in the fields for the alert.

④ Click **OK**. When circumstances occur that meet the alert criteria, the alert appears in the Investing Center.

INTRODUCTION

You can use alerts to warn you if you go over or under a specified figure. For example, with your cash flow accounts, you might use an alert to let you know if your balance drops below your checking account minimum. Alerts appear at the top of the Cash Flow Center window so you can easily spot them when they occur.

TIP

Alert Prompt Box
If you'd rather set a more obvious alert, choose the **Urgent** option in the Alerts Center window. With this option activated, the alert appears as a prompt box. Click **OK** to close the box and continue working with Quicken.

TIP

Remove an Alert
To remove an alert you no longer want, reopen the Alerts Center window and deselect the check box beside the item to which an alert is assigned.

Downloading Stock Quotes

Start

1 Click the **Investing Center** link on the Account bar.

2 Type the stock quote you want to look up.

3 Click **Go**.

4 Establish your Internet connection, if needed, and then Quicken opens the integrated Web browser and displays the quote. Close or minimize the browser window.

INTRODUCTION

You can view stock quotes and even download them into Quicken. The Investing Center window includes a handy tool for grabbing stock quotes and viewing them in the integrated browser window. Or if you want to download quotes you've already entered into your investment accounts, you can activate the Update Now feature. This task shows you how to perform both methods.

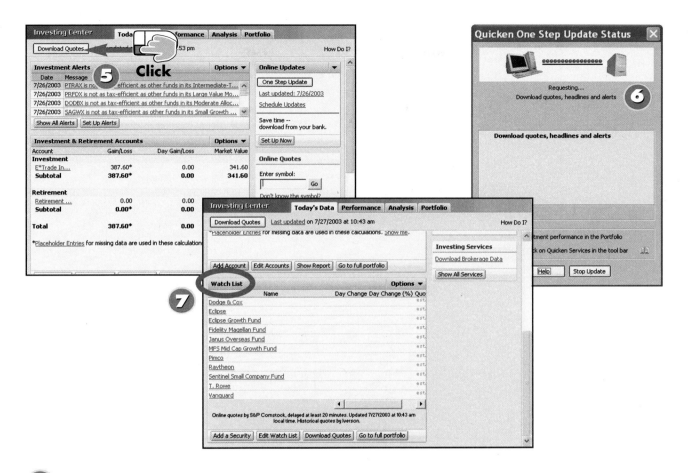

5 To download a stock quote into Quicken, click the **Download Quotes** button.

6 Quicken downloads the latest quotes and adds them to your securities Watch List.

7 Scroll down the page to view your securities in the Watch List area.

End

Add to the Watch List
You can add other stocks to your watch list and track their progress. Click the **Add a Security** button below the Watch List and fill in the ticker symbol and name. Download the current quote and tell Quicken to add the stock.

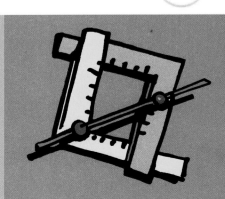

Viewing Securities and Reports

Start

1. Display your investment portfolio and click the security you want to view.

2. Quicken opens Security Detail View window. This window displays transaction history, details about the security, and the current quote.

3. To view a report for the security, click the **Report** button.

You can view details about any investment account security and analyze your data with a report. For example, you can view details about the value and performance of the stock. You can print out reports to study your data away from the computer, or you can save your reports to use later.

Defining Securities

A *security* is a single investment that has a share price, such as stocks or bonds. In most instances, you own a number of shares in a security and determine the total value by multiplying the number of shares by their per price amount.

4 Quicken displays a report you can print out by clicking the **Print** button.

5 Click the **Close** button to exit the Report window.

6 Expand the Security Detail View window again if it's minimized and click **Close** to exit the window.

End

Customize It
You can click the **Customize** button in the Report window and customize the items displayed in the report. To save the customized settings and view the report again, click the **Save Report** button, type a name, and click **OK**.

Using the Retirement Calculator

Start

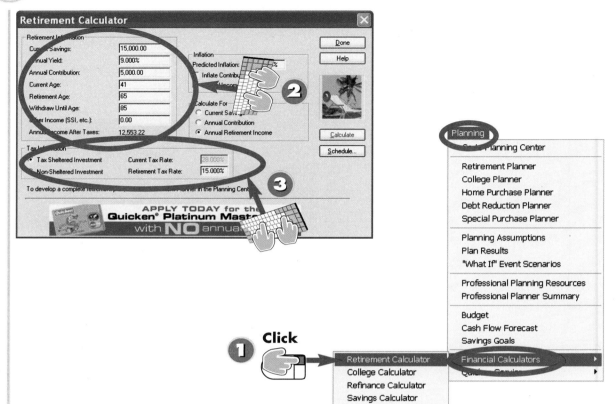

Click

1. Click **Planning**, **Financial Calculators**, **Retirement Calculator**.

2. Quicken opens the Retirement Calculator dialog box. Type in the retirement information, including an annual yield and a contribution amount.

3. Select any tax information that might apply to the investment.

HINT

Calculators Link
You can also access Quicken's calculators through the Planning Center window. Click the link for the calculator you want to open.

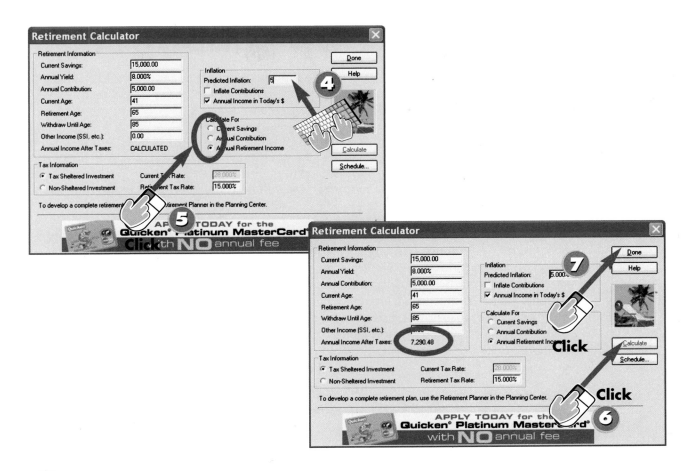

(4) Enter your projected inflation data.

(5) Select whether you want to calculate for Current Savings, Annual Contribution, or Annual Retirement Income.

(6) Click the **Calculate** button and the Retirement Calculator displays the results.

(7) When you are finished calculating retirement savings, click the **Done** button to close the Retirement Calculator.

End

Other Calculators

Quicken offers other calculators you can use to make financial calculations, including the Savings Calculator, the College Calculator, the Refinance Calculator, and the Loan Calculator. See the Part 9, "Tracking Loans," to learn about the Loan and College Calculators.

Setting Up a Budget

If you want to monitor your spending, creating a budget is a necessary task. Budgets help you understand where your money goes, as well as plan for future purchases. A budget also makes it easy to forecast your financial future.

The Budget tool is used to create a budget in Quicken. For fast results, you can let Quicken create a budget for you based on your income and expenditures, as long as you have several months' worth of transactions already recorded in Quicken. Or you can choose to create a budget manually, by defining which categories to track and entering budget amounts yourself.

Budgets are based on categories and subcategories that classify each transaction in an account. Categories are organized into groups. By default, Quicken creates three groups for categories: Discretionary, Income, and Mandatory Expenses. The *Discretionary* group is for optional expenses, such as dining out or entertainment. The *Income* group is for earned income, such as salaries, dividends, and interest. *Mandatory Expenses* are all the expenses you cannot avoid, such as a mortgage payment, a car payment, and utilities. You can add new groups, if needed, but you'll probably find that most of your income and spending fall into these three default groups.

After creating a budget, you can generate a report that shows you exactly how you are doing in terms of keeping up with the budget.

The Budget Window

You can use the other tabs to adjust the budget amounts or set up another budget.

The Summary tab shows a graph of your budget.

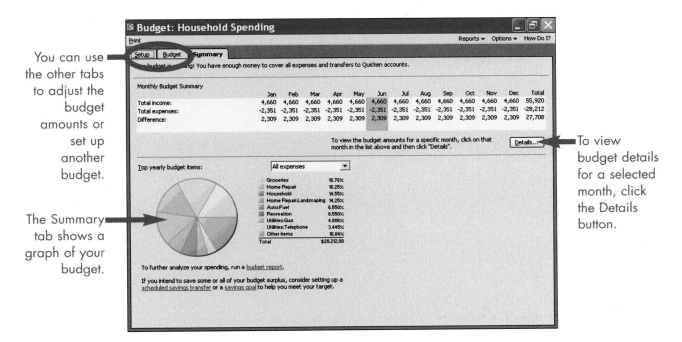

To view budget details for a selected month, click the Details button.

Creating a Budget

Start

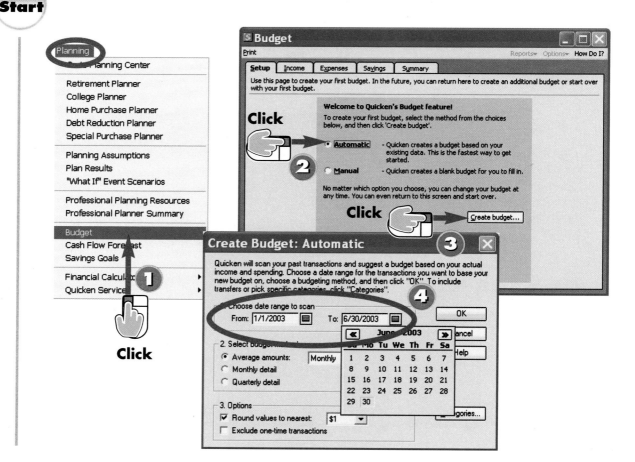

1 Click **Planning, Budget**.

2 The Budget window opens. To let Quicken create a budget based on your previously recorded transactions, click **Automatic**.

3 Click the **Create Budget** button.

4 The Create Budget: Automatic dialog box opens. Choose the range of data that you want to include in the analysis of your income and spending habits.

An accurate budget can help you pin down specific categories where you'd like to reduce spending, as well as anticipate discretionary dollars. With Quicken's Budget tool, you can create a budget based on your current financial data or you can create a budget from scratch.

Choosing Categories
For best results, you should include all the categories used in your scheduled and memorized transactions in the budget, as well as any other categories you use frequently for transactions.

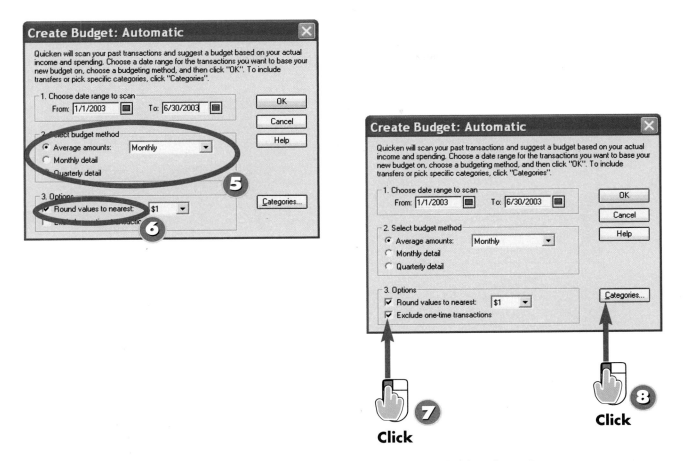

Click **7**

Click **8**

5 Leave the **Average Amounts** option selected to create a budget based on average amounts. Select from the other options to base the budget on actual amounts instead.

6 Leave the **Round Values to Nearest** option selected to round up to the nearest $1, $10, or $100.

7 To exclude any one-time transactions that can affect the accuracy of your budget, click the Exclude One-Time Transactions option.

8 Click the **Categories** button.

See next page

How Many Budgets?
Quicken gives you the capability to create multiple budgets. You can set up a budget to show only certain categories, such as a budget for car expenses or a budget to track how much your child is spending at college. Follow steps 1–3 of this task to start a new budget. The Create Budget dialog box that appears offers you an opportunity to assign a unique name to additional budgets you create. Type a distinctive name for the budget before continuing to define the budget details.

Creating a Budget Continued

Choose Categories

Include in Budget

Select the categories and accounts that you want to include when creating your budget.

Category/Account	Type	Description
✔ FROM IFCU Checking	Bank	
✔ FROM IFCU Savings	Bank	
✔ FROM E*Trade Brokerage	Invest	
✔ FROM IRA	Invest	
✔ Allowance	Expense	Cash withdrawal from bank ac...
✔ Auto	Expense	Automobile Expenses
✔ Fuel	Sub	Auto Fuel
✔ Insurance	Sub	Auto Insurance
✔ Loan	Sub	Auto Loan Payment
✔ Service	Sub	Auto Service
Bank Charge	Expense	Bank Charge
Check Printing	Sub	Check Printing Char
Overdraft Charge	Sub	Overdraft Charge
Cash	Expense	Misc Cash
C	Expense	Charitable Donation

OK | Cancel | Help

Click 10

Create Budget: Automatic

Quicken will scan your past transactions and suggest a budget based on your actual income and spending. Choose a date range for the transactions you want to base your new budget on, choose a budgeting method, and then click "OK". To include transfers or pick specific categories, click "Categories".

1. Choose date range to scan
   From: 1/1/2003   To: 6/30/2003

2. Select budget method
   ⦿ Average amounts: Monthly
   ○ Monthly detail
   ○ Quarterly detail

3. Options
   ☑ Round values to nearest: $1
   ☑ Exclude one-time transactions

OK | Cancel | Help | Categories...

Click 11

Quicken 2004 for Windows

ⓘ Your new budget has been fully created.

OK

Click 12

⑨ The Choose Categories dialog box opens. Deselect the categories you do not want included in the budget.

⑩ Click **OK**.

⑪ Quicken returns you to the Create Budget: Automatic screen. Click **OK** to have Quicken begin building your budget.

⑫ Quicken prompts you that your budget setup is complete. Click **OK**.

Your budget should be as on target as possible, but it's not necessary to estimate every monthly expense to the penny. The best approach is to enter a round number for each category in the first month of the budget and "fill" that number to subsequent months. You can go back and adjust values for one-time events, such as a month when you expect to receive a bonus or a month when you expect a car insurance payment. As you build your budget, watch the budget figures calculated at the bottom of the Budget window.

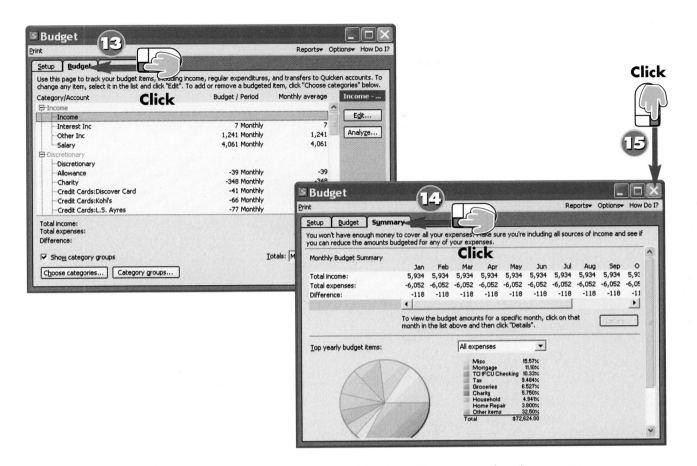

13 Click the **Budget** tab to view your completed budget. You can make changes to budget items, if needed.

14 Click the **Summary** tab to see an overview of your budget.

15 Click the **Close** button to close the Budget window.

End

Minimize and Maximize
You can minimize any window you open in Quicken by clicking the window's **Minimize** button. When minimized, the window appears as a button at the bottom of the Quicken program window. To maximize it again, click the button.

Editing a Budget

Start

(Planning)

Go to Planning Center

Retirement Planner
College Planner
Home Purchase Planner
Debt Reduction Planner
Special Purchase Planner

Planning Assumptions
Plan Results
"What If" Event Scenarios

Professional Planning Resources
Professional Planner Summary

Budget
Cash Flow Forecast
Savings Goals

Financial Calculators
Quicken Services

Click

1

Click

3

Budget: Mortgage

Print   Reports▾ Options▾ How Do I?

Setup | Budget | Summary

Use this page to create and manage your budgets. Using the tools below, you can create an additional budget or start over with your current one.

— Current Budget —
Name: **Mortgage**

To open or create an alternate budget, use the controls below. To continue using your current budget, click one of the tabs above.

Start over...
Rename...

— Other Budgets —
Budget Name   Description
Budget 2
Household Spending

Open
Rename...
Delete

2 **Click**

— Create Another Budget —
You can create additional budgets in Quicken to try out different scenarios or to track separate sets of categories, such as personal vs. business.

Budget: Household Spending

Print   Reports▾ Options▾ How Do I?

Setup | **Budget** | Summary

Use this page to track your budget items, including income, regular expenditures, and transfers to Quicken accounts. To change any item, select it in the list and click "Edit". To add or remove a budgeted item, click "Choose categories" below.

Category/Account	Budget / Period	Monthly average	Gifts
Trash Removal	-14 Monthly	-14	
Utilities	0 Monthly	0	Edit...
Utilities:Electric	-37 Monthly	-37	Analyze...
Utilities:Gas	-113 Monthly	-113	
Utilities:Sewer	-26 Monthly	-26	
Utilities:Telephone	-81 Monthly	-81	
Utilities:Water	-16 Monthly	-16	
Unassigned			
Unassigned - Other	0 Monthly	0	
Gifts	-25 Monthly	-25	
Home Repair:Landscaping	-335 Monthly	-335	
FROM IFCU Savings	750 Monthly	750	

Click

4

1 Choose **Planning, Budget**.

2 The budget window opens. Click the **Setup** tab, select the budget you want to edit, then click the **Open** button.

3 Select the budget item you want to edit.

4 Click the **Edit** button.

You can open a Quicken budget and make changes to the amounts and categories as your budget needs change. For example, you may need to switch from average amounts to specific monthly details, depending on your spending patterns.

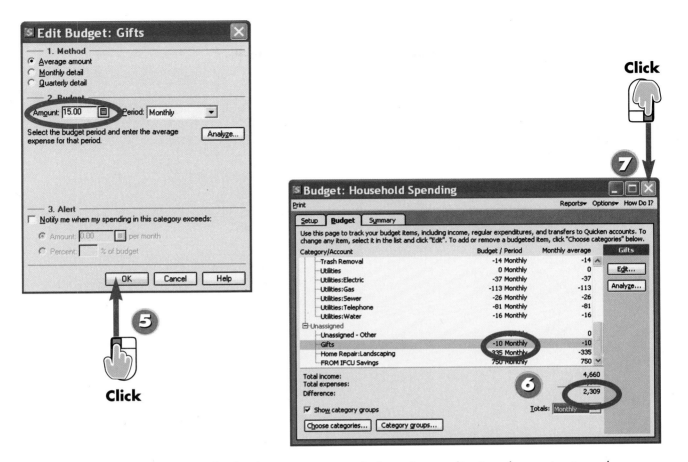

Click

Click

5 Make your changes to the budget item as needed, such as adjusting the amount, and then click **OK**.

6 Quicken saves your changes and applies them to the budget.

7 Click the **Close** button to exit the Budget window.

End

Delete a Budget
You can remove a budget you no longer need. See the next task to learn how.

Print a Budget
To print the current information shown in the Budget window, click the **Print** button in the upper-left corner of the window.

Deleting a Budget

Start

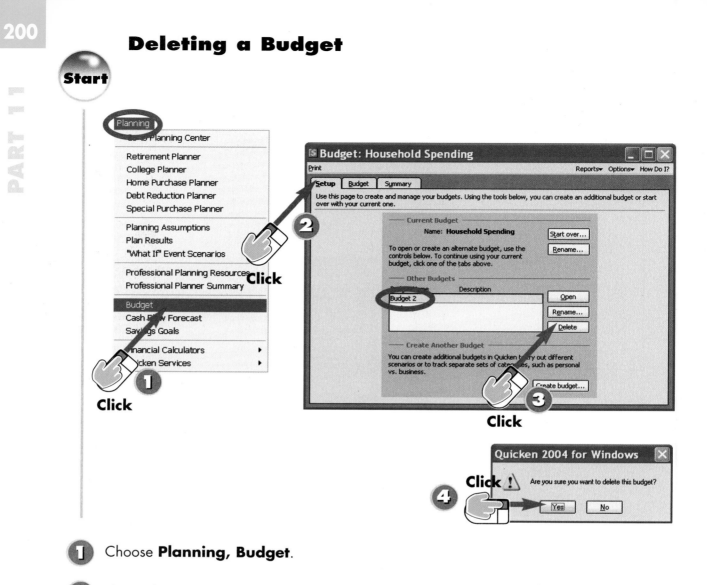

1 Choose **Planning, Budget**.

2 The Budget window opens. Click the **Setup** tab.

3 Select the budget you want to remove and click the **Delete** button.

4 Click **Yes** and Quicken removes the budget.

End

You can delete a budget you no longer need. For example, you may have created a budget to help you save up for a specific item and have reached your goal.

Setting a Budget Alert

Start

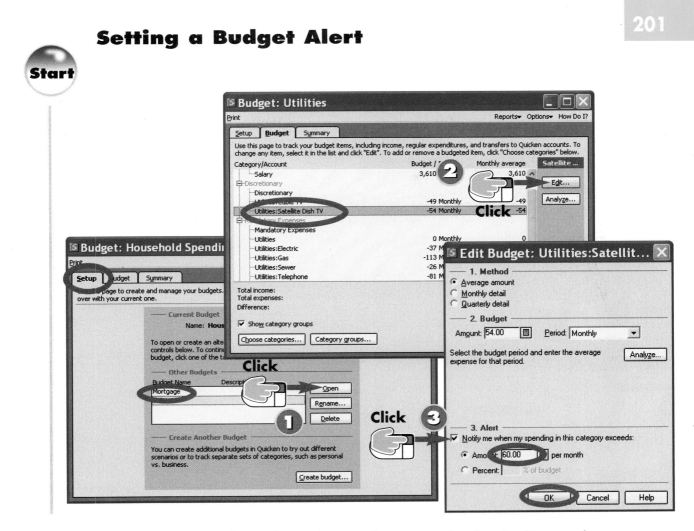

① Choose **Planning, Budget**. The Budget window opens. Display the **Setup** tab, select the budget you want to edit, and then click **Open**.

② Select the category for which you want to set an alert, and click the **Edit** button.

③ Click the Alert check box, set an amount for the alert and click **OK**. Quicken activates the alert and if you exceed the amount, a warning prompt box appears.

End

INTRODUCTION

You can set up an alert that tells you if you exceed a budget amount for the month. For example, your budget may include a category for miscellaneous expenses. You can set up an alert that warns you if you exceed a set amount, such as $200. If you do exceed the set limit, Quicken displays a prompt box warning.

Options Menu
You can also click the **Options** menu in the Budget window and select **Set Up Alerts** to create a budget alert.

Creating a Budget Report

Start

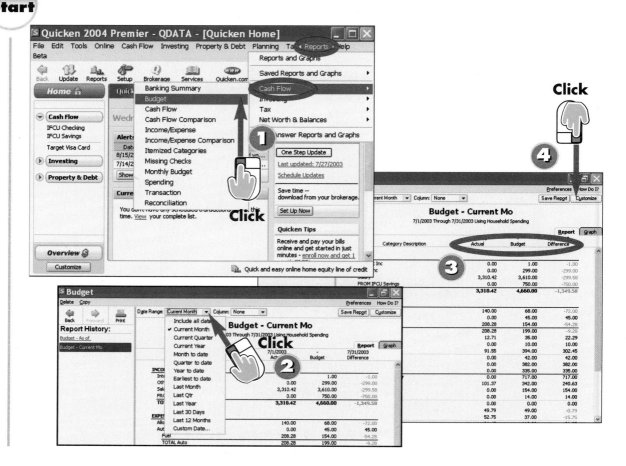

1 Click **Reports**, **Cash Flow**, **Budget**.

2 The Budget Report window opens. Click the **Date Range** arrow to select the dates you want to display in the report.

3 Review the **Actual**, **Budget**, and **Difference** columns to see how you're doing.

4 To customize the report, click the **Customize** button.

INTRODUCTION

After you set up your budgets, you can later open a budget in the Budget window and generate and print a report. The report shows you how actual income and expenses compare with the budget amounts you entered. You can choose either the Budget Report, which shows the year-to-date budgeted and actual figures, or the Monthly Budget Report, which compares monthly budgeted versus actual amounts for each category.

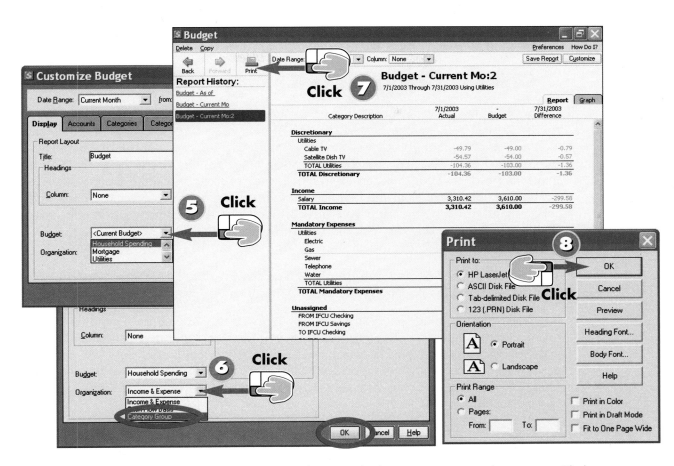

5 If you have several budgets, you can choose which one to view in the report. Click the **Budget** arrow and select the budget.

6 To change how the budget is organized in the report, click the **Organization** arrow, choose a method, and then click **OK**.

7 Quicken updates the report. To print the budget report, click the **Print** button.

8 The Print dialog box opens. Click **OK** to print using the default settings.

Save It
You can click the **Save Report** button in the budget report window and save the report to a Quicken center. To see the report again, display the center to which the report was assigned.

Family Affair
Share budget results, especially the easy-to-understand graph, with everyone in the household. You might convince skeptics to join you in your quest for better budget management.

Report Adjustments
You can modify a Budget report just like any other. See Part 5, "Balancing Accounts," to learn how to modify a report.

Using Quicken's Planning and Organizing Features

Quicken offers a multitude of tools and features to help you plan for future events and goals, as well as organize and keep track of your assets. For example, the Planning Center is a page that you can use to view information about events that ultimately affect your finances. Such events include such things as weddings, the purchase of a home, the birth of your children, retirement, and so on. Individual planners, like the Home Purchase Planner or the Retirement Planner, can help you calculate costs and set financial goals by assisting you in recording detailed information about the event. Quicken's planners are very easy to use and walk you through each phase for recording important financial information.

You can also find planning and organizing features on both the Property and Debt and the Planning menus on the Quicken Menu bar.

In addition to planning, you can use Quicken to assist you with an inevitable yearly event—taxes. Quicken can lend a hand as you plan and prepare for tax time all year round. You can estimate your taxes using existing tax-related data you recorded in Quicken, using data you import from TurboTax, or using data you manually enter. Quicken's tax tools make it relatively painless to determine how much taxes you owe or how much of a refund you can expect.

The Tax Center

The Projected Tax area shows your tax information.

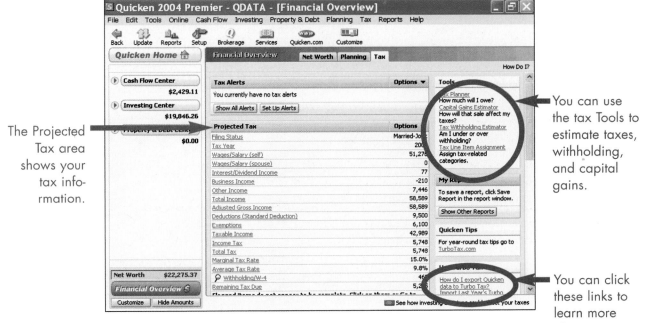

You can use the tax Tools to estimate taxes, withholding, and capital gains.

You can click these links to learn more about using Quicken with TurboTax.

Viewing the Planning Center

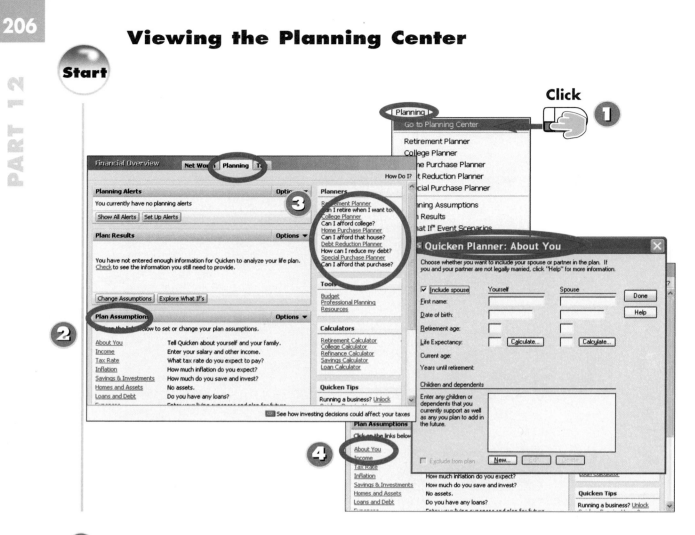

 Choose **Planning**, **Go To Planning Center**.

2 Quicken opens the Planning Center window. The Plan Assumptions area displays information about you and your finances and links to enter more information.

3 All of Quicken's built-in planner tools are listed in the Planners area.

4 You can click a link to open a dialog box for entering detailed information for goals and events.

End

Quicken's Planning Center provides access to a variety of planners, such as the Tax Planner and the Retirement Planner, as well as specialized calculators and other tools to help you make the most out of your financial goals and plans. After setting up a plan, you can view up-to-date information on the Planning Center page to find out how well your plan is working.

Viewing the Tax Center

Start

Click

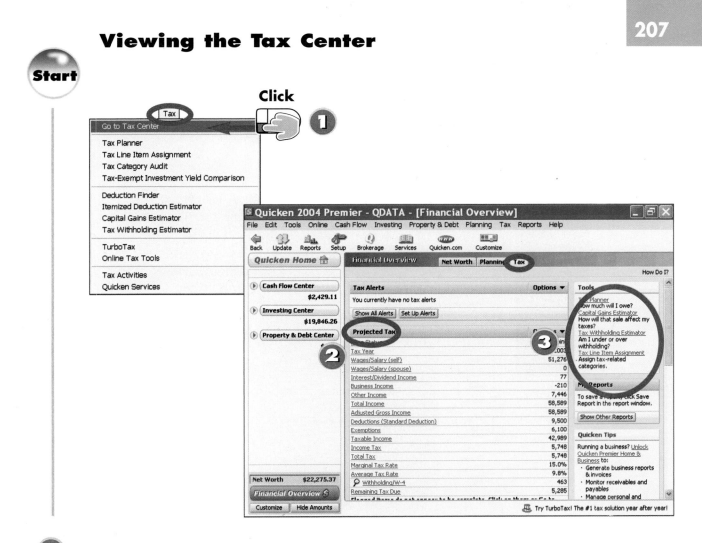

1 Choose **Tax**, **Go to Tax Center**.

2 Quicken opens the Tax Center window. The Projected Tax area summarizes your tax information. Be sure to scroll down to view all the information.

3 You can access Quicken's tax tools in the Tools area on the right.

End

INTRODUCTION

You can use the Tax Center to access a variety of tax-related tools and features in Quicken. The page offers several areas for viewing tax-related data, such as a tax calendar, tax-related expenses, taxable income, and more. Take time to explore all the features to find out which ones will be of most benefit to you.

HINT

Planning Center
You can also access the Tax Center from the Planning Center page; just click the **Tax** tab.

Estimating Taxes Using the Tax Planner

Start

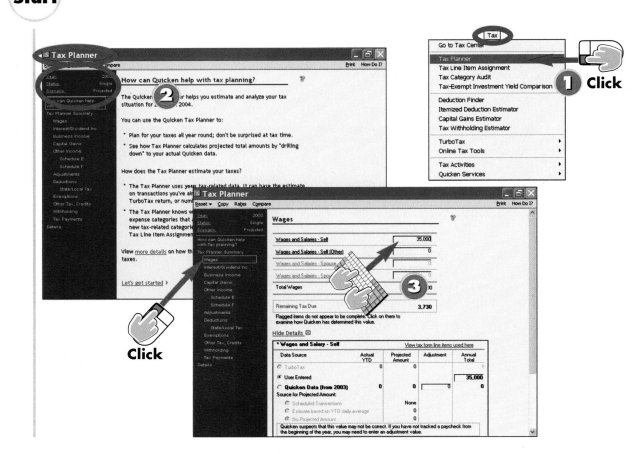

Click

Click

1. Choose **Tax, Tax Planner**.

2. Quicken opens the Tax Planner window. Check to make sure the correct tax year and filing status are displayed.

3. Click the **Wages** link and type in your wages. You may need to click the **Show Details** link to view all the settings.

You can use Quicken's Tax Planner to estimate your federal taxes. The Tax Planner can help you estimate the amount you owe or the amount of refund you can expect. You can enter data into the Tax Planner using three methods: You can manually enter the data, use Quicken data already earmarked by tax-related categories, or download the data from TurboTax. The steps in this task focus on manually entering your own tax data into the Tax Planner.

TIP

TurboTax?
When you first start the Tax Planner, you may encounter a dialog box asking if you want to download TurboTax data. You can choose to do so if you already use TurboTax to calculate your taxes.

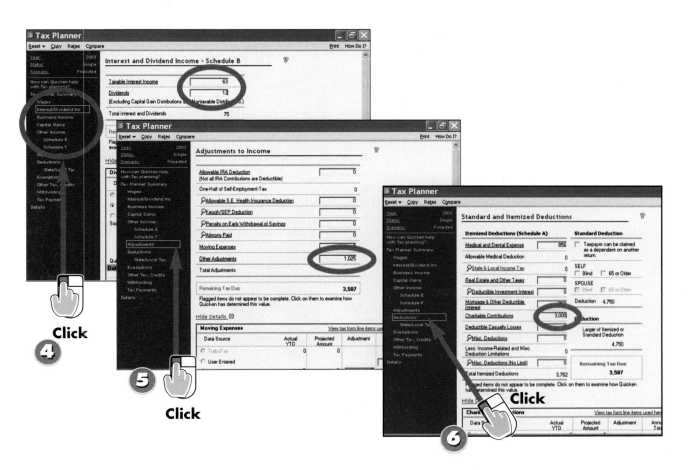

Click **4**

Click **5**

Click **6**

4 Click the **Interest/Dividend Inc**, **Business Income**, **Capital Gains**, or **Other Income** links to record any income you receive from other sources.

5 To make any adjustments to your gross income, click the **Adjustments** link and add any changes.

6 To calculate itemized deductions, click the **Deductions** link and estimate your deductions for expenses.

See next page

TIP

Using Quicken Data
If you've been faithfully recording tax-related transactions in Quicken, the program estimates your taxes based on previously recorded entries. When Tax Planner annualizes a category, it projects a full-year total for that entry based on the sum of the amounts for transactions entered to date. You can override any of the information by clicking a form link and changing the data.

TIP

Download Tax Data
To import a TurboTax data file from a previous tax return, click **File**, **Import**, **TurboTax**. Select the file you want to import and click **OK**. Quicken asks you to confirm the data.

Estimating Taxes Using the Tax Planner
Continued

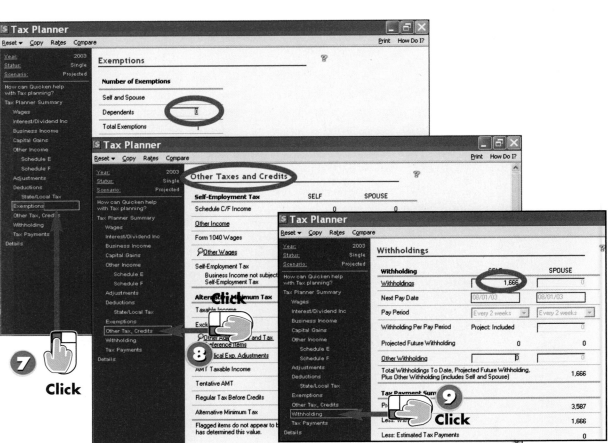

 Click the **Exemptions** link and specify the number of dependents you want to claim.

 Click the **Other Tax, Credits** link to enter any other taxes you intend to pay in addition to federal income tax.

 Click the **Withholding** link and record how much money you have paid through federal withholding.

To enter data into the Tax Planner, you can use the links in the left pane of the Tax Planner window to open forms for recording data. You can randomly view forms by clicking a link, or you can proceed through each form in order by clicking the Next link that appears at the bottom of each form.

Viewing Scenarios

You can use the **Scenario** link in the Tax Planner window to enter data for different tax scenarios and save the scenarios. You can then use the **Compare** button at the top of the Tax Planner window to compare your scenarios.

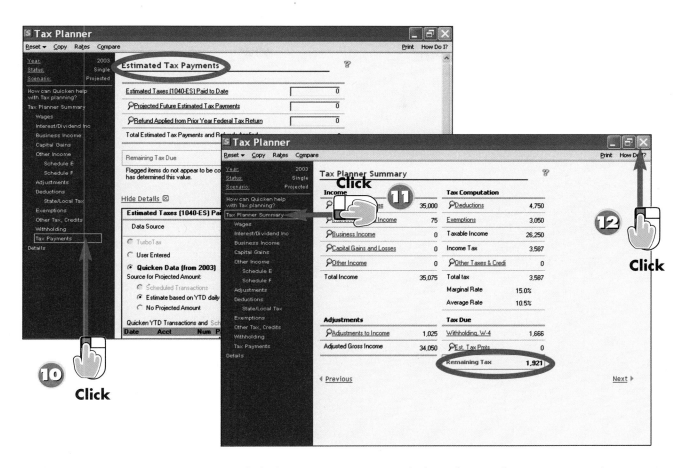

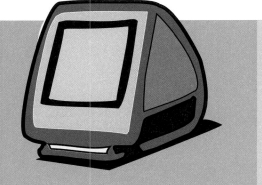

10. If you pay estimated taxes, click the **Tax Payments** link and record your estimated payments.

11. After completing each form, as needed, click the **Tax Planner Summary** link. You can review your estimated taxes.

12. When you finish using the Tax Planner, click the **Close** button to close the window.

Starting Again
When you exit the Tax Planner and later restart it, the Planner displays any tax-planning information you previously entered. To start fresh again, click **Reset** and click the appropriate reset setting in the list.

Tax Report
To display the report of all tax-related income and expense transactions, choose **Reports**, **Tax**, **Tax Summary**.

Setting Up Tax-Related Categories

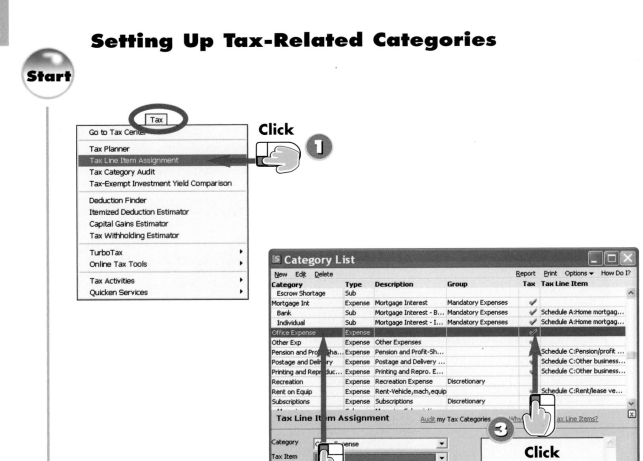

1. Click **Tax**, **Tax Line Item Assignment**.

2. Quicken opens the Category List window. Click the category you want to mark as tax related.

3. Click the **Tax** column and Quicken adds a checkmark to indicate that the category is tax related.

INTRODUCTION

For Quicken to track federal tax information accurately, you must select the transaction categories to identify tax information and the correct tax form and line associated with the item. After you identify tax-related categories, Quicken can display a report showing all transactions using these categories. Use this information to reduce your tax preparation time.

The Tax Center
Access all of Quicken's tax features in the Tax Center page. Click **Tax**, **Go to Tax Center**. To edit tax-related categories as shown in this task, you can click the **Tax Line Item Assignment** link. To open the Tax Planner, click the **Tax Planner** link.

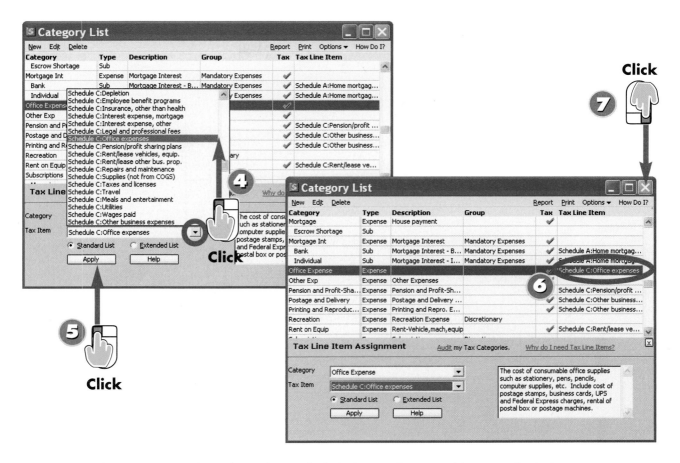

4 Click the **Tax Item** drop-down list and click the tax form and line to which the category applies.

5 Click the **Apply** button.

6 Quicken applies the form to the category.

7 Click the **Close** button to close the Category List window.

End

Category Check
By default, Quicken identifies many categories as tax related, such as the Salary and Charity categories. You should double-check to ensure all tax-related categories are marked properly, especially if you've created any categories or subcategories.

Finding More Tax Deductions

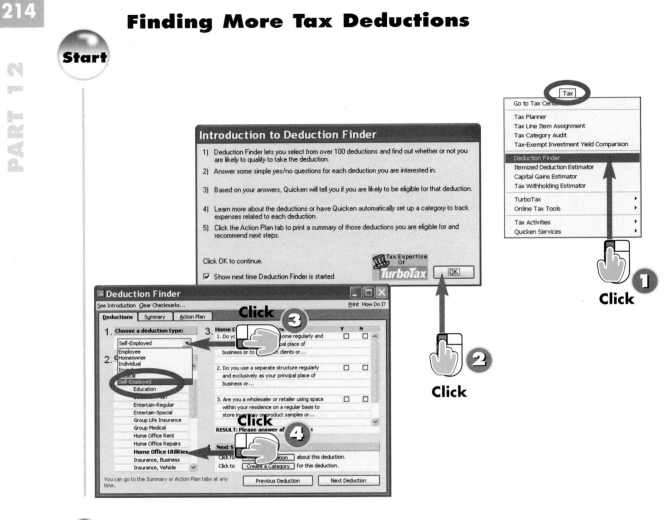

① Choose **Tax**, **Deduction Finder**.

② If you see the Introduction to Deduction Finder dialog box, click **OK**.

③ Make a choice from the **1. Choose a Deduction Type** drop-down list.

④ Click a choice under **2. Choose a Deduction**.

You can use Quicken's Deduction Finder to look for potential tax deductions; you may find that you should have been itemizing your deductions all along! The Deduction Finder asks you a series of questions. You respond to the questions to find deductions for which you may be eligible—called your action plan.

Oops!
You can click the **Clear Checkmarks** button at the top of the window to clear all your answers and start again.

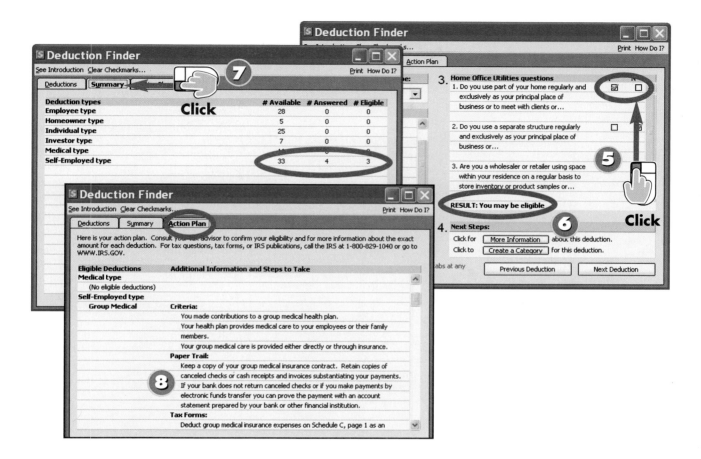

5 Click the **Y** or **N** check box to respond to each of the questions listed.

6 Quicken evaluates your answers. Repeat steps 3–5 to research additional deductions.

7 Click the **Summary** tab to review a tally of available deductions.

8 Click the **Action Plan** tab to review your action plan. When finished, click the **Close** button.

More Info

HINT

To learn more about a deduction, click the **More Information** button at the bottom of the Deduction Finder window.

The Action Plan

TIP

The Action Plan tab in the Deduction Finder window lists potential deductions for you. Review each of these deductions and click the **Print** link to print the action plan for tax time.

Organizing Emergency Records

Start

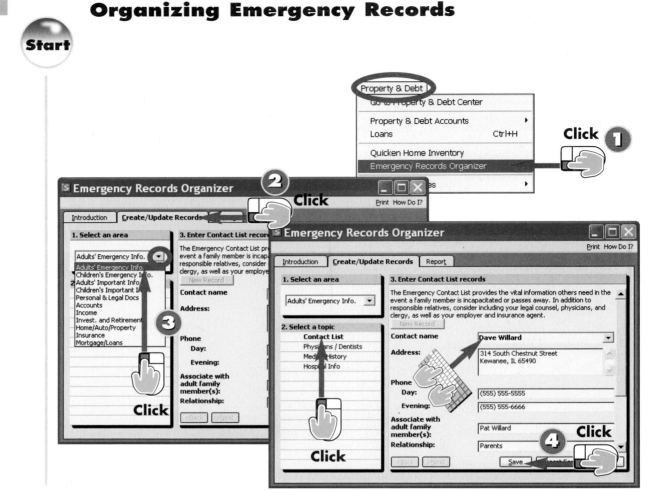

1. Choose **Property & Debt, Emergency Records Organizer**.

2. Click the **Create/Update Records** tab.

3. Make a choice from the **Select an Area** drop-down list.

4. Click a **Select a Topic** choice, enter record information, and click **Save**.

INTRODUCTION

Quicken's Emergency Records Organizer tracks information about people to contact in case of emergency, medical history information, locations of legal documents, details about property you own, and so on. Start by entering a record for each piece of information, as follows.

HINT

Privacy Alert
The records you enter might contain very sensitive or private information. To keep it secure, create a new Quicken data file, enter the Emergency Records Organizer information, and assign a password to the Quicken file.

TIP

Editing a Record
To find a particular record, click the **Next** or **Back** button on the **Create/Update Records** tab. Make your changes and then click **Save**.

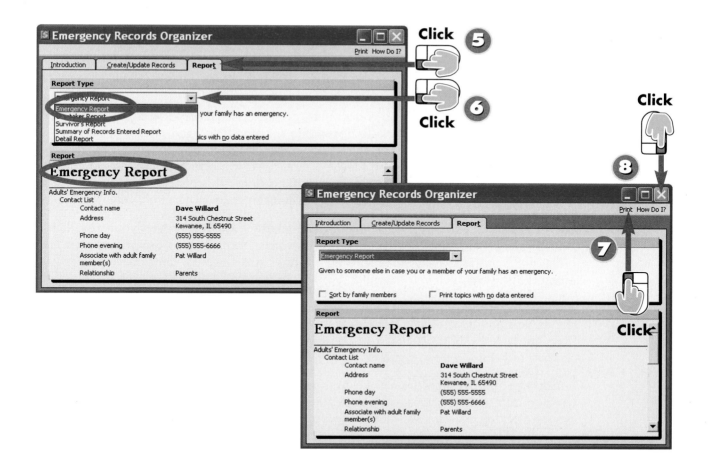

5 After repeating steps 3 and 4 to add all records, click the **Report** tab.

6 Select a report type. The report appears at the bottom of the tab.

7 Click **Print** to print the report.

8 Click the **Close** button to close the Emergency Records Organizer window.

End

Update
TIP

You should update your emergency information at least twice a year or whenever you make a change, such as opening a new bank account. To delete a record, display the topic and click the **Delete** button.

Organize Household Items
TIP

Quicken has another tool you can use to organize assets in your home. Choose **Property & Debt, Quicken Home Inventory** to open the Home Inventory database to list items, their value, and replacement costs.

Managing Quicken Data Files

As you add data to your various accounts, all the data is stored in a Quicken data file. Not only does the file include transactions, categories, and other information, but the file also includes setup information about the file, such as account types. In the course of building your Quicken file, you may need to perform some file management techniques, such as importing or exporting data. This chapter shows you several methods you can use to manage your Quicken data more effectively.

Security is also part of the Quicken 2004 package. You can protect your data files from unauthorized usage by assigning passwords. You can also assign passwords to individual transactions to make sure no changes are made to items previously entered into your Quicken accounts.

Another important part of protecting your data file is to back it up often. This chapter shows you how to create a backup file and restore the file, if you ever encounter a problem with the original file. You can also learn how to create a year-end file to archive old data in your accounts.

In addition, you can create more than one data file to use in Quicken 2004. You can use two different data files to track separate checking accounts, or you might keep a file for tracking investments that is separate from your checking and savings data.

Password Protect Quicken Data

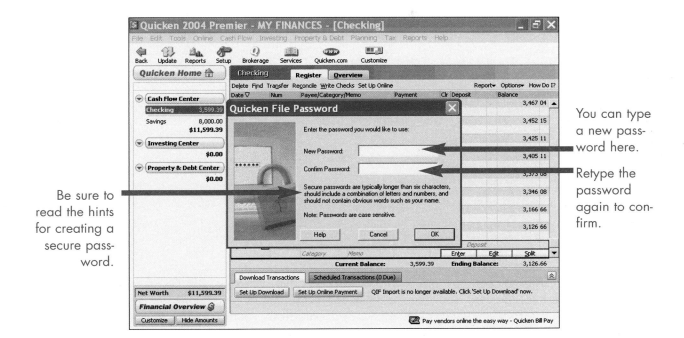

You can type a new password here.

Retype the password again to confirm.

Be sure to read the hints for creating a secure password.

Assigning a Password

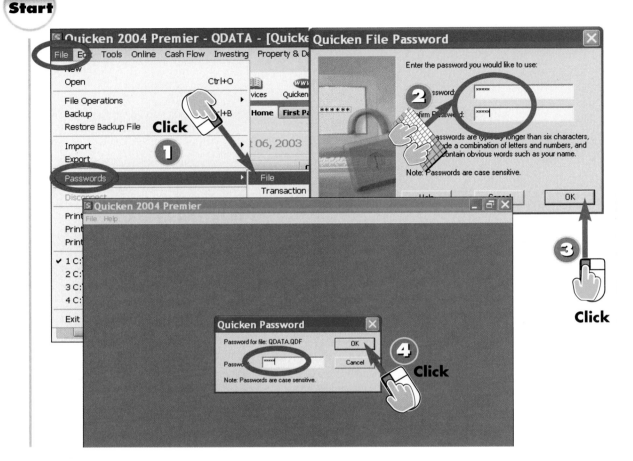

1. Choose **File**, **Passwords**, **File**.

2. Enter your password into the **New Password** and **Confirm Password** text boxes.

3. Click **OK** to finish assigning the password.

4. The next time you open the Quicken file, the Quicken Password dialog box appears. Enter the password and click **OK**.

Protecting Transactions
Quicken also allows you to assign passwords to protect all the transactions in a file that occurred before a certain date that you specify. To assign a transaction password, click **File**, **Password**, **Transaction**.

Changing or Removing a Password

Start

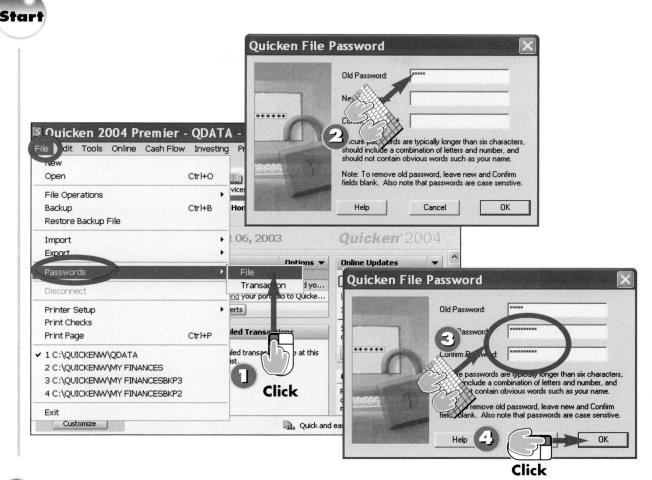

1. Choose **File**, **Passwords**, **File**.

2. Enter the old password into the **Old Password** text box.

3. Enter the new password into the **New Password** and **Confirm Password** text boxes.

4. Click **OK** and the password is changed.

End

INTRODUCTION

When a file already includes a password, you can change or remove that password at any time. You have to use the old password to change passwords, though, so jot your password down in a confidential location if you fear you'll forget it.

HINT

What's the Word?
You have to choose a password carefully. Too obvious, and others can guess it. Too obscure, and you'll forget it. Steer clear of family names or numbers. Instead use a favorite thing, such as a song title.

TIP

Removing Passwords
To remove a password, open the Quicken File Password dialog box and remove any passwords from the **New Password** and **Confirm Password** fields. Leave the fields blank and click **OK**.

Backing Up Your Quicken Data

Start

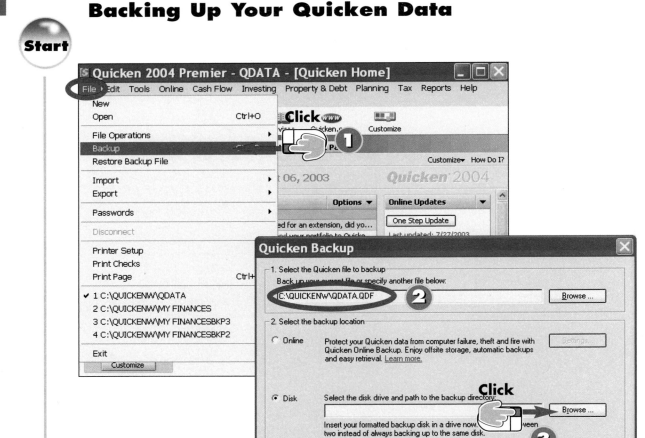

1. Insert a blank, formatted disk or CD-ROM into the appropriate drive and choose **File**, **Backup**.

2. The Quicken Backup dialog box appears. Make sure the current file is listed.

3. Select **Disk** and click the **Browse** button.

TIP

Online Backup
If you sign up for Quicken Online, for a small fee you can back up your data file for storage on Quicken's protected data center. To use the service, click the **Online** option in the Quicken Backup dialog box and follow the instructions.

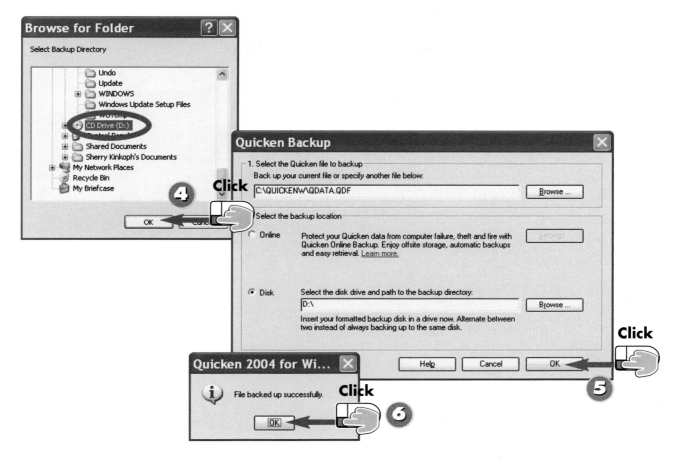

The Browse for Folder dialog box opens. Select the folder or drive for the backup and click **OK**.

Click **OK** and Quicken begins backing up the data file.

When the backup is complete, click **OK**.

End

How Often?
You should back up your Quicken data file at least once a month, after you reconcile your main checking account with your statement. If you have a lot of accounts or enter many transactions per week, you can back up weekly.

Restoring a Backup File

Start

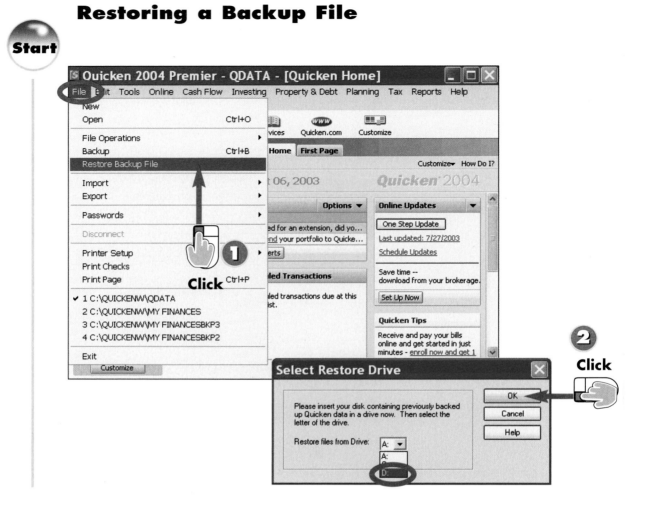

1 Insert the disk containing the backup file and choose **File**, **Restore Backup File**.

2 Select the disk that holds the backup file from the **Restore Files from Drive** drop-down list. Click **OK**.

Backup Files

TIP

See the previous task, "Backing Up Your Quicken Data," to learn how to create a backup file on an external disk.

3 The Restore Quicken File dialog box opens. Click the backup file you want to use (probably QDATA.QDF) and then click **OK**.

4 Click **OK** when the message asks if you want to overwrite the current file.

5 Click **OK** when the message tells you that the restore operation worked.

End

The Right One

TIP

The backup filename matches the name of the original file, such as QDATA.QDF. If you've stored backup copies for multiple Quicken files in the same location, be careful to select the right one.

Online Restore

TIP

If you signed up to back up onto Quicken's Web servers, you must use another method to get your data. Click **Start**, **Programs**, and **Quicken Online Backup**. Then click the Retrieve View tab and select from the retrieval options.

Creating Another Quicken Data File

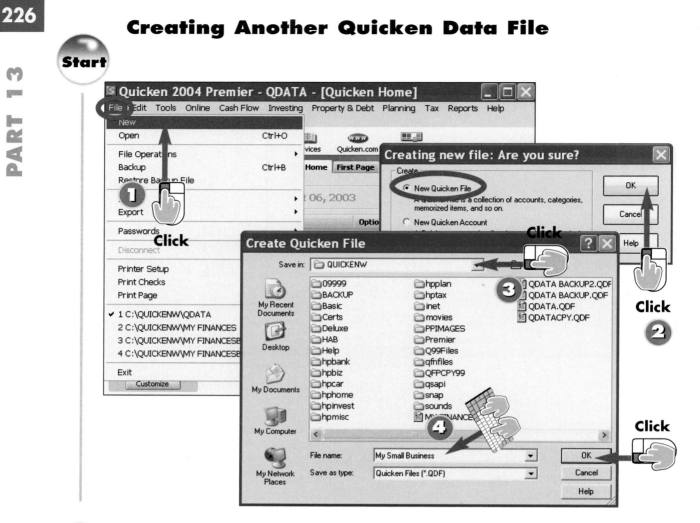

1 Choose **File**, **New**.

2 In the Creating New File: Are You Sure? window, leave the **New Quicken File** option selected and click **OK**.

3 If you want to choose a different drive or disk for the new file, use the **Save In** drop-down list and double-click a folder.

4 Enter a name into the **File Name** text box and click **OK**. Then work through the new account setup as you learned in Part 2, "Setting Up Accounts."

INTRODUCTION

Quicken enables you to create multiple data files. Each Quicken data file you create uses the QDF filename extension (Quicken data format). Quicken adds that extension to the filename for you. This task shows you how to create a new Quicken file and how to open a particular file when you need it.

TIP

Adding an Account
When you create a new Quicken file, Quicken immediately (after step 4) displays the Create New Account dialog box so you can add an account into the new file. Create the type of account you'd like, as described in Part 2.

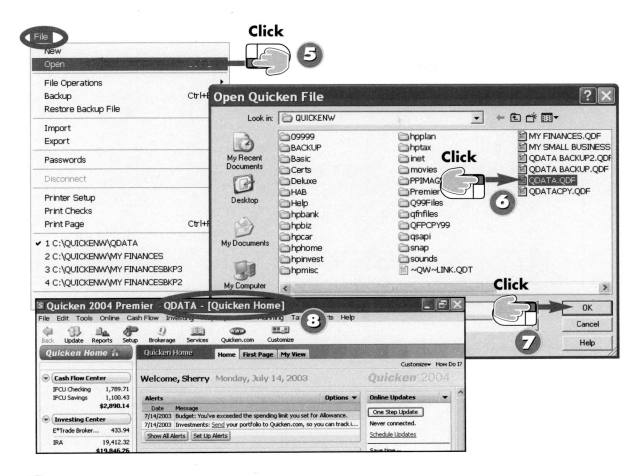

5 To open another Quicken file, choose **File**, **Open**.

6 The Open Quicken File dialog box appears. Choose the file you want to open.

7 Click **OK**.

8 Quicken opens the data file.

Take a Backup

Always back up the current Quicken data file before you create a new file or open another file. See the task "Backing Up Your Quicken Data" to review the steps for backing up.

Creating a Year-End Data File Copy

Start

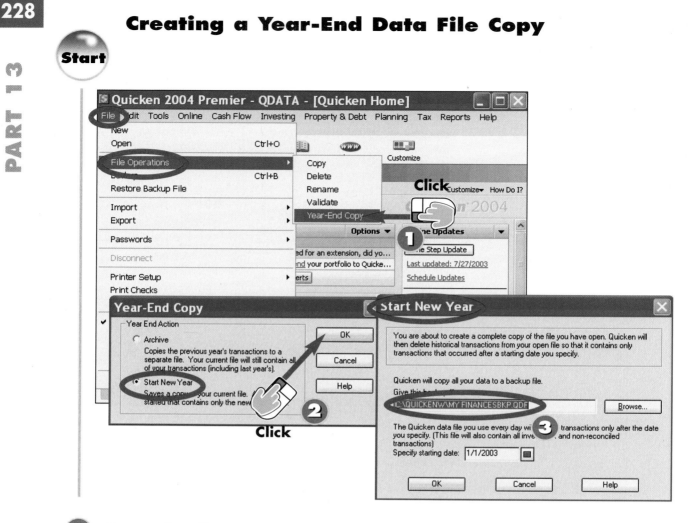

1. Choose **File**, **File Operations**, **Year-End Copy**.

2. The Year-End Copy dialog box opens. Click the **Start New Year** option and click **OK**.

3. The Start New Year dialog box opens with a default filename already assigned. You can type a new destination and filename, if needed.

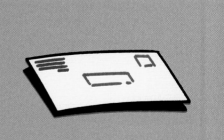

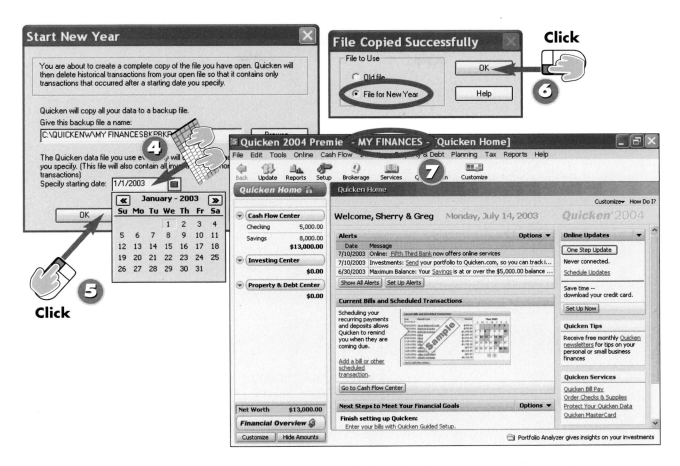

4️⃣ Type a starting date for the current file or click the calendar icon and select a date. Quicken will archive all transactions recorded prior to the date that you enter.

5️⃣ Click **OK**.

6️⃣ Quicken archives the data and asks you which file you want to remain open: the new file or the archive file. Make your selection and click **OK**.

7️⃣ The file opens in the Quicken window.

End

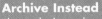

TIP

Archive Instead
This task shows how to save the previous year's data and start a new year of Quicken data. If you prefer to archive the data instead, the Archive File dialog box appears in step 3, allowing you to save the data in a specified archive file.

HINT

Fast Transfer
You can use the import and export features in Quicken to transfer information from an older Quicken file into a new file.

Exporting Data

Start

Quicken 2004 Premier - QDATA - [Quicken Home]

File Edit Tools Online Cash Flow Investing Property & Debt Planning Tax Reports Help

New
Open   Ctrl+O

File Operations   ▶
Backup   Ctrl+B
Restore Backup File

Import   ▶
Export   ▶   QIF File
Passwords   ▶

Discard

Printer
Print
Print

✔ 1 C:\Q
2 C:\Q
3 C:\Q
4

Exit

Click **1**

06, 2003

Options ▼   Updates ▼
One Step Update

QIF Export

QIF File to Export to:
C:\QUICKENW\Checking   Browse...   OK
                                                 Cancel
Account to Export from: Include Transactions in Dates:
king   ▼   1/31/2000 to: 7/18/2003   Help

Export
Transactions
Memorized Transactions

QIF Export

QIF File to Export to:
C:\QUICKENW\Checking   Browse...   OK
                                                 Cancel
Quicken Account to Export from: Include   Dates:
IFCU Checking   ▼   to: 7/18/2003   Help
<All Accounts>
IFCU Checking
IFCU Savings   **Click** **3**
E*Trade Brokerage
IRA   Account List   Category List
                           For Macintosh Users   Security Lists

1 Choose **File**, **Export**, **QIF File**.

2 The QIF Export dialog box opens. Click inside the **QIF File to Export To** field and type a name for the new export file.

3 Click the **Quicken Account to Export From** arrow and choose which account you want to export.

QIF Export

QIF File to Export to:

C:\QUICKENW\Checking   Browse...   OK

Quicken Account to Export from: Include Transactions in Dates: Cancel

IFCU Checking ▾   1/31/2000 ▦ to: 7/18/2003 ▦   Help

Include in Export
- ☑ Transactions   ☐ Account List   ☑ Category List
- ☐ Memorized Transactions   ☐ For Macintosh Users   ☐ Security Lists

Click 4

6

Click

QIF Export

QIF File to Export to:

C:\QUICKENW\Checking   Browse...   OK

Quicken Account to Export from: Include Transactions in Dates: Cancel

IFCU Checking ▾   4/29/2000 ▦ to: 7/18/2003 ▦   Help

Include in Export
- ☑ Transactions   List
- ☐ Memorized Transactions   ☐ Fo   Lists

5

April - 2000

Su	Mo	Tu	We	Th	Fr	Sa
						1
2	3	4	5	6	7	8
9	10	11	12	13	14	15
16	17	18	19	20	21	22
23	24	25	26	27	28	29
30						

4 Select which items you want to export, such as **Transactions**.

5 If you're exporting transactions, adjust the **Include Transactions in Dates** entries as needed.

6 Click **OK** and Quicken exports the data.

End

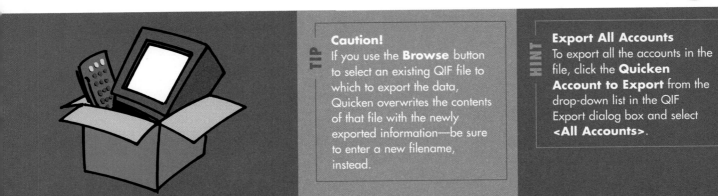

TIP

Caution!
If you use the **Browse** button to select an existing QIF file to which to export the data, Quicken overwrites the contents of that file with the newly exported information—be sure to enter a new filename, instead.

HINT

Export All Accounts
To export all the accounts in the file, click the **Quicken Account to Export** from the drop-down list in the QIF Export dialog box and select **<All Accounts>**.

Importing Data

Start

1. Choose **File**, **Import**, **QIF File**. The QIF Import dialog box opens.

2. Click the **Quicken Account to Import into** arrow and select the account type.

3. Click the **Browse** button.

4. The Import from QIF File dialog box opens. Select the QIF file you want to import and then click **OK**.

INTRODUCTION

When you import data, Quicken adds the new data to the data already in the file. If you have data in separate Quicken files and later want to combine it in one account, you can export the data from one account and import it into the other. Before you start, open the file into which you'd like to import information.

Import Limit

In Quicken 2004, you can only use the Import command 20 times to import QIF files from other sources. To learn more, click the **More Info** link in the QIF Import dialog box.

Backup

It's a good idea to back up your data file before importing new data.

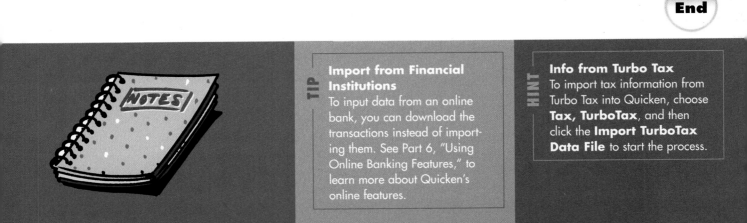

5 Select which items you want to include in the import, and then click **OK**.

6 Quicken imports the data. Click **OK**.

7 Click the **Accept All** button to move the imported data into your register.

End

Import from Financial Institutions
To input data from an online bank, you can download the transactions instead of importing them. See Part 6, "Using Online Banking Features," to learn more about Quicken's online features.

Info from Turbo Tax
To import tax information from Turbo Tax into Quicken, choose **Tax, TurboTax**, and then click the **Import TurboTax Data File** to start the process.

Glossary

A

account   A Quicken account represents each savings, checking, credit card, or investment account you have in the real world. You use each Quicken account you create to hold the transactions for that account and calculate the current account balance.

Account bar   A pane on the left side of the Quicken window that offers shortcut links to your accounts.

Account List   An alphabetized list of accounts in a Quicken data file. Select the account to work with from the Account List.

Account Overview   When you click the Overview tab in the account register, Quicken displays Account Overview information, including basic account information, recent account statistics, and graphs. You can update account information in the Account Overview or click links to perform operations pertaining to the account.

alert   A special warning or message you set up to appear. For example, you can set up Quicken to alert you when a checking account balance falls below a particular amount, such as the minimum required by your bank.

asset   Something you own that has value that you can track, such as a car, a home, jewelry, or electronics.

B

back up   Creating an extra copy of your Quicken data file on a particular date, to preserve your data in case the original file becomes damaged. See **Restore**.

balance   When you've cleared all transactions while reconciling the account and the difference between the Cleared Balance and the Statement Ending Balance is 0.00, the account is balanced.

brokerage account   An account set up to track securities through a brokerage.

browse   Move from Web page to Web page by using the integrated browser software.

browser   See **Web browser**.

budget   An expense and income plan you create in Quicken. Quicken can then compare your budget to actual expenses and income you enter, showing the difference left for savings and other purposes.

C

capital gain   The amount you earn from selling an investment for more than you paid for it.

capital loss   The amount you lose from selling an investment for less than you paid for it.

category   A label used in Quicken to identify an income or expense, so Quicken can report on how you spend your money and where it comes from. See **subcategory**.

Category List   A window in Quicken where you can edit and add new categories for tracking transaction amounts.

checking account   A Quicken account that corresponds to your real-world checking account. You can enter payments (bills) into the checking account and use Quicken to print checks to pay those bills.

cleared balance   The total amount of cleared transactions.

cleared transaction   A transaction you check off while reconciling your account, indicating that the transaction has been executed by your bank or financial institution. You can mark a transaction as cleared when your account statement (from the bank or financial institution) shows the transaction. See **reconcile**.

credit card account   An account set up to track credit card debt in Quicken.

D

data file   See *Quicken data file*.

deposit   A transaction for money added into a Quicken account.

download   The transfer of a file from one computer to another, often using a modem and telephone line.

E

EasyAnswer Report   A type of Quicken report that focuses on a very narrow range of information, such as how much you're saving or the total payments (amounts) assigned to a particular expense category.

ending balance   The current account balance that Quicken calculates by adding and subtracting transaction amounts from the opening balance you specified when you created the account. See *statement ending balance*.

F

field   In a register program, one piece of information you enter for a transaction, such as the *payee*.

Financial Activity Centers   Areas in Quicken that group features for particular aspects of financial management, including Cash Flow, Investing, and Property & Debt.

find   Search for and display one or more transactions that match criteria settings you specify.

font   The particular design of the characters in a report. Each font has a name, such as Arial or Times New Roman. You select the font by name to apply it to a selection.

G

graph   A visual representation of the entries in one or more Quicken accounts.

group   Classifies similar categories and subcategories, such as those that represent discretionary expenses.

H

Home page   See *Quicken Home page*.

hyperlinks   Specially formatted text, buttons, or graphics you click on a page to display (jump to) a different page or feature.

I–J

insertion point   The flashing vertical mark that indicates where typed text appears in a field or dialog box.

Internet   The worldwide network of computers that stores and transfers information.

Internet account   Dial-up or network Internet access you purchase from an Internet Service Provider. When you obtain an account, you receive an account name and password you use to connect and log on. After you connect to your Internet connection, you can use Quicken's online features and services.

K–L

liability   Something you owe, such as a mortgage.

liability account   An account set up to track loans and payments to lenders.

links   See *hyperlinks*.

M

memorized report   A customized report you've saved for reuse.

memorized transaction   A saved transaction you can reuse or copy into your register and update as needed. QuickFill can automatically save transaction information for each new payee or Paid By entry you make in an account. You can also use the Memorized Transaction List to add and work with memorized transactions.

Memorized Transaction List   The list that stores your memorized transactions.

N-O

new transaction line   The next available line in a register. Enter the next new transaction in this line.

online banking   Setting up Quicken to transfer information from your bank or financial institution directly into a Quicken account.

opening balance   The balance you enter when you create a new account, based on the most recent statement balance for the real-world account tracked by the Quicken account.

P

payee   The recipient of the funds from a check or withdrawal transaction or the source that paid you the funds for a deposit transaction.

postdate   Entering a future date for a check transaction, so you can print or pay the check at a later date.

Q

Quicken Bill Pay   An online payment service you can use to pay your bills from any checking account. You must sign up to use the service for a small fee.

Quicken data file   A file that holds Quicken accounts. Although a Quicken file can hold multiple accounts, you might want to create a separate data file for each person using Quicken, to keep information separate.

QDATA   See *Quicken data file*.

QIF   An acronym for Quicken Interchange Format, a file format supported by older versions of the Quicken program.

Quicken Home page   This initial window displayed by Quicken includes handy lists and reminders.

QuickFill   A feature that memorizes a transaction for each new payee (creating a memorized transaction) and enables you to quickly fill in that transaction information when you begin typing the payee's name in a new transaction.

R

reconcile   Comparing a Quicken account with the paper account statement from your bank or financial institution. Reconciling involves clearing and adjusting Quicken transactions to make them match the statement so that ending balances for both the Quicken account and the statement are identical.

recurring transaction   See *scheduled transaction*.

register   An account register holds the entries for your account. The register for bank accounts (for example, checking and savings accounts) looks very similar to your paper checkbook register.

reminders   A feature that reminds you to use an upcoming scheduled transaction. Reminders appear when you start Quicken. You control how far in advance a reminder appears.

Reminders List   The list of dates on which you've specified that Quicken should remind you of an upcoming scheduled transaction. See *reminders*.

report   Specially summarized or grouped information in Quicken. You can print the report after displaying it.

restore   Using a backup copy of your Quicken data file to replace the current version if it becomes damaged.

S

scheduled transaction   A check or payment transaction or deposit (such as a pay deposit) that happens at regular intervals. Quicken reminds you of each scheduled transaction and enters the transaction information for you, if you want.

Scheduled Transaction List   The list of scheduled transactions you've entered in Quicken.

scroll   Viewing a different area in a file or list. Usually accomplished by clicking a scroll bar on the side or bottom of the window.

split   Assigning more than one category or subcategory to a transaction to reflect accurately the purpose of the expenditure or the source of the income. You specify the portion of the transaction that falls into each category or subcategory.

statement ending balance   The ending balance from your paper bank statement, to which you compare your Quicken transactions when you reconcile your account.

subcategory   A subdivision of a Quicken category used to identify an expense or income transaction more precisely. See *category*.

T–U

Tax-deferred   An account that is not taxable.

tax estimate   A calculated estimate of your federal taxes, based on approximate values you enter at the time of calculation or on Quicken data you've entered previously.

Tax Planner   A Quicken feature you use to generate a tax estimate.

tax-related category   A category you identify as tracking either a taxable income or expense. Quicken uses the information from tax-related categories to generate tax reports and estimates.

toolbar   The toolbar appears along the top of the active window in Quicken, well below the menu bar for the Quicken application itself.

transaction   A bill (check), deposit, transfer, withdrawal, or ATM action you record in a Quicken account.

transaction group   A list of transactions you collect under a group name and schedule in the Scheduled Transaction List. You can select a transaction group to enter all of that group's transactions in the register simultaneously.

transfer   A transaction that withdraws money from one account and deposits it into another account.

TurboTax   A popular tax preparation program also made by Intuit, the makers of Quicken.

V

void   Marking a transaction as no longer valid, but leaving it in the register with the check number intact so Quicken correctly numbers subsequent checks.

W–Z

Web (World Wide Web)   A subset of computers on the Internet storing information you can display graphically by using a Web browser.

Web browser   A program that enables your computer to display graphical information downloaded via modem from the World Wide Web. Quicken includes an integrated browser you can use to browse the Web.

window   Holds a particular type of information within Quicken; for example, the Memorized Transaction List window.

A

transactions

U-V

W-Z